Red Tobruk

Red Tobruk
Memoirs of a World War II Destroyer Commander

**Captain Frank Gregory-Smith
RN DSO*, DSC***

Edited by Dominic Symons

Pen & Sword
MILITARY

First published in Great Britain in 2008 by
Pen & Sword Military
An imprint of
Pen & Sword Books Ltd
47 Church Street
Barnsley
South Yorkshire
S70 2AS

ISBN 978 1 84415 862 1

A CIP catalogue record for this book is
available from the British Library

Typeset in 10pt Palatino by Mac Style, Beverley, East Yorkshire
Printed and bound in the UK
By Biddles

Pen & Sword Books Ltd incorporates the Imprints of
Pen & Sword Aviation,
Pen & Sword Maritime, Pen & Sword Military,
Wharncliffe Local History,
Pen & Sword Select, Pen & Sword Military Classics, Leo Cooper,
Remember When, Seaforth Publishing and Frontline Publishing

For a complete list of Pen & Sword titles please contact
PEN & SWORD BOOKS LIMITED
47 Church Street, Barnsley, South Yorkshire, S70 2AS, England
E-mail: enquiries@pen-and-sword.co.uk
Website: www.pen-and-sword.co.uk

Contents

Introduction

In 1922 William Frank Niemann Gregory-Smith was sent to Dartmouth Naval College, the school for Royal Navy officer cadets. He was twelve years old and had grown up in the suburbs of Manchester and the hills of Shropshire. There was no family history of service in the Royal Navy nor any significant connection with the sea; just an imaginative only-child with a head full of maritime history, inspired by stories of the Royal Navy's past glories. Gregory-Smith had asked to go to Dartmouth and his parents agreed, thus starting a naval career that would stretch until his retirement in 1960.

Red Tobruk is the story of Gregory-Smith's experiences at sea during the Second World War, told in his own words. At the heart of *Red Tobruk* lies the story of HMS *Eridge*, Gregory-Smith's first command. This humble escort destroyer served in the Mediterranean from May 1941 to August 1942, when the Mediterranean Fleet fought some of the most intense periods of action experienced by the Royal Navy in the entire war. The Royal Navy struggled with the Italian Navy, German U-Boats and E-boats, and the Luftwaffe for control of this sea. The sea routes to North Africa were critical to the outcome of the struggle on land, where the Axis armies faced the forces of the British Empire fighting for control of the Middle East. If the Middle East had been lost, then Britain and her Navy would have lost their main supply of oil and Britain's chances of survival would have been even more precarious. The determination and ferocity with which both sides fought for control of the Mediterranean is a testament to the importance of this struggle, and evident in HMS *Eridge*'s constant fight to survive attacks from bombers, U-boats and E-boats.

Gregory-Smith's naval career spanned one of the greatest eras of change Britain has ever known. In 1922 the country was recovering from the traumas of the Great War though it remained confident of its role as one of the superpowers of the day; the British Empire still covered a quarter of the globe and ruled around a quarter of the world's population. The Royal Navy, which protected trade between Britain and her colonies and projected British power across the globe, was still the largest navy in the world. But within a generation the Empire and her merchant navy had disintegrated, and the Royal Navy had become a navy of small ships. The change was so sudden and so dramatic that subsequent generations can easily forget the world outlook of Britons born into Empire. But this was the world that the men who fought in the Royal Navy in the Second World War were born into – the world as it was for Gregory-Smith during the carefree days of service before the war clouds began to gather.

Dominic Symons, November 2007

CHAPTER ONE

Come Aboard to Join, Sir

May 1927

To this nervous seventeen year old cadet Portland was looking even more depressing than usual and not even the presence of an Atlantic Fleet Battle Squadron could conceal the drabness of the little dockyard town, nestling in the shadows of the grim Borstal establishment. The ships were all veterans of the Battle of Jutland and my own ship, the battlecruiser HMS *Tiger*, was easily distinguishable by her three funnels and long slim hull. In the still evening air, bugle calls and the trill of bosun's pipes carried clearly across the harbour, reminding me that I was about to become a very small cog in the world's mightiest navy. It was a humbling thought which made me feel horribly inadequate. I wanted companionship during the ordeal but, for some unknown reason, no other new cadets were waiting for the evening boat.

The jetty was quite deserted except for a bored policeman who answered my anxious questions in curt monosyllables. Hurt by his indifference, I swaggered along the jetty, hoping to persuade him that my brand new dirk and uniform were concealing a mariner of some experience. I doubt if I succeeded. I certainly did not deceive myself and, by the time HMS *Tiger's* boat arrived, I was firmly convinced that no other profession in the world had such a terrifying initiation as this forthcoming boat trip, which proclaimed with such utter finality that one was leaving the land for the sea for the rest of one's working life.

The Coxswain shook his head on being asked if he had conveyed any other cadets so, with rising anxiety, I followed my luggage into his boat, which promptly headed towards HMS *Tiger*, every thud of its propeller emphasising that I was exchanging a boy's life for a man's. By the time the boat glided smoothly alongside the gangway, I was such a bundle of nerves that I forgot all advice about climbing aboard in a dignified manner and scuttled up it like a startled rabbit.

From the gangway's upper platform, the quarterdeck looked so vast that it was difficult to accept that this was only one section of a single ship. Nevertheless, the open space between the gangway and turret seemed to be filled entirely by gaping quartermasters, bosun's mates, corporals, call boys, side boys, messengers and buglers, beyond whom stood the officer of the watch whose eyes, to an oversensitive imagination, appeared to be bulging in shocked surprise at my sartorial untidiness. Feeling more insignificant than ever, I stumbled past the reception committee. With my legs tangling with my wretched dirk I saluted the officer of the watch and stuttered, 'C-come aboard to join, sir.'

I half expected him to snarl, 'You're a day late! Consider yourself under arrest!' But, to my surprise, he accepted my hesitant report with an encouraging smile. A feeling of profound relief at having overcome this first hurdle immediately swept over me. The quarterdeck staff looked human, all of a sudden, and the side boys, at a curt command from the quartermaster, nipped down the gangway to fetch my luggage. A minute later, I was following a messenger into the superstructure where, for the first time, I became aware of that faint but bitter sweet smell of humanity, cooking, oil fuel and bilges. This smell haunts all those who go down to the sea in ships. The messenger lead me to the small, dark gunroom behind the ship's armour plating where the cadets lived. Our chests were stowed in an open passageway and our hammocks slung in a hot airless space above one of HMS *Tiger's* eight boiler rooms. It was in constant use at night but we were kept so busy that we were invariably too tired to notice the noise and traffic.

Next day, the ship sailed for Portsmouth. HMS *Tiger* was leaving harbour in company with the battleships HMS *Benbow* and HMS *Marlborough*. It was an informal departure without guards and bands but, even so, this the first movement of one's first ship, was a thrilling experience. Perhaps it was even more exciting than the similar movement, years later, of one's first command, because it was a novelty; the thud of the anchor coming home, the rising whine of the turbines, the beat of the propellers, the rapid exchange of signals, the bugle calls and bosuns' pipes all combined to emphasise that one was being absorbed into the finest service in the world. Moreover the quiet orders of Captain Gordon Campbell VC and the sight of three heavy ships manoeuvring into close formation, without fuss or shouting, confirmed that such a claim was not without foundation.

By the start of 1928 I was newly promoted to midshipman and joined the County class cruiser, HMS *Cumberland*, then commissioning for two years of service in the Far East and fitting out in Chatham dockyard. We sailed for Hong Kong on 26 January 1928. At nightfall, when we turned towards Ushant, St. Catherine's light was flashing brightly off our starboard beam. Half an hour later, only its loom was visible and most men off-watch had gathered on deck to watch their last link with England, branding it in their memories, until that, too, sank below the horizon. Two years would pass before that light rose out of the sea again and, for the whole of that period, our company of 700 would be entirely isolated from wives, families and girlfriends. It was a sombre thought and an unnatural silence brooded over the ship. Our excited anticipation of the future had been temporarily eclipsed by a feeling of sadness at the prospect of this long separation.

But the Navy did not allow its midshipmen to remain idle and after two busy years patrolling the China Station from Japan to Singapore we sailed for home. Our journey home took us to Malta's Grand Harbour where the heavy ships of the Mediterranean Fleet were preparing for their annual manoeuvres with the Atlantic Fleet. The destroyers looked so alike: same shade of grey paint, steel burnished, brass brightly polished, guns at the same elevation; yet each one possessed its own individuality like the crews who manned them. They were businesslike too, ready at a few hour's notice to operate anywhere in the world. As I watched the controlled activity on their decks, I knew where my future lay.

As we neared England a full gale was blowing out of the south-west, bringing with it heavy seas and drenching rain. We rounded Ushant without even sighting its light and crossed the Channel in a heavy, beam sea. Then, all of a sudden, England rose up on the horizon ahead. It was raining heavily, of course, but the hills of Devon were looking incredibly green after the barren rocks and deserts of the Middle East. The paying off pendant was broken for the last time and the ship proceeded slowly up the Sound and Hamoaze into Plymouth, passing battleships, carriers and cruisers before we secured alongside a wharf. We were home at last.

Behind us lay the happiest and most care-free years of our lives; ahead lay manhood, commissioned rank and responsibility. It was a sobering thought and most of us were in a pensive mood when we landed. To celebrate our return to England we went to Nicholson's Saw Dust Bar which, in those days, was the centre of the naval bachelor's life in Plymouth. Everyone, sooner or later, gravitated there. It was our first visit to an English pub for more than two years and, under the influence of its cheerful atmosphere, we soon warmed up, imbibing, until closing time, an imprudent mixture of draught beer and Plymouth gin which encouraged us to treat lieutenants as equals and then, as the evening wore on, as inferior beings.

'My dear, how pale you look,' my mother said next day when she met my train. 'I expected you to be brown and sunburnt.'

After passing my seamanship exams I was promoted from Midshipman to Sub-Lieutenant in 1930. I dearly wanted to be appointed to a destroyer and even visited the Admiralty in London to request this. But, ten days later, I was appointed sub-lieutenant on the battleship HMS *Warspite*, the flagship of the Second Battle Squadron serving in home waters. I promised myself that never again would I ask for a particular appointment and I never did.

The Captain gave me plenty of opportunities to handle the ship and on such occasions one felt like a keeper in charge of a great monster, which meekly obeyed orders to go faster or slower or to turn to port or to starboard. But like all monsters HMS *Warspite* was liable to take control of herself and unless counter action was taken at precisely the right moment, her momentum would carry her far from her intended position. Judgement was needed to estimate that precise moment and that required constant practice.

The sea lanes in the North Sea and Channel were amongst the busiest in the world and ships – ocean going, coasters, drifters and trawlers – were always in sight. Trawlers fished separately but the presence of drifters was indicated by a forest of masts rising steadily above the horizon, until they developed into dozens of fishing vessels lying to leeward of their long nets. At night the navigation and fishing lights of these vessels looked like those of a small town dumped in the North Sea. Of the ocean-going ships sighted, most were flying the Red Ensign. We steamed through only a section of the world's shipping lanes but on seas and in harbours all over the world our preponderance was clear; the Merchant Navy, under the protection of the Royal Navy, formed the links in a chain binding the mother country to her Empire. To a young naval officer, inspired by maritime history, it seemed inconceivable that the Empire and the great ocean going merchant fleet flying the Red Ensign would one day be a vestige of its former glory. They both seemed immortal!

But the days of peaceful duties were coming to an end. By 1935 I was a first lieutenant on one of the Great War's three funnelled destroyers and international tension was growing inexorably. Throughout the summer Italian troops had been massing along the borders of Abyssinia: Mussolini had left the world in no doubt that he intended to conquer the country. The British Foreign Secretary had answered Mussolini's threats by urging the League of Nations to impose sanctions and pledging Britain's support if they did so. His speech, proving that some effort was at last being made to deter unprovoked aggression, was received with relief, tinged perhaps by a little apprehension.

A few nights after the Foreign Secretary's speech, Portland harbour became alive with the familiar sounds of a fleet preparing for sea – curt commands, bugles, bosun's pipes, sirens, clanking cables, whining derricks, hawsers creaking through blocks, noisy boat loads of libertymen recalled from leave. Shortly afterwards, the ships steamed singly between the breakwaters and disappeared into the mists of the Channel. The fleet was bound for the Mediterranean to show the world that Britain was standing by her word: that we were standing once more between a powerful aggressor and his weaker victim. Unfortunately our destroyer was detailed for submarine training duty in Portland. We felt utter disappointment as we idled away 3,000 miles from the centre of activity.

Italy invaded Abyssinia in October 1935, an act of defiance which surely had to be punished. But the Government, by then, had no intention of becoming involved in a war with Italy and contented itself with interminable discussions about the imposition of sanctions. The combined fleets were still based in Alexandria but it was now clear that, in spite of all the fine oratory, Mussolini's challenge would not be accepted.

I sailed for Alexandria on the fleet destroyer[1] HMS *Foresight* towards the end of March 1936. When we reached Alex the harbour appeared to be crammed with battleships, battlecruisers, carriers, cruisers, destroyers, submarines and depot ships, forming a fleet which was probably larger than any concentration of British ships in the Second World War. It was a magnificent spectacle. Although no one, now, had any illusions about the prospect of intervention, the fleet was still on a semi-war footing and the Commander in Chief, Admiral Sir W.W. Fisher, was determined to take full advantage of the temporary removal of restrictions on fuel consumption. He worked the ships without respite until they were more than ready to meet the enemy they would never fight. The only place the fleet did encounter the Italians was at Port Said. This was not a popular station owing to the constant passage of Italian transports whose passengers, elated by the easy victories over a poorly trained and badly equipped Abyssinian enemy, had shown their contempt, by word and gesture, for the Royal Navy which, according to the boastful claims of their propaganda, feared the valiant Italian Fleet. During the summer, the Abyssinian war reached its inevitable conclusion with the complete conquest of Abyssinia. Britain's role had not been one of which we could be proud. Having thrown down the gauntlet against aggression, we had spent the following months trying to pick it up, merely succeeding in throwing Italy into the arms of Germany. Consequently we were delighted when the fleet was ordered to disperse.

But peacetime duties did not return. Almost as soon as we were back in Devonport another emergency was upon us. The Spanish Civil War had just broken out because the Spanish army, led by General Franco, had rebelled against the socialist government in July 1936. Units of the 4th Destroyer Flotilla hastened to the North Spanish coast to protect British shipping; they were to be kept busy. The next few weeks was the era of 'Potato' Jones, and merchant seamen of similar ilk, who defied the rebel's blockade of Republican ports and thereby caused numerous confrontations between British and Spanish warships. Their exploits had considerable glamour and appealed to the British public. Nevertheless, the claim of the leftish press that these men were defending democracy must have amused those concerned who, for the most part, were merely merchant adventurers trading where the profits were highest. The press made a great fuss of these maritime incidents and their descriptions made us envy those ships at the centre of the excitement.

By September 1937 HMS *Foresight* was involved in its second spell on the Spanish coast and the situation had noticeably changed. The policy in Spain was non-intervention, agreed by all the major European powers. But it was already clear that only Britain and France were keeping this agreement. Germany, in particular, was intervening and had already carried out the forerunner of so many similar raids in the years ahead – the terror bombing of Guernica. Few people at the time readily accepted the Republican reports of devastation because Franco's propagandists immediately claimed the communists had dynamited the town. This argument was willingly swallowed because we wanted to believe that the Germans would fight cleanly whereas it was common knowledge that the communists would stop at nothing. By late 1937 intervention was occurring on a massive scale; Germany and Italy were not only using the war to test new weapons, they were supplying Franco with the technicians to use them. Russia, although not providing manpower, was giving similar aid to the Government and volunteers from all over the world were streaming to their assistance in the International Brigades. The left and right wings of the world hurled accusations of Fascist or Communist aggression at each other. To us, both charges seemed correct. It was all foreign interference in a domestic quarrel.

CHAPTER TWO

Dunkirk

Through 1938 the crisis in Czechoslovakia grew as Hitler agitated aggressively over the plight of the Sudenten Germans. War seemed imminent. But with the agreement of Britain, France and Germany at Munich, that September, the war clouds seemed to clear. As the crisis ended I was unexpectedly appointed First Lieutenant of the destroyer HMS *Jaguar*. She was one of the new J class, the first of an entirely new generation of larger and more powerful destroyers armed with: six 4.7-inch power-driven dual purpose guns; ten twenty-one-inch torpedo tubes; anti-submarine equipment; close range anti-aircraft weapons and advanced control systems. HMS *Jaguar* had recently been launched at Denny's yard in Dumbarton and a nucleus of officers and ratings would spend the next twelve months watching her inanimate steel hull gradually developing into a fighting ship.

Being associated with the gradual growth of a fighting ship was a novel experience and any preconceived ideas about shipbuilders' unwillingness to work were quickly dispelled. Denny's work force was a tough but friendly team which worked cheerfully and continuously through wet and cold – and the weather that winter was bad – usually clad in nothing more substantial than an overall. Thanks to their efforts, the bare, steel hull rapidly developed into a ship. At a yard like Denny's, the officers were allowed considerable latitude in certain aspects of the ship's construction which kept us pleasantly occupied. This, naturally, gave us an even keener interest as the living spaces took shape and the weapons and machinery were progressively installed. Nothing, we thought, would be more pleasant than a peacetime commission in such a fine ship and, in the immediate aftermath of Munich, this seemed probable.

But the prospects of a peacetime commission faded swiftly with the German occupation of Czechoslovakia in March 1939. After that, the war clouds gathered thick and fast. Germany occupied Memel; Italy invaded Albania and Britain guaranteed support to Poland, Greece and Romania. Nevertheless, we continued to enjoy ourselves throughout that warm, threatening summer. We had the whole of the Western Highlands on our doorstep, with mountains to climb and lochs to fish.

HMS *Jaguar's* captain joined at this time. He was Lieutenant Commander J.F.W. 'Beppo' Hine, a large, ungainly man with an ugly though not unattractive face which, at the least excuse, would be transformed by a broad grin. He was an old destroyer hand and, together, we made the final preparations before commissioning, knowing that war was now a certainty. We were in the shipyard on Sunday, 3 September, when Chamberlain made his gloomy announcement that hostilities had commenced following Hitler's invasion of Poland. Immediately afterwards, the air raid sirens sounded and, for the first of thousands of occasions, we heard that dismal warning.

HMS *Jaguar* commissioned on 12 September. She had a west country ship's company, a curious mixture of elderly reservists and mere boys which James Wood, the Second Lieutenant, and Francis Bruen, the Sub-Lieutenant, brought from Devonport. That same evening – even before the newcomers had found their way around the ship – we sailed from the Clyde. None of us slept that night, not because we were expecting to meet an enemy but because everyone was anxious to learn about his action station and how his weapon worked. Thus, all that night and the following day, we exercised action, defence and cruising stations until every man onboard at least knew what he was supposed to do, if not how to do it.

This was rectified during the next fortnight at Portland, the working up base, where we carried out torpedo and gunnery exercises by night and day, hunted submarines and performed every known drill or evolution. The work up was very similar to a peacetime crash programme. The weather was perfect and it was a pleasure to be at sea in such a fine ship. The wardroom settled down well together and the seriousness of the work up was relieved by some peacetime skylarking. In fact that fortnight was the nearest HMS *Jaguar* ever came to peacetime service and everyone was determined to make the best of it before we reached our war station. We had assumed that would be with the main fleet at Scapa Flo so we felt slightly affronted when we were ordered to the Immingham, on the Humber, where Vice Admiral Edwards-Collins was forming a striking force consisting of the 2nd Cruiser Squadron and our 7th Flotilla.

Our care-free life lay behind us: the unknown lay ahead and not even the least imaginative on board could help feeling apprehensive. Quite rightly, we soon discovered. The purpose of the Humber striking force was to intercept German surface sorties into the southern portion of the North Sea; thrice during the next fortnight, the force, having hurriedly raised steam, proceeded eastwards at full speed. The weather was steadily worsening as the autumn days slipped by and a high speed sweep along the Norwegian coast, before returning to either Rosyth or the Humber, was a painful experience for ships' companies who had not yet found their sealegs. So bad was the promulgation of information that the destroyers never had the slightest idea what we were supposed to be hunting. Not until many years later did I learn that the second sweep was to search for the German battlecruiser *Gneisenau* and a mixed force of cruisers and destroyers which had been reported at sea. In fact the German sortie had been no more than a feint to draw our surface forces into a submarine and bomber trap. This was partially successful as the striking force became the target of spasmodic and unsuccessful bombing attacks.

HMS *Jaguar*, having developed an electrical defect, missed these attacks but provided a target for other bombers when returning alone to Rosyth. She was still about 100 miles east of the Firth when a look-out yelled, 'Aircraft approaching from astern.'

Having intercepted bombing reports from the 2nd Cruiser Squadron, we were already closed up at action stations when the control tower quickly picked up two aircraft in its sights. They might have been anything – Heinkels, Dorniers, even friendly Blenheims – but our intuition warned that they were hostile and a noticeable air of tension gripped the ship. So much had been claimed by air power propagandists about the superiority of bombers over ships that the queasiness at the pit of one's stomach could be excused – we were the guinea pig about to put theory into practice.

'Full speed ahead together,' growled Beppo. 'Open fire the moment they turn towards us.'

The ship plunged into a rough sea, flinging solid water across the bridge, while the bombers were gaining bearing. Reaching the quarter, the aircraft swung inwards and, a minute later, HMS *Jaguar* fired her first salvoes, shuddering under the impact. Immediately afterwards our close range weapons joined in, pumping out a stream of high explosive and adding to the fiendish din of gunfire and shell bursts. The bombers flew steadily towards us and passed overhead, just as a mushroom of black water erupted about 500 yards away.

'Bombing, sir,' Wood, the Second Lieutenant, called out.

The bombers circled the ship like cats watching a mouse. Any hope that they had expended their bombs was promptly extinguished when they once more turned towards us.

'On a bombing course,' yelled Wood.

'Hard a starboard,' growled Beppo. 'And for god's sake don't keep reporting the obvious.'

Once again the ship shuddered from the concussion of her gunfire and once again the bombs exploded about 500 yards away, the shock waves, even at that distance, slamming against the hull. The bombers then flew several circuits around the ship, presumably hoping to spot signs of damage, before turning towards the horizon. They left us with profound feelings of relief and satisfaction. We could now confirm that the bomber was not quite the lethal weapon its supporters claimed. On the other hand, our anti-aircraft gunnery was nothing to boast about. In fact, the main armament, having a maximum elevation of only forty degrees, had already proved itself to be practically useless against high level attacks.[2]

Our offensive role seemed to be forgotten and, for the next two months, the 7th Flotilla was employed on a variety of duties: covering the Norwegian convoys; escorting cable ships cutting the continental cables and steaming far out into the Atlantic to join troop convoys. Officers and ratings alike were on duty for more than twelve hours at a time, most of them in positions exposed to the wind, rain and sea, which frequently surged across the upper deck in a solid mass of turbulent water while the ship plunged, wallowed, rolled and yawed on the different legs of her zigzag courses. Broken periods below deck were too short to gain precious sleep, remove wet clothes or even to have a decent wash. The messdecks stank of unwashed humanity, stale air, food and vomit; they were littered with the contents of drawers and lockers, which violent motion had torn from their stowages, and with sou'westers, seaboots and oilskins lying where their weary wearers had dropped them. Food, crockery and the men themselves were frequently flung across the messes when a heavy sea hit the beam. Our senses were numbed by the endless swoosh and crack of heavy seas which seemed to be punishing us daring to take on a human foe as well as the elements. Our first task on returning to harbour was to make the messdecks habitable but time seldom permitted any attention to the salt-caked hull and upperworks. The ship's appearance would have shocked the builders who had taken so much pride in making her.

Exhausted through lack of sleep and without any compensating results, every man onboard became a stern critic of the conduct of the war at sea. 'How will the enemy ever be brought to battle?', we wanted to know. At every reported movement along the Norwegian coast, the Battle Fleet promptly steamed towards Iceland, directly away from the threat. The Commander in Chief, Admiral Sir Charles Forbes, was, of course, arranging his fleet to intercept a breakout into the Atlantic. In spite of that, his single mindedness was scornfully dismissed by the epithet 'one way Charlie'. We were even more irreverent towards our own Admiral although he, at least, had satisfied our offensive spirit by invariably leading his force directly towards the reported movement. He was the 'Sea Pig'!

The flotilla returned to Immingham on Christmas Eve, after a rough passage escorting a convoy of iron ore ships from Narvik. Our Christmas mail was waiting and the knowledge that we would spend Christmas in harbour had such an exhilarating effect that we forgot our exhaustion.

In the initial weeks of 1940 the Admiralty seemed unable to decide how to employ the flotilla and we carried out the most ludicrous tasks for fleet destroyers. But, however trivial the assignment, it was always in waters threatened by submarines, aircraft or mines so our degree of readiness could never be relaxed: we were always short of sleep. To add to our troubles, the weather was bitterly cold – almost arctic. Even our own Humber was blocked by ice flows and patrolling in the face of easterly gales, which cut like a knife, was sheer misery. Then, at long last, the expected air offensive started against east coast shipping. Fortunately, instead of concentrating against selected targets, the enemy dispersed his attacks between the Thames and Rattray Head so his successes were less than they might have been. Nevertheless, fighter escorts over the sea had not yet been organised so we suffered increased losses.

Once again HMS *Jaguar* was sent off on some lone mission, on completion of which she proceeded to Scapa to refuel. The defences there were still incomplete and the fleet was operating from Loch Ewe so HMS *Jaguar* was the only fighting ship present. It was an eerie sensation being alone in that vast enclosure of water and we were glad to leave. At least we thought we were leaving until Beppo made one of his inexplicable errors and the ship, instead of passing through the Hoxa gate, ended up in the anti-submarine boom – an enormous fly caught in a gigantic web.

'Oh Christ!' Murmured Beppo. 'I've done it again.'

The boom defence people were incensed. Having spent three months laying the boom, working night and day in appalling weather conditions, they now had to cut most of it away to extricate one careless destroyer. Their feelings were expressed in vivid terms and they had a real job on their hands because their boom was in a proper mess. Having picked up the hauling-in wire with our propellers, we then swung broadside half over the boom so the huge supporting cylinders were lining both sides of the ship. Apart from being cold, the weather was stormy and the ship rolled incessantly. Each time she rolled, one or more of the cylinders would crash against the side, causing the whole hull to shudder. Down below, it sounded as if a team of giants was striking the plating with huge sledge hammers.

We remained in that blasted boom for a week, at the end of which our senses were deadened by the everlasting hammer blows against the hull.

The cheers, when the last wire was cut away, were so deafening that they must have been heard in Wick. We sailed immediately- after some insincere well-wishes from the entire boom defence organisation. Our plating looked like corrugated sheets and we soon discovered that the ship was leaking like a sieve. But the powers that be had little sympathy and innocently believing HMS *Jaguar* had enjoyed a week's unscheduled idleness, decided that we should make it up by extra seatime. Except to fuel, we scarcely saw the inside of a harbour, let alone a pub. The weather was still bad; we were wet and cold on deck and wet and cold below. We began to get on each other's nerves.

The trouble was we were suffering from the utter boredom of exercising sea power. We had been running incessantly, except when one of Beppo's minor miscalculations had put us out of action, for six months; but, for all our efforts, we'd only had one brief encounter with a couple of aircraft. In fact we were doing ourselves an injustice as, on one of the cable cutting expeditions, we had seriously damaged a submarine. This success only became known at the end of the war, by which time HMS *Jaguar*, and most of those responsible for damaging the submarine, were lying in a watery grave off Mersa Matruh. But the war at sea was anything but phoney. The first sinking of the campaign at sea had occurred within hours of the declaration of war: the destruction of the first U-boat ten days later. By mid-March 1,250,000 tons of shipping had been sunk, mostly by submarine and mine (the unseen enemies) and half of these losses had occurred in our operational area off the east coast. The enemy, too, had suffered losses but, in our biased opinions, nothing commensurate with the effort expended by hundreds of British ships. Nevertheless, our ships, by their mobility across the seven seas, were exerting the invisible pressure of sea power and the enemy's own ability to operate was being inexorably and relentlessly contained and eroded. But such high strategy was beyond our brains. All we saw was an ever increasing number of victims of the enemy's mining campaign each time we left the Forth or the Humber. All our destroyer losses had occurred in our operational area and the fear of damage by mine or torpedo was ever present each time we put to sea. Yet we had nothing to show for incessant steaming, overwork and too little rest in dreadful weather conditions. It seemed such a waste of a powerful destroyer designed to operate with the Battle Fleet. But if we had so operated, we would have achieved little more. We had been steeped in a naval history which highlighted the great naval battles of the past without too much emphasis on the dreary blockades and patrols which had preceded the Quiberon Bays, St Vincents and Trafalgars. The Home Fleet had yet to fight its Narviks, Bismark, North Cape and Bering Sea and, for us, the prelude had grown tiresome.

Human bodies were obviously as much in need of a rest as the ship so we were glad to learn that she would be refitted in Hull in mid-March. True, it was not a popular port; neither was it a place which a west country ship's company (expecting no more than seven days leave to each watch) would have selected, as there were hundreds of miles across England to travel home. But, at least, it was dry land and an opportunity for leave: like schoolboys we ticked off the passing days and prayed that we survived to enjoy it. We were off the Norwegian coast when the welcome signal 'carry on in execution of previous orders' was received and we headed thankfully for the Humber. We were still 100 miles to the eastward when the wireless office bell buzzed on the bridge. The duty signalman hauled up the signal, read it and uttered an audible gasp of dismay.

'What's the matter?' growled Beppo.

Speechless, the signalman thrust the signal into Beppo's hands. He read it in silence and then handed it to me, his eyes expressing far more than mere words could ever convey. It was from the Admiralty curtly cancelling Hull and diverting us to the Caledon shipyard at Dundee, a full 300 miles further from the west country.

The reason for the signalman's consternation was only too clear. Devonport was far enough away from Hull but Dundee would add another twelve hours, at least, to the travelling time – taking a hell of a slice out of our seven days leave. We knew only too well what our men's reaction would be and, indeed, the messdecks were buzzing like a hive of angry bees as the news percolated from the wireless office. Consequently, the ship's company was not in the most cheerful frame of mind – their expressions suggested a major maritime disaster – when the ship passed the Bell Rock and entered the Tay estuary. It was a cold, raw day with frequent snow squalls which did not improve the appearance of the estuary towns and countryside and our disappointment was unrelieved when the ship finally berthed.

No one could be sent on leave until we knew exactly how long the ship would be in dockyard hands, so we agitated for an early refitting conference. At that, the shipyard manager welcomed us to the Caledon but went on to say that the yard had never before refitted a fighting ship so he would apologise in advance in case we were not handled as swiftly as in one of the recognised naval yards. Beppo solemnly retorted that no one would object to a couple of extra days leave to make up for the additional travelling, after which we went through the defect list in detail.

At the end, Beppo posed the vital question: 'How long?'

The shipyard manager glanced through his notes and pondered for a few moments. 'At least six weeks,' he finally stated.

It was beyond the wildest dreams of those who had only expected a fortnight. As soon as the news reached the messdecks, Dundee instantly changed from a dour Scottish town into a gay, inviting city. The gloom was replaced by smiles and singing and the men eagerly discussed how they planned to spend their three weeks at home and a similar period in Dundee. The ship's company soon found that not only the Caledon but the town itself was glad to see us and we were rapidly swept up in a whirl of gaiety and riotous living, which utterly refuted the libel of Scotch meanness. Bruen, through his friendship with one of the cruiser HMS *Edinburgh's* sub-lieutenants, Peter Sime, made the initial moves for the wardroom's entry into Dundee society. Bruen and Sime came onboard one evening for a drink. The wardroom, by then, was in a shocking state, the corrugated plating on one side having been replaced by a canvas screen through which the easterly winds cut like a knife. Anyway, we were huddled round the fire, drinking a hot toddy to keep out the cold, when the Quartermaster interrupted us.

'Excuse me', he said. 'The dockyard police have rung to say that two ladies are waiting at the gate.'

Bruen jumped to his feet. 'Oh God,' he exclaimed. 'I'd forgotten all about 'em. We only came onboard to ask you to sign their passes.'

'You're not bringing girls onboard,' I exploded. 'The wardroom isn't fit for a pig to enter.'

'Oh, Peter's sister won't mind,' Bruen airily retorted.

The pair departed with the passes while I made the habitable section of the wardroom reasonably tidy, before returning to the fire to mutter silent curses about Bruen's stupidity. In a short while we heard two female voices expostulating vigorously about the thoughtlessness of those who kept girls waiting in the cold while they filled themselves with drink.

'This is my sister, Jean,' Sime muttered in an off-hand, almost shamefaced, manner as he re-entered the wardroom.

I looked at her and my heart gave a great bound. She was a slim, petite brunette with a pair of shapely legs and ankles, not at all what her indignant complaints had suggested and my manners were temporarily forgotten.

'If only you'd remove yourself from the fire, other people would have a chance of warming themselves,' she unexpectedly remarked.

I apologised meekly and withdrew. Nevertheless, any girl whose first remark to a total stranger was so worded deserved detailed consideration and I watched her closely. Having adequately expressed her opinion of Bruen's behaviour, she was soon displaying the cheerful, vivacious side of her nature and I felt my pulse quickening.

I became increasingly intrigued by Jean. She, too, seemed not unaware of me and appeared pleased when I rang her and suggested dinner. After that, we met daily. I took her to dinners and dances which persuaded her, quite falsely, that I was a dancing enthusiast, although experience of my technique should have corrected that impression at our very first dance. She, too, was not entirely guiltless and, by accompanying me on various cross-country rambles, wrongly convinced me that she would be entirely at home on some of the least accessible Bens. But, in spite of the misunderstandings, my desire to take advantage of her steadily faded as my interest increased. I was blacklegging on the glorious brotherhood of naval bachelors. I was falling in love.

On 8 April Germany invaded Norway and the British people felt a thrill of relief. The phoney war was over at last and Germany had thrust out an arm which surely could be lopped off, during the course of which the main fleets must make contact. We listened eagerly to the news bulletins and cursed our inactivity during the two battles of Narvik and in various other skirmishes up and down the Norwegian coast. But, even though the enemy's major units were at sea, the Battle Fleet failed to intercept and, once more, the amateur strategists had some excuse for disappointment. 'One way Charlie' had again gone the wrong way! Even worse, the exposed arm was tougher than expected and it was the British, not the Germans, who were being hurled back into the sea. Soon ships damaged during the evacuation were flooding into Dundee: our disappointment at not being there alongside them quickly diminished after hearing their hair raising accounts of operating in the fjords under the enemy's complete air superiority.

The end of the refit, which had once seemed so remote that one never troubled to contemplate returning to the war at sea, swiftly arrived. Before sailing, the ship's company held a farewell dance to thank the good people of Dundee for their kindness and hospitality. It was an uproarious affair. Two days later we sailed down the Tay. I was not the only one to leave my heart behind. At least six other members of the ship had found their future wives.

HMS *Jaguar* next spent a short period in Scapa and then joined a strike group consisting of the aircraft carrier HMS *Ark Royal* and ten fleet destroyers. By then southern and central Norway had been evacuated but the British and French still held an area around Harstadt. From that base the allied army was assaulting Narvik, hoping to hold the port long enough to destroy the harbour installations in order to slow down the flow of Swedish ore to Germany. HMS *Ark Royal's* task was to provide air support for the ground forces from an area well inside the Arctic Circle. For the first time since the commencement of hostilities HMS *Jaguar* was being correctly employed with a heavy fleet unit and we were delighted to make our debut with the famous *Ark Royal*, sunk so frequently according to German propaganda. She was a restless lady to escort – zigzagging constantly at high speed, altering course at irregular intervals and accelerating to full speed every two hours or so to operate aircraft. Coping with these frequent alterations, in addition to normal station-keeping, gave the bridge and engine room teams little peace. But miraculously the sea, in contrast to its normal state in that part of the world, and to the appalling conditions of the past winter, was like a mill pond. The sun shone in a cloudless sky, dipping below the horizon for no more than a few hours each night to produce a brief twilight.

We never spotted an enemy and not even the constant movement of HMS *Ark Royal's* aircraft, and the daily report of their successes and losses, could associate those tranquil waters with war. Nevertheless, ships were being sunk not so far away. Allied forces were being evacuated when the German navy struck against weak, scattered groups, disorganised even further by the evacuation. If only they had encountered our powerful well knit force, the result, surely, would have been vastly different. Every three or four days the destroyers refuelled in Harstadt, where the burnt-out wrecks and battered buildings around the landlocked fiord reminded us of some of the grimmer realities of war. But it was no more than a temporary lesson, forgotten as soon as we reached the placid waters of the open sea.

We knew, of course, that the German offensive had opened on the Western Front, that their armies were rolling relentlessly westward and that Holland had already surrendered. But we also remembered that the Allies had halted a similar thrust in 1914 and dismissed the present drive, in the optimistic belief that the British and French were merely waiting for the enemy to over-reach himself before launching their counter attack. Unfortunately our optimism was unfounded.

In late May a curt signal ordered HMS *Jaguar* and HMS *Javelin* to proceed with all despatch to Scapa and, having bid farewell to HMS *Ark Royal*, we steamed southwards at twenty-five knots. In Scapa, the total absence of ships indicated the scale of naval operations mounted but that grim, northern bastion was too remote for one to think seriously of a disaster on land. Yet the German armoured columns were still advancing through France and the low countries, and their spearheads, were daily drawing closer to the Channel ports.

No sooner had we fuelled than the Admiralty ordered both ships to Harwich. Here we were no longer remote from the Continent and the atmosphere was tense. The harbour was crowded with supply ships: troops, waiting for a passage to the Low Countries, were everywhere. But people were growing alarmed and rumours were seeping through the Belgian ports. Rumours that were even worse than reality and that was bad enough with the Germans already hammering at Boulogne. Minor evacuations were in progress and, hourly, we awaited orders to assist. Instead, on 27 May, HMS *Jaguar* was ordered to patrol off the Thames Estuary, a dreary stretch of water at the best of times. But after the great ocean spaces of the North Atlantic, we felt stifled by the endless shoals and by the rusting, twisted victims of the mining campaign. The sky itself looked leaden, as if warning of even greater disasters than the Belgian surrender, which was announced that day. But, for some illogical reason, this news upset us less than the sight of some pathetic, khaki clad figures drifting face downwards in the current, still in their now useless life jackets. These men had entrusted themselves to the sea but, somehow, we had failed them.

On the following afternoon, HMS *Jaguar* was ordered to the beaches to the eastward of Dunkirk where we were told, 'A few British troops are awaiting evacuation.'

Assuming these to be stragglers cut off by the Belgian surrender, we increased to full speed and soon sighted the huge pall of smoke at Dunkirk which was to become so familiar. Our first sight of the coastline did nothing to correct our mistake. The beaches stretched eastward from Dunkirk as far as the eye could see and the waiting troops looked utterly lost amongst so much sand. To reach them, we had to pass through the main concentration of shipping off the port. Jutting into the water near the mole were lines of lorries placed end to end, marking pathetic attempts to construct jetties on which small boats could berth. A number of these were ferrying troops to waiting ships, amongst which we gloomily noted the burnt out hulls of several wrecks. We anchored opposite the largest group of soldiers and lowered our motor boat and whalers. While doing so, a semi-naked swimmer was spotted splashing towards the ship and, a few minutes later, we were embarking our first passenger. This turned out to be an officer who told us that his platoon was ready for evacuation. We suggested that he might wish to return with our boats to identify his men but he proved unreceptive to the proposal. That was the beginning of an anxious, frustrating period. No matter how many trips made by our boats, which could carry no more than a handful of men, the numbers ashore never seemed to diminish and, judging from the miscellaneous collection that embarked, the waiting platoon was still ashore. Their officer, however, reckoned he had discharged his responsibility and, having swallowed a double whisky, was now sound asleep in the wardroom. Unfortunately, we had no time to remind him of his duty. HMS *Jaguar*, being outside the anti-aircraft defences of Dunkirk, was a tempting target for the many high level bombers which, either singly or in pairs, kept gliding out of the sun, often located only by their rapid high pitched acceleration after bomb release. We had been more or less immune from aerial attack for eight months but now, when denied the protection of speed and mobility, we were the target for an unending succession of attacks and the experience was most unpleasant. Our guns, with fifteen seamen away in boats, were undermanned but, even with full crews, they would have found few opportunities to engage our assailants before bomb release. By sunset we had embarked so few men that we'd accepted we would have to remain there overnight, when a peremptory signal ordered us to proceed forthwith to Dover. We had endured a belly full of bombing that day and everyone heaved a sigh of relief, without bothering to think about possible reasons for our recall.

On reaching Dover, HMS *Jaguar* was ordered to join three other fleet destroyers, HMS *Grenade*, HMS *Gallant* and HMS *Greyhound*, to carry out an evacuation from inside Dunkirk harbour, the theory being that ships would be loaded quicker from a jetty than from open beaches. That meant devoting most of the night to taking onboard ammunition and fuel. Being denied sleep provided too much time to think about the previous day and to contemplate the morrow. We had been through a bad time off Dunkirk but had been far too busy to feel afraid. Now, during the long, silent hours of the night, we could appreciate that war had hit us with a vengeance and that another trip was unlikely to be any better. The thought of danger is often more unnerving than the reality of it (when one is too occupied to worry) so we were quite relieved when the four ships slipped at dawn.

The division negotiated the swept channel in single line ahead as the sun was peeping above the horizon, warning of another hot, windless day. Once clear of the channel, we increased to twenty-five knots and, shortly afterwards, a large number of aircraft with fixed undercarriages appeared high overhead, turning in a tight semi circle.

'Air raid warning state?' Beppo grunted.

'All clear, sir,' the yeoman of the signals shouted back.

We wanted to believe those planes were friendly; that the enemy could not evade our fighter and radar defences so close to our own shore. But the only British aircraft with the remotest similarity were Lysanders; the improbability of such a large concentration of reconnaissance planes had struck us even before four of them gave a semi roll, causing the sun to glint briefly on their fuselages, and dropped in vertical dives. Our worst fears were confirmed. They were Stuka dive bombers, the most frightening aerial weapon in existence.

One was immediately above us. Beppo glanced quickly at it, estimating its angle and direction of dive.

'Full ahead both engines,' Beppo ordered. 'Hard a port.'

The telegraphs rang urgently; the ship surged forward and heeled stiffly outwards, turning towards her attacker, forcing it into an even steeper dive. In the same instant, the main armament opened fire, surrounding the ship with a barrage of high explosive. Owing to the guns lack of elevation, the space between the ship and the bomber looked horribly naked until the close range weapons began to pump out a stream of explosive tracer, which burst with a rippling bang, bang, bang.

Down dived the bomber. Above, others were peeling off to follow their section leaders, each of which was accelerating onto one of the destroyers, their engines screaming under the stress. Until that dive, they had looked no more dangerous than slow, unwieldy monoplanes. Now they showing their true colours. At a review, their vertical dive would have been breathtaking and exhilarating; now, it looked horribly obscene. The plummeting aircraft looked determined to dive into us. But, suddenly, it zoomed upwards and, for a brief moment, the full span of its wings hovered above the bridge, like a huge bird of prey. Then it climbed swiftly back into the high heavens just as three columns of black water jerked out of the sea astern. The bombs burst with an ear-splitting crack; shock waves slammed against the hull and the ship shuddered as if hit by a gigantic hammer. The other planes followed in swift succession. As one group of splashes subsided, another took its place: the shock waves and shuddering never ceased. Our own guns continued to blotch the sky with high explosive. The noise of accelerating engines, gunfire, bomb and shell bursts was indescribable, tearing at the senses so much that only well drilled gun crews could go through the motions of loading and firing. In fact, they continued to fire automatically even after the final attack and several seconds elapsed before we realised they were firing at nothing. The sky above, except for shell bursts, was empty. Unfortunately our bark had been very much worse than our bite.

'Let it be clearly understood,' growled Beppo as he rang the ceasefire gongs, 'That, henceforth, every plane sighted is hostile until it proves it's friendly.'

The noise of gunfire dwindled away and, for a few seconds, the ship was covered by an eerie silence, abruptly broken by the engine room telegraphs as Beppo began to manoeuvre the ship back into station. By then, the division, having taken avoiding action, was separated by several miles and each ship was hastening to reform on the leader. But one, HMS *Gallant*, kept dropping astern, constantly turning in a series of circles.

'Steering gear jammed by near miss,' she signalled.

Being useless for our purpose, the leader ordered *Gallant* back to Dover. She was still visible astern, thrashing around like a wounded mastodon, when the great pall of smoke above Dunkirk was sighted. Shortly afterwards, we reached the buoy marking the end of the Dunkirk swept channel and, as we turned into it, huge columns of water straddled the division with an explosive crack. The dive bombers had so alerted us that we immediately assumed another aerial attack and all the guns, without waiting for orders, were promptly aimed skywards while their look-outs anxiously scanned the heavens.

'It's a shore battery', yelled the Gunner's Mate.

He was right, of course. The battery, presumably ranged on the mark buoy, was too far inland for us to detect its position or to retaliate, for fear of hitting our own troops. Neither could we zigzag owing to the narrowness of the channel, which confined us to a steady course under a hail of well aimed salvoes. It was an unnerving experience and we were thankful when a spur of the sandhills hid us from the battery's observation post. By then we were near the entrance to Dunkirk harbour which offered a most uninviting spectacle. To the westward, the water area was littered with the hulls of burnt out wrecks. Facing them was the mole which looked reasonably intact but, beyond it, several jetties and warehouses were nothing but great heaps of rubble. Behind these lay the town of Dunkirk, battered beyond recognition, while a great blanket of smoke, from burning oil installations, hung like a pall over the whole area. Every few seconds, a thick eddy kept billowing low across the harbour, reducing visibility to a few yards and stinging our nostrils with the stench of burning.

Any ships caught by bombers in the harbour would be sitting targets and our one desire was to get in and out as quickly as possible. But, first, we had to wait for our consorts to berth and the delay, short as it was, was quite long enough for that dreadful scene of desolation and destruction to become indelibly printed on our minds. It seemed an eternity before HMS *Grenade* ordered us to enter. As soon as she had done so, HMS *Jaguar* moved ahead at slow speed and was passing between the moles when a cross eddy caught her, sweeping her towards the wrecks. The water there was so shallow that the rudder was virtually useless and Beppo had to manoeuvre at full power to avoid the wrecks, then swing the ship towards her berth. The delay, again, was negligible but nerves were on edge and many an impatient glance was cast at the bridge while the HMS *Grenade's* berthing party relieved their feelings with some unprintable comments about Beppo's ship handling.

While we were securing HMS *Jaguar*, the Piermaster, Commander 'Beaky' Armstrong, strolled along the mole as casually as if he was taking the air on Brighton Pier, and gave some quiet instructions about the embarkation. Even before he had finished, the first troops began to trickle towards us; then more and more were pouring onto the mole until a solid phalanx was moving along it, not in recognisable formations but in a confused conglomeration of infantry, gunners, tank crews, engineers and base troops. Their leading files were approaching the destroyers when I joined Beppo on the bridge. As I reached him, an ominous throb in the southern skies dragged my eyes upwards and my heart missed a beat at the sight of about fifty Heinkel heavy bombers, weaving steadily northwards. Within seconds, every anti-aircraft gun around Dunkirk had opened fire, blotting out the noise of the bombers which were dipping successively into gentle glides towards their point of bomb release. Our own guns were below the level of the mole so we could do nothing but watch while the bombers were rapidly closing. Then the bombs began to fall in shallow water with a rippling 'whoomph', 'whoomph', 'whoomph' which reached progressively towards the mole, proving only too clearly that it was their target. The soldiers flung themselves to the ground as each stick fell closer, tossing up tall columns of blackened water which towered high in the air before plunging downwards in a welter of muck and spume. The extending line of bursts was creeping rapidly towards HMS *Jaguar* until a stick burst against the mole's outer face, flinging up a shower of stones and concrete.

We dropped to the deck and waited fearfully, scarcely daring to breathe, for the next stick would surely hit us. But instead of the shriek of bombs followed by a shattering explosion and an eruption of fire and smoke, we heard only the unbroken thud-thud of anti-aircraft guns which suddenly fell silent. Then one by one the pulsating throb of the retreating bombers became audible once more. Thick dust was rising from the new crater but, incredibly, that seemed to be the only damage caused by at least 200 bombs.

The soldiers picked themselves up and, without troubling to remove the new accretion of dust, resumed their weary plod towards the ships. But the sight of their white ensigns reminded them that Britain and, possibly, even home leave were only a few hours away; their glazed eyes staring fixedly out of dirty, grey faces glistened with a new borne hope while their shuffling feet unconsciously picked up a jauntiness which was almost recognizable as the rhythm of marching men. Having scrambled onboard, they sank, exhausted, to the deck, expecting no more than a space in which to rest their weary limbs and doubly grateful, therefore, for the tea and sandwiches we served. The embarkation was now proceeding so smoothly that we were hoping to clear the harbour before the next attack when the heavy clump of tired, plodding feet was drowned by gritty, raucous voices. A minute later, the root of the jetty was invaded by a noisy ill-disciplined rabble swaying drunkenly from side to side and carrying, instead of rifles, looted fishing rods, tennis rackets, wine and brandy. We watched glumly while they staggered along the mole and prayed that the military police directed them to another ship. But we were out of luck and their leaders were halted abreast HMS *Jaguar*.

'Is that mob to come onboard?' A petty officer demanded indignantly from the focs'le.

'Yes,' Beppo tersely replied. 'And get that drink off them.' Aside to me, he added, 'God help us if those are typical of the Army.'

Realising their bottles were forfeit, it was amazing how cunningly the newcomers concealed them while seamen were pushing and dragging them onboard. As soon as they had embarked, HMS *Jaguar*, her decks crammed with about 350 troops and one dog, backed stern out of the harbour. While turning, the loud hailers blared a warning for troops to lie on the decks until given permission to move. But the bottles were out again and a chorus of derisive cheers from the focs'le greeted this sound advice. Before leaving, the Piermaster had informed us that shore batteries were bombarding the western channel so we steamed east at slow speed to avoid swamping the armada of small boats, the numbers of which had greatly increased since the previous day, which were ferrying troops from the beaches to a curious collection of fighting ships, cross channel steamers, coasters, Dutch schuyts and trawlers. The sea was like a mill pond and the sun blazed out of a cloudless sky. For a change there was no air raid warning and we felt much happier now that we were clear of the claustrophobic harbour. I had just decided to confiscate the liquor when, without the least warning, the sky turned black with low flying bombers. Some were heading towards the mole; others towards HMS *Jaguar*.

'Full ahead together,' Beppo grunted into the voice pipe.

The ship was beginning to surge forward when two Junkers JU 88 bombers, their engines screaming like tormented spirits, swooped out of the sun. There was no time for controlled fire and Bruen, in the director, was still yelling 'barrage independent' down his telephone when their bombs exploded in our wake. Even before a solid wall of water had collapsed onto the quarterdeck other aircraft were pouncing from different directions. The pom-poms and oerlikons had already thudded into action and the heavier guns were pumping out high explosive, surrounding the ship with a curtain of steel. But the bombers hurtled through it, synchronising their attacks so accurately that we knew we were pitted against a first class team.

More bombs began to fall. The ship lurched violently off course; then a heavy explosion on the opposite side flung her back again. Poor old HMS *Jaguar* kept shuddering under an endless succession of attacks which seemed to go on and on for ever; one lost count of their number and brains were deadened by the shriek of engines, the crack of guns and the crump of bombs. Even so, the gun crews and control parties carried on automatically, keeping the guns firing doggedly, refusing to be swamped by the weight and viciousness of the attack. A cloud of black smoke enveloped the ship which was being so jolted by near misses.

Then, unbelievably, it was over. The towering columns of water suddenly subsided; the smoke drifted away more slowly but, between the rifts, we could see our assailants vanishing behind the sand dunes. One by one the guns fell silent and a strange, unnatural stillness descended. I could feel the ship losing speed and, for a few seconds, imagined Beppo had given an engine order. But when I looked behind the bridge, the wireless yards and aerials were hanging judas across the funnel and director, both of which were peppered like a colander. Bruen, his clothing dappled with blood, was climbing unsteadily out of his now useless director. But my mind still tried to reject the obvious even when I saw the bridge telegraphist lying across his shattered set and hawking a horrible, gasping, rasping sound through a jagged slit in his jugular. Then the safety valves lifted, drowning all other sounds with the vicious roar of escaping steam. We had been hit.

Scarcely daring to look, I glanced over the bridge casing at the focs'le; the sight which met my eyes propelled me down the bridge ladder. As I left the superstructure, I caught a brief glimpse of a mushroom of dense smoke – the funeral pyre of HMS *Grenade* which had been caught in the harbour – towering above the mole we had just left. Then I was in the charnel house of dead, dying and wounded. This was my first contact with death and, for some illogical reason, I had always expected dignity and serenity in man's final departure. But these men had died brutally and violently around the forward mounting; their blood and guts were dribbling into the scuppers; their shattered bodies and severed limbs lying amongst the scattered, pathetic remnants of their loot, which looked so utterly out of place amid the carnage. Even worse were the wounded. Their torn off limbs were indistinguishable from those of the dead but their mouths were capable of emitting animal like moans which were horrible to hear.

An ashen faced captain of the forward gun stumbled over the casualties of his own crew and waved his arm vaguely towards the focs'le.

'They tried to get below when the bombing started,' he mumbled. 'They wouldn't lie down.'

This was no time to ponder over the stupidity of other men and I hurried to the messdecks which were being swiftly but calmly evacuated. A quick inspection confirmed no direct hits but that every compartment had been holed by large, jagged lumps of metal; shivers of daylight were filtering through the gashes, augmenting the dim secondary lighting – now our only source of light – to spotlight fractured pipes, severed cables and shattered basins. The decks were littered with clothing, food, broken lockers and smashed crockery over which a dirty scum of oil and water was sloshing wearily from side to side. The atmosphere was hot and airless and the smell of blood tainted the messdecks where seamen and soldiers were lying in the ugly, ungainly attitudes of death. The whole hull was shuddering as steam, our precious life blood, roared into space.

The tough reliable figure of the Chief Bosun's Mate, who was in charge below, emerged out of the gloom. 'Everything's under control,' he growled. 'There was a bit of panic on the watchkeeper's messdeck but a guards' sergeant soon settled that'.'

'What did he do?' I automatically asked.

The petty officer laughed grimly. 'Threatened to shoot any man who stood up without orders. And he meant it.'

The damage control parties were doing everything possible – plugging holes near the waterline or stuffing them with hammocks, replacing electric cables, patching or isolating leaking pipes – so I moved on to the stokers' messdeck. Its only occupant was a motionless, crouching soldier, staring fixedly at the deck, as if he was praying.

'On deck, soldier,' I called.

He took no notice. I shouted again, louder this time, but he still remained in his curious, unnatural posture and, going closer, I spotted something sticking out of his back. In the uncertain light, it looked remarkably like the point of a bayonet.

Before I could investigate, I saw, through a great, circular hole, another destroyer coming alongside so I returned to the upper deck. The pale, shaken troops were now mustering under their own officers and non-commissioned officers: the wounded were being helped or carried to the waist. Lying beneath the bridge was a moaning, shuddering pioneer with a bloody tourniquet covering the shattered stump of his thigh. One of the first aid men was giving him a shot of morphia after which I helped to carry the poor fellow from the focs'le. He was a dreadful sight, covered in blood from head to toe which made him look less human than some victim of a slaughter house. I thought, at first, that the blood was flowing entirely from his leg but, on laying him down, I noticed his neck was pierced by a small, round hole which only a small calibre bullet could have made.

The first aid man pointed at it accusingly and growled, 'One of his mates did that. Tried to put 'im out of 'is misery.'

The troops and about fifty wounded were transferred as quickly as possible to the other destroyer's already overcrowded decks, leaving

HMS *Jaguar* alone with her own company and too many silent, motionless figures. While the destroyer was casting off, the deadening roar of our steam began to diminish and finally died away in a choking gurgle, leaving an eerie silence brooding over the ship – which was lying in the water like a waterlogged tree trunk. She had no power, the control system was completely out of action and the heavy guns could only be moved by hand, a method which was far too slow to provide even the minimum protection in the event of another attack.

I took another turn round the upper deck. The gun crews were replenishing ammunition lockers, replacing defective parts and preparing some sort of defence by loading the guns into the sun, the most likely direction for an attack. In contrast, the torpedo-men were immobilising their armament. The depth charge primers had already been removed and, while I was passing, the torpedoes were jettisoned. They could not be fired to seaward, owing to offshore shipping, so the Gunner was firing them into the shallows where they exploded in a succession of terrific 'bangs', much to the consternation of troops waiting higher up the beach. I noticed for the first time, and without the least emotion, that the Gunner was also wounded.

I returned to the messdecks and, almost immediately, the ship trembled under the opening salvoes of a continuous barrage. The repair parties dropped to the deck, gazing blankly into space until the close range weapons chattered into action. For all they knew, the ship was about to become the target of another concentrated attack. Then the ship shuddered from a more distant explosion and shock waves slammed against the hull. We began to count the slowly moving seconds, waiting for the next stick to fall. But, to our relief, the firing dwindled away and the hands, grinning sheepishly at each other, picked themselves up one by one and carried on with their work in a silence. Most of the holes had now been plugged or patched and the only natural lighting was filtering down hatchways or ammunition chutes, leaving the messdecks in a ghostly twilight in which men looked grossly distorted. The atmosphere was hotter and stuffier then ever and the sickly stench of blood lingered everywhere.

As I re-emerged into the sunlight, the barrage suddenly recommenced. Even above the thunder of the guns, a vicious whistle, like an express train leaving a tunnel, was clearly audible and, a moment later, the hull bucked as another stick exploded alongside.

'What the hell's the RAF doing?', a seaman snarled.

Not a single friendly aircraft had been sighted throughout that long, hot, horrible day but, even so, this grumble would have died away had it not been for a news bulletin picked up on a portable radio. This gave a laudatory account of fighter and bomber operations over Flanders but scarcely mentioned the naval evacuation. As it ended, a growl of anger rumbled round the ship, sparking off a bitter complaint which was to be repeated frequently in the years ahead by many more ships. Later, these feelings were exacerbated by the RAF's apparent determination to hog the limelight at the expense of other services. But, at Dunkirk, the RAF was conducting a whole series of operations far from their bases and criticism was doing them scant justice. Nevertheless, it was quite impossible to persuade men who were not only mourning their own dead but had seen other ships being hit and set ablaze, that their predicament would be even worse if not for these unseen operations. They simply did not believe it. Like justice, air support had to be seen to be believed.

Bruen was squatting against the superstructure. His face was as white as chalk, its pallor being heightened by two feverish red blotches on his cheeks. He looked as it he was suffering from shock.

'What are you doing here?' I exclaimed in surprise. 'You should've left with the wounded.'

Bruen summoned a weak smile. 'I thought I might be of some use.' I looked at the idle gun crews and torpedo-men and laughed without mirth. 'Not many are doing anything useful at the moment. You'd better rest in the wardroom.'

'I can't,' he mumbled, 'There's a drunk down there.'

Angrily, I hurried to the wardroom. Lying beneath the table was one of our elderly pensioners and, in the dim light, Bruen's diagnosis seemed not uncharitable. I dropped to my knees, intending to shake him, and felt something damp soaking my trousers. Instinctively feeling it, I was horrified to find my fingers covered with a red, sticky mess. It was blood. I examined the motionless body more closely and immediately saw how wrong we had been. The poor fellow, mortally wounded, had obviously crawled to the wardroom first aid post only to find its team has left to help the wounded on deck. I had seen about seventy casualties that afternoon but that man's death, alone and untended, upset me far more than any other; I suddenly felt bitterly angry with the 'drunks' whose behaviour had conditioned my mind to accept such an unjust accusation without question.

The sun was beating down mercilessly on our steel box. In the stifling heat of the engine and boiler rooms, 'Baldy' Rothwell, the Chief Engineroom Officer, his artificers and stokers were struggling to isolate the steam pipe which had caused our loss of steam. They, at least, had work to occupy their minds whereas those on deck had nothing but their thoughts. Inevitably mine kept reverting to our late passengers and the more I thought about them, the less I felt like making allowances; they were drunken hooligans, imagination had unhesitatingly converted all of them into 'drunks' who, by now, were probably in England, boasting of their experiences. At the time, I had paid little attention to the first aid rating's remark about the pioneer's wound but, on reflection, I could recall no other hole in the hull or upperworks which small arms fire could have caused. His accusation, therefore, had some credibility. The wounded pioneer was no longer onboard but the soldier who I believed had impaled himself, like Saul, on his own bayonet could, at least, be examined and I hurried to his messdeck, stumbling over discarded rifles and kitbags, the flotsam of a hurried departure. But, by then, his body had been removed and laid out decently on deck; when I saw the twenty-five still, silent figures, each covered by a strip of bloodstained canvas, my bitterness evaporated. I was alive and should be thanking God instead of disturbing the dead. An enquiry might have established that his death had been caused by an unusually shaped splinter which, in the uncertain light, had looked like a bayonet. On the other hand, it might have confirmed that he had killed himself and that, if publicised, would achieve nothing except bring unnecessary distress to his family. It would be better, by far, to leave the poor fellow in peace.

The minutes ticked imperceptibly away. From time to time single bombers swooped out of the heavens to be greeted by a ragged defence but we were spared another mass attack, thank God. After each raid, the gun crews could occupy themselves for a few minutes by replenishing their spent ammunition before resuming their long, endless wait for the next attack. But, at long last, the sun sank slowly into the sea and, for a time, a ribbon of red sky glowed along the western horizon, as if the countryside behind Dunkirk was aflame. By then, we were reconciled to a night in an E-boat area but, shortly after sunset, thick, black smoke began to rise sluggishly from the funnel, forming a seamark which must have been visible for miles. Audibly cursing Baldy and his team, look-outs anxiously scanned the slowly darkening sky and a long, nerve wracking period followed, as day seemed so reluctant to surrender to the night. But night eventually fell and the guns were prepared to repel E-boats which had already been reported and were, in fact, to gather a rich harvest that night. In spite of that, we were feeling much more optimistic now that the ship was returning to life. First the dynamos began to hum; then power returned to the gun mountings and, finally Baldy clambered wearily out of the stifling boiler room and filled his burning lungs with cool, clean air before reporting that the main engines were ready. Beppo immediately ordered 'obey telegraphs' and a ragged cheer rippled round the ship when the turbines started to revolve. Every thud of the propellers carried us nearer home and, sometime during the middle watch, HMS *Jaguar* limped painfully into Dover harbour and disembarked her dead.

Of the four fleet destroyers which had left Dover in company, only one had returned with troops. One, HMS *Grenade* had been sunk and the other three more or less seriously damaged. HMS *Jaguar* was suffering from fractures to oil pipes, water mains, soil pipes, hydraulic mains, urinals and lavatory bowls, the contents of which were oozing into her messdecks and storerooms causing her to stink like an Augean stable. In spite of the efforts of her repair parties, her hull and upperworks were still punctured by several hundred holes, some big enough to put an arm through, and those near the water line had to be properly patched before she could return to Immingham for full repairs. So, while the hard pressed dockyard employees were making the ship watertight, her company cleaned up the messdecks, sorted out the equipment left by the army and repaired the damage to their own clothes and hammocks. Temporary repairs took several days, during which an endless procession of ships, many showing signs of damage, entered harbour and discharged their weary troops. It was a depressing sight but good for us. If we had gone at once our opinion of the British army would have been tainted for ever by those miserable men who, even without the suspicion of suicides and wounds deliberately inflicted, had convinced us that we knew why the British Expeditionary Force had failed where their fathers, twenty-five years earlier, had succeeded. Every service contains a few black sheep which it can absorb without detriment to the whole. We had met some of those people who, in all probability, would have been forgotten had we disembarked them without being damaged. But we had not.

We had lost too many shipmates – discharged dead in cold, unsentimental naval terms – while drunken stragglers had escaped scot free. This had coloured our views of the far greater number of orderly, well behaved troops onboard and of the entire British army. Consequently our morale benefited from our sojourn in Dover, where we witnessed thousands of battle-weary but disciplined troops landing in perfect order and thereby gained a truer picture of the British army in adversity. These men would fight honourably if Hitler invaded Britain, which every amateur strategist was already forecasting would be his next target.

Our unsuccessful attempt at Dunkirk had persuaded the Admiralty that the fleet destroyers were too valuable to risk and, in due course, the survivors were withdrawn, those damaged heading for various dockyards. Back in Immingham, HMS *Jaguar* was immediately docked and three days leave given to each watch. After an endless wait for a free line, I contacted Jean and asked her to join me at my parents' house in Staffordshire. She gladly accepted but met with considerable opposition from her mother who was under the mistaken impression that we were intending to spend an immoral weekend together. It was wonderful to see Jean again and we quickly became engaged. That same afternoon Italy declared war but not even that miserable event could mar our happiness.

The three days passed all too quickly and I returned to Immingham, wondering if and when we would meet again, by a succession of incredibly slow cross-country trains. The initial preparations for repelling an invasion were already visible. Sign posts and station name boards were coming down. Railway officials were reluctant to announce the names of their stations and it was difficult to discover when to change trains. It was like travelling through a strange and slightly hostile country.

There were other and more important changes too. The J and K class destroyers had been thrown into a hat, so to speak, and half had already left for the Mediterranean while the remainder, based on the Humber under Lord Louis Mountbatten, were to form one of the four anti-invasion flotillas. Mountbatten drove us hard but he was always fair; his own ship, HMS *Kelly*, had suffered battle damage often enough for him to understand the traumatic experience, as a result of which he was always most tolerant with HMS *Jaguar*.

The flotilla raised steam each night in readiness to frustrate any raids on east coast shipping. But, if convoys were at sea, which was a nightly occurrence in that area, it sailed to escort them between Flamborough Head and Cromer or vice versa. It was a frustrating task. Thanks to the narrowness of the swept channel, convoys had to proceed more or less in single line and were frequently stretched over more than twenty miles of channel. In such conditions, ships in one section were often unaware of an attack on another. Air raids on these convoys were frequent but, by chance HMS *Jaguar*, although in constant use as an escort, was seldom directly involved: her worst experience was a night bombing attack. Being bombed by an unseen enemy which, presumably, could see its target, was not a pleasant experience.

Very little time was spent in harbour and much of that time had to be devoted to giving my ten cents worth of long distance advice to Jean about our wedding. This would have to take place at a date which would remain unknown until only a day or two beforehand, providing, of course, leave was granted. HMS *Jaguar's* Australian Doctor, 'Slasher' Simpson, agreed to be my best man but such uncertainty was most unsatisfactory for Jean and her mother, who had complete responsibility for other arrangements, such as the wedding dress, cake, champagne and other non-perishables. The church, parson and invitations would have to wait for a more definite date.

Shortly after our return to Immingham, the flotilla was transferred to Plymouth to counter the German destroyers now operating in the Western Channel. We made a daylight passage through the Straits of Dover, an area dominated by shore batteries and in which the enemy's air power had been recently flung against coastal shipping. We were expecting anything to happen. The sky above was full of vapour trails from British and German fighters but, unknown to us, the enemy had just switched to inland targets and we got through without firing a single shot. Every beat of the propellers was taking us away from the narrow, mine infested channels of the east coast and, as we approached the west country, the HMS *Jaguar's* manning district, one could feel the spirits of the ship's company rising. Although our overall strategy was defensive, we guessed our tactical role would be offensive and, in the more open approaches to the Channel, a clash with the enemy destroyers inevitable. Moreover, the enemy would be near their families and, although they would see little of them, they would at least be fighting on home ground.

We were involved immediately in an offensive operation. Apart from its military value, it was also to be a morale boosting affair and the British press was invited to send reporters, who sat in at the briefing at which it was disclosed that the battleship HMS *Revenge* and our 7th Flotilla was to bombard Cherbourg.

The bombarding force sailed eastward in the early evening. Off Portland Bill the ships turned south, arriving off Cherbourg during the middle watch. HMS *Revenge's* opening salvoes were greeted by a wonderful aerial pyrotechnic display – searchlights, flares, tracers and shell bursts. The garrison had obviously mistaken shells for bombs and several minutes elapsed before the coastal batteries opened fire to seaward. They soon found the range and several eleven-inch shells plunged close to the destroyers, which had gone inshore to bring the harbour area within range of their main armament. As soon as the bombardment was completed, the force steamed northward at HMS *Revenge's* best speed, which seemed incredibly slow. Meanwhile gigantic splashes towered amongst the ships and overs shrieked overhead like express trains.

After that, we turned to night sweeps along the French coast, hoping to intercept invasion barges moving to their embarkation ports. To our surprise, we found no coastal movement whatsoever. Later, we learnt that the Germans had postponed their intention to invade and, as a consequence, had stopped the transfer of barges to the more westerly ports at which bigger ships would be needed in the uncertain Autumn weather.

One Saturday in mid-October, HMS *Jaguar* came into port to clean boilers allowing me a small window of leave. It was not the most opportune occasion for a wedding. Jean and I were at opposite ends of the country and most of the four days leave would be occupied in travelling. But any amateur strategist could foresee that the flotilla might soon join their consorts in the Mediterranean. If we were to be married it had to be now. So, as soon as the ship was secured, I rushed to the Yacht Club to put through a telephone call. But my enthusiasm and exuberance was dampened by wartime delays and it was not until after midnight, six hours later, that a line to Dundee was free.

'How about getting married on Monday?' I asked Jean.

Jean immediately agreed and turned me over to her mother who proceeded to point out the practical difficulties of fixing a wedding in less than forty hours, with a Sunday intervening. However, having made her point, she cheerfully accepted the fact that she was about to gain a son-in-law and I hurried back to the ship. Having alerted Slasher, I retired to bed, satisfied with a job well and truly done.

It was a miserable journey. The train was crowded and crawled slowly through Devon and Somerset, stopping at every station. There was no restaurant car and Slasher soon showed the symptoms of a dangerous complaint – thirst.

'You'll get a drink in Bristol,' I consoled him. 'It'll be opening time when we get there.'

'You'll be lucky,' remarked one of Job's comforters seated opposite. 'It's Sunday. Pubs don't open until seven o'clock.'

The train reached Bristol at half-past six and pulled out again at five to seven. Slasher was almost weeping with frustration at being so near, yet so far from a drink.

Half an hour later, the train pulled into a dreary, unnamed ill- lit station. Slasher was on the platform before the train had stopped and was racing towards the buffet. It was shut!

'What time does this bloody place open?' he yelled.

'It don't, mate,' a voice called out of the darkness. 'You're in Wales. Pubs don't open Sundays.'

Slasher climbed back onboard and the train crawled on, eventually swinging north towards Shrewsbury. But at quarter to ten the train was still in open countryside: Slasher's despair was pitiful to behold, as each minute ticked by towards ten o'clock closing time. The next few minutes seemed endless but at one minute to ten the train chugged slowly into Shrewsbury. We were both out as soon as our coach reached a platform. No buffet – it was on another platform. Pushing through the passengers and piles of mail, we raced over the footbridge and hurled ourselves at the dim but welcoming sign. As we reached it, the light suddenly went out and the door was slammed in our faces. We were too late!

'This is the first time in seven years I've spent a teetotal day,' Slasher grumbled. 'Never again ask me to be your best man.'

I assured him that would be unnecessary and led him disconsolately back to our carriage.

When a wintry dawn began to filter through the windows, I took a stroll along the crowded corridors. Near the rear, I thought I heard a familiar voice and, sure enough, it was my mother upbraiding the guard for having locked a communicating door and complaining bitterly that Hitler had deliberately laid on a special raid to inconvenience her. Nevertheless, it was a magnificent effort to undertake an uncomfortable journey at such short notice and I was glad to see her.

At Perth we transferred to a local train which reached Dundee hours after the scheduled connection with the London express. Jean was at the station, having met every connection for the past few hours. By then, she was almost frantic with worry and the prospects of a wedding were hourly growing bleaker. However, gay Lochinvar had come out of the west and the best man at last did his duty by providing a bottle of champagne.

We were married in Dundee Cathedral on 14 October 1940, a gloomy winter's afternoon. Following the ceremony was a brief reception and then we were back at the station to begin a most unusual honeymoon. Its first night was spent in a station hotel at Edinburgh; the second at Crewe and the third in an air raid shelter beneath Plymouth Station. I had barely time to install Jean with an aunt, who shared her rations with an elderly terrier, before it was back to sea.

We returned to our old routine of abortive sweeps along the French coast. It was a trying time for those with families in Devonport or Plymouth because the blitz had started. From seaward, anti-aircraft fire and fires blazing in the target area were clearly visible so those with families naturally wanted assurance that they were safe. Apart from this worry, life was as hard as ever. We were still keeping watch and the watchkeeping officers seldom saw their cabins. Off duty, they snatched an hour or two's sleep on the wardroom settee or in one of the armchairs.

Then, towards the end of 1940, I was unexpectedly appointed to take command of HMS *Eridge*, one of the new Hunt class escort destroyers. She was building on the Tyne but, for all I knew, she might already be preparing for sea so I packed my kit in readiness to jump ashore as soon as we returned to Plymouth. I said my farewells onboard before entering harbour and then, as soon as the ship was secured, nipped over to the HMS *Javelin* to bid farewell to Mountbatten.

'I know the master of the Eridge hunt,' were his parting words. 'Write to him and give him my regards. He'll probably send you a mask or a brush.'

Farewells said, a feeling of profound regret at leaving such a fine ship swept over me. It was to be another year before I saw her again. Most of my old ship mates were still onboard but, soon afterwards, Beppo was tragically killed by friendly gunfire during a dusk torpedo bombing attack on the Mediterranean Fleet. The ship herself only outlived her first captain by a few months and, as in life, was being incorrectly employed at her death. She was sunk on the same day as the Battle of Sirte. But, instead of being with the main fleet on that heroic occasion, she was escorting a Tobruk convoy when a submarine's torpedo hit and sent her to the bottom with the majority of her ship's company.

Having rejoined Jean we made a tedious cross-country journey to Newcastle where I was surprised to learn that HMS *Eridge* would not be completed before the New Year. So Jean and I were given an unexpected gift of several weeks together in a city which, so far, had suffered only an occasional minor air raid. The revolving doors of the Station Hotel, spinning like a gigantic top from a bomb blast, were considered serious enough to provide the staff with a subject for conversation for weeks. Newcastle seemed determined to be normal. Its theatres, cinemas and restaurants were always full, in stark contrast to those in poor, battered Plymouth. We would obviously enjoy our welcome bonus.

But it was not all play and no work in Newcastle. I spent several hours each day at Swan Hunter's shipyard where a small team of officers and senior ratings were performing the same role as their HMS *Jaguar* counterparts at Denny's. The officers were the First Lieutenant, a serious minded young officer and two warrant officers, the Chief Engineer, Mr V Lee, and the Gunner, Mr W Ward. The two warrant officers were nearer forty than thirty: the Gunner was well built, hale and hearty and the Chief was a quiet, unassuming, rather frail man who looked older than his age. He was supposedly suffering from stomach trouble but, as he never complained, not even the Doctor could confirm it.

In January 1941, the nominal lists were received and the First Lieutenant, the Gunner's Mate, Petty Officer F.L. Blandford, and the Coxswain, Petty Officer Oake, were happily engaged in planning the watch and quarter bills. The Coxswain, a tall man, was so slim that, in the months ahead defaulters were to grumble that he could hide behind a funnel guy to detect their misdemeanours. The Chief and his Chief Engineroom Artificer, were similarly engaged with their own department.

By the New Year HMS *Eridge* had grown to look like a warship which suddenly became alive with the arrival of her 170 officers and ratings. The latter were mostly 'hostilities only' with a leavening of regulars and, as they dumped their kit onboard, in many cases with obvious trepidation, it was apparent that most were joining their first ship. She was also my first command and I was sufficiently apprehensive about my own ability to feel sorry for these raw youngsters whose lives were being entrusted to an untried captain.

Our remaining officers consisted of the Surgeon Lieutenant, Lee Abbott, the Doctor, and two sub-lieutenants. Sub-Lieutenant W. McCall, a Royal Navy Volunteer Reserve officer had just completed a short gunnery course so he was the obvious choice for gun control officer. That left navigation, anti-submarine warfare and fighter direction for Sub Lieutenant Nisbet Glen, a regular officer, now known as the Pilot. All these duties could be controlled from the bridge but it was a heavy responsibility for young, inexperienced shoulders to bear though shortage of officers left no choice. I was also shocked to learn that, out of four seamen officers, only one had a seagoing-watchkeeping certificate. We were all worried by our inexperience and ability to cope. No one could help me but ten years in destroyers and similar ships had given me enough practical experience with which to train and encourage others. Unfortunately patience was not one of my virtues. In the past this had not been too obvious but now, aggravated by my own self doubts and the knowledge that the buck stopped with me, control might be far more difficult.

We eventually bade farewell to the Tyne and spent a month working up in Scapa's usual appalling weather. We then joined a North Atlantic escort group based at Londonderry, but our time in the North Atlantic coincided with a quiet period. Convoys were sometimes bombed by long range aircraft and submarines were often reported in the vicinity, though no attacks developed. But even these calm conditions tested my patience, especially with those reacting slowly or with uncertainty. The main sufferers were those who spent most of their time on the bridge – the Pilot, and Brewer, the Yeoman of Signals. Brewer was a toughened individual but the Pilot was a quiet, sensitive lover of classical music and was clearly upset by my attitude. That only seemed to goad me.

We suffered one loss. The First Lieutenant was so sea sick that he was virtually useless at sea. We could not afford a passenger so he had to go. Lieutenant George Evans, his relief, soon proved to be a cheerful, reliable character with an explosive streak of aggression. He was considerate enough to warn potential targets of his temper by flicking out the tip of his tongue, like a fly catcher devouring its victim. Evans' arrival was preceded by that of the inevitable dog and cat. Pets played an important part in life onboard ship. They reminded men, confined in a tough, male world, of their family and provided an outlet for the affections of animal lovers. Scruffy, the non-descript dog, appeared from nowhere and rapidly became one of the ship's institutions, sleeping in his own little hammock and having his personal model lamp post. He was expected to land with any libertyman who required his company and his temporary hosts were mortally offended if Scruffy refused to drink his quota of beer.

The cat had merely strolled onboard because she liked the look of the ship. Having inspected every compartment, she rightly decided that my cabin was the most comfortable and would retire there whenever she needed a rest from her human friends. I enjoyed her company until she began to take it for granted that she had precedence over my bunk and chairs. Her disillusionment evoked outrage but she was far too fond of comfort to be sufficiently strong minded to surrender her squatter's rights. Thenceforth peaceful coexistence was frequently marred by her forcible eviction when the number of chairs was insufficient to accommodate both human beings and a cat.

In May 1941 HMS *Eridge* sailed for the Clyde, where she joined three other 'Hunts' – HMS *Farndale*, HMS *Avonvale* and HMS *Heythrop*, under Commander 'Shorty' Carlill, to operate initially from Gibraltar and then Alexandria. At the last moment, HMS *Heythrop* was delayed but the others sailed as planned. The ship's company disliked leaving home waters, even though they seldom saw their families, and were even more despondent when their first fleeting visits to Gibraltar proved that wartime conditions in the overcrowded fortress were different to those described by the regulars onboard. Moreover, the transfer brought no relief from North Atlantic convoys and only twice during the next six weeks did the three ships meet in Gibraltar. The second of these meetings occurred just before joining a Malta bound convoy, Operation SUBSTANCE. For security reasons, the ship's company could not be briefed about the convoy before sailing and the cancellation of an eagerly awaited self maintenance period was their first intimation that something was brewing.

CHAPTER THREE

Slow Boat to Gib

A t daylight, Sunday, 21 July 1941, the remnants of the night were still lingering amongst the pens and jetties. In this uncertain light, every berth in the long, narrow harbour, lying in the shelter of the mighty rock, seemed occupied by heavy ships and destroyers, all of which were involved in the familiar activities of a fleet preparing for sea. At the South Mole, the battlecruiser HMS *Renown's* seaboat was being hoisted at the run, its falls creaking through wooden blocks until halted by a stentorian 'high enough'. In the centre of the harbour, the cruiser HMS *Hermione* was already riding by a slip rope and her cable was clanking slowly through the hawse pipe. Beyond her, the pens were too indistinct to distinguish individual destroyers but each time one of them tested her sirens, the rock flung back a high pitched, agitated, whimper.

HMS *Eridge* was leading the fleet and would have to pass between two columns of heavy ships, all of which would be pointing or turning towards the entrance in readiness for their own timed departures. Consequently, the area of clear water would be diminishing rapidly so delay on our part would not only complicate our own movement but might seriously impede these bigger vessels. A quick getaway was imperative.

Officers, signalmen and look-outs were waiting, motionless and silent on HMS *Eridge's* open compass platform. Evans stood, slightly apart, alongside the director control tower whence he could be seen and heard by the seamen handling the berthing wires. A flag signal fluttered slowly to HMS *Renown's* yardarm and the little group stirred, as if waking from a doze. Brewer focused his binoculars and, without even checking the signal manual, called out, 'Proceed in execution of previous orders. Executive to follow.'

I nodded and called over my shoulder, 'Ring on main engines. Obey telegraphs.'

The Pilot repeated the order down the voice pipe. In response, telegraphs whirred in the wheelhouse, bells clanged indistinctly in the bowels of the ship and were answered, a moment later, by a loud, impatient jangle below the compass platform.

'Main engines rung on, sir,' the Coxswain's sing song voice floated up the pipe.

Silence again descended on the compass platform and, for the third or fourth time, I mentally rehearsed our imminent move from our berth at the southern end of the dockyard to the open sea.

'Executive signal, sir,' Brewer's bellow again shattered the silence.

'Let go forward, let go aft, hold on to the springs, slow astern starboard.'

The focs'le and quarterdeck men hauled in the berthing wires which slapped briefly against the hull. The turbine began to revolve with a high pitched whine; its propeller gripped the water and the ship dropped back on to the spring, straining against it until her bows swung away from the jetty, as if glad to do so.

'Let go spring, half ahead port.'

The ship shuddered and began to turn smoothly towards the centre of the harbour. At that moment, the fog which had been threatening since first light, decided to have one final fling before the rays of the still unseen sun became too hot and rolled relentlessly across the harbour, hiding one ship from another. The Pilot was bent over the chart table.

'Don't dither, man,' I called impatiently. 'Fix the ship while you can still see and start a stop watch.'

Even while speaking I was cursing myself for being so quick tempered. I tried to excuse myself by arguing that manoeuvring in a fog bound anchorage is such a tricky business that even a man with the patience of Job would be irritated by anyone reacting so slowly to a rapidly worsening situation. It was a feeble excuse and I knew it. That made me even more angry with myself but I vented it on the Pilot, constantly nagging him about his timekeeping while the bows cut slowly through the fog. We felt, rather than saw, the vast bulk of HMS *Hermione* closing the starboard bow. We heard the hum of her dynamos and the steady flow of circulating water until both were briefly silenced by the clang of her telegraphs high overhead and the mounting whine of her turbines. On the opposite side a flurry of water, flowing towards the centre of the harbour, indicated that the aircraft carrier HMS *Ark Royal* was already swinging clear of the South Mole. Ahead of us, the sternwards movement of a destroyer backing out of the pens was being marked by impatient blasts on her siren, which grew rapidly closer until we momentarily expected to sight her stern parting the fog ahead.

The Pilot, stopwatch in hand, announced that it was time to turn. I swung the ship towards the entrance, praying that he was right or that no unexpected current had delayed our progress, and waited anxiously until an excited voice shouted from the murk covering the focs'le, 'Breakwater light fine off the port bow, sir.'

The ship was edged further to starboard until a deeper, more reassuring voice, hailed, 'Detached mole to starboard, sir,' and then steadied on a course. Soon afterwards, a gentle, unhurried pitch told us that she was moving into the open sea at precisely the time ordered. I caught the Pilot's eye and grinned apologetically at him.

HMS *Eridge*, moving slowly southward, had the sea, at first, to herself except for some distant sirens on the starboard bow where our convoy was feeling its way through the Straits. But as more ships cleared the harbour, spread out and began creeping ahead towards their approximate positions, the fog became so filled with the wail of sirens that HMS *Eridge* seemed hemmed in by protesting monsters. The convoy's signals, also, were growing more distinct and it was now possible to distinguish the deeper note of the merchant ships from the higher pitched blasts of their escorts. Consequently, it was reasonable to assume that Vice Admiral Sir James Somerville would give the convoy plenty of searoom by turning Gibraltar Force H to the eastward as soon as it had cleared Europa Point. It was also quite evident, from the tone of her siren, that HMS *Ark Royal* was close to our starboard beam and would be swinging towards us once the turn commenced. I tried to edge to port but a long wail, like a road hog's impatient demonstration, warned that another destroyer was close abaft our port beam, holding us against the heavy unit. The manoeuvring wave chattered briefly and unintelligibly; then faded away. The operator swore impatiently and fiddled with his controls. HMS *Ark Royal's* siren screamed again but thanks to the vagaries of sound in fog, it was impossible to estimate her exact position. The bridge team stared to starboard trying to see through the fog and waiting anxiously for the next blast which definitely sounded closer. I told myself not to imagine things; that it would be absurd to take action until convinced that our heavier neighbour was closing. Besides, her sound signal would be repeated in a couple of minutes; I tried to look unconcerned while the seconds were ticking away so slowly that the interval seemed endless. But when the siren wailed again, it was still impossible to guess its distance or direction.

The radar operator's bell tinkled. 'Ship crossing ahead from starboard to port,' he called. 'Range 1,000 yards.'

'Have you received that signal?' Petty Officer Godfrey demanded impatiently from the wireless office.

'Not on the manoeuvring wave,' Brewer retorted.

'The Admiral's ordered a turn to 090 degrees,' the unseen voice urgently called. 'The executive's been made.'

I swore to myself. The other ships had obviously commenced the turn and a brief mental picture of the heavy carrier swinging rapidly towards us seemed so vivid that, instinctively, I called to the wheelhouse, 'Full ahead together, steady as you go.'

A column of thick, black smoke erupted briefly from the single funnel. The ship trembled slightly, like an animal poised to pounce, and then surged into full power. A huge, menacing presence, rather than an identifiable shape, slipped down our starboard side and dropped astern. Seconds later the siren howled again, dead in our wake, where HMS *Eridge* would have been had she not accelerated.

The hands were being piped to defence stations. That meant that half the ship's company would be at action stations while the other half rested. By then the fog had vanished as quickly as it had come. For a time it had held its own against the sun. But the latter's rays gradually sucked up more and more of the cloying moisture until the fog suddenly gave up the unequal struggle and lifted, like a theatre's curtain. There, against a back drop of North African mountains, lay the main group of the convoy. Force H at once began to close and, for the next thirty minutes, ships were breaking formation and criss-crossing each other's tracks to reach their final screening positions. HMS *Eridge* was stationed on the port bow of the convoy and, when she was in station, I spoke to the ship's company over the public address system.

'Malta is desperately short of supplies and the admiral has ordered that the convoy must get through whatever the opposition,' I told them. 'I know that every man onboard will do his best to ensure the success of the operation.'

'I'm sorry you've been kept in the dark and our few days in harbour have been postponed. The first, of course, was a security measure applicable to all ships while the postponement will be no more than temporary, after which you will enjoy your run ashore all the better for the knowledge of a job well done.'

'For the benefit of those below, HMS *Eridge* is on a semi-circular anti-submarine screen of some twenty destroyers. The convoy of six large merchant ships from the peacetime Australian and South American trade routes is three miles inside the screen. Stationed around the convoy is an anti-aircraft screen of the battleship HMS *Nelson* and cruisers HMS *Edinburgh*, HMS *Manchester*, HMS *Arethusa* and HMS *Manxman*. Some miles astern is the battle cruiser HMS *Renown*, flying the flag of Vice Admiral Sir James Somerville who is in overall command. HMS *Ark Royal* and the cruiser HMS *Hermione* are acting independently to allow the carrier to operate her aircraft without hindrance.'

'When we reach the Sicilian Narrows, HMS *Nelson* and some destroyers will join HMS *Renown's* group which will proceed to a position from which HMS *Ark Royal's* aircraft can attack Italian bomber bases. The force making the final dash to Malta will be commanded by Rear Admiral Syfret, flying his flag in HMS *Edinburgh*. HMS *Eridge* is part of that force.'

'Good luck to you all.'

During the first dog watch, Leading Cook Hardy, a keep fit fanatic of fine physique, carried his weights to the focs'le where he proceeded to give the bridge watchkeepers and the gun crew at the forward mounting a demonstration of weight lifting. He looked quite professional but that did not silence some gratuitous advice from A gun's crew. Hardy was not amused. The less active of those off-watch were resting in the warm sunshine, some dozing, some reading but mostly in small, animated groups. Since commissioning, the weather had been our worst enemy and men were bored with so much activity bringing so little reward. But now the ship was engaged in something different with an objective understood by everyone. The supply of Malta had always aroused a fierce enemy reaction and the groups were eagerly discussing their own involvement in the fighting ahead.

Day slowly gave way to a dark moonless night. Sometimes the ship seemed to be entirely alone until a sliver of white foam from a bow wave warned of the presence of a nearby ship. The hours of darkness brought no relaxation to our routine but the darkened ship was now wrapped in a deeper silence, broken only when the gun crews carried out a practice run or, at more frequent intervals, when the lookouts or watch were relieved. I never left the compass platform at night, having learned by bitter experience the folly of using my cabin; the short ascent of the bridge ladders, no matter how dim their illumination, left one ill prepared for the darkened compass platform, besides those few seconds could be vital in an emergency. By resting in a sickbay chair, I could doze quite comfortably through the normal noises of the ship although anything unusual aroused me at once. Moreover, that indefinable grape vine which links men together without the need of speech told me that the ship's company appreciated their captain's constant presence on the bridge and that knowledge was ample reward for any extra discomfort.

That night and the following day, while the mountains of Morocco were giving way to the hills of Algeria, passed without incident. But the enemy was aware of the convoy and HMS *Ark Royal's* fighters were in frequent contact with shadowing enemy aircraft.

Such immunity could not be expected on the third day, still one sunrise from Malta, and the fleet closed up at action stations long before dawn. McCall, wondering how long he would have to remain in his cramped seat, clambered into the director, carried out a test run with the guns and then made himself as comfortable as possible to await daylight. The captains of the guns checked and rechecked their ready use ammunition and fuses. Leading Seaman Rayner, at the pom-pom, trained and elevated his weapon through its full limits and then examined the ammunition belts. Able Seamen Forbes and Stone tested their oerlikons in a similar manner. Damage control and repair parties were dispersed around the ship. Both boilers were connected and galley fires drawn. HMS *Eridge* was ready for action.

Now that the moment of decision was at hand many men, who had experienced only excited anticipation since leaving Gibraltar, were feeling a little apprehensive. HMS *Ark Royal*, several miles astern, had flown off her fighter patrols, one of which was circling high above the convoy. The sun was still below the horizon when this patrol hurtled eastward at full throttle. Seconds later a large number of torpedo bombers flipped above the horizon, split into two groups and rapidly closed the convoy from both bows. Instantly the screening destroyers adjusted their courses to bring to bear as many guns as possible and laid down a barrage, a ragged crescendo of gunfire swiftly merging into a continuous cacophony. Shell bursts, splashes and cordite fumes quickly blurred the horizon and partially obscured the bombers. One, just skimming the sea, burst out of the haze and flew between HMS *Eridge* and her neighbour. Rayner managed a short burst with the pom-pom. He could clearly see the pale, strained face of her gunner, a man with only seconds to live, as he swung his weapon and peppered the upperworks with a few ineffectual rounds. Then the bomber was through the screen and the battleship HMS *Nelson's* guns opened fire with a mighty crash. The aircraft staggered and a tongue of flame, leaping from the fuselage, swiftly expanded into a great ball of fire amid which the bomber suddenly disintegrated.

Adjacent destroyers had ceased firing and were manoeuvring back into their screening positions. Ships on the far side of the convoy were still heavily engaged but, in the murk, it was impossible to see if the attackers were the first or a following wave of torpedo bombers. Suddenly, a vivid flash was followed by a pillar of black smoke.

Brewer studied it through his binoculars and remarked almost casually, 'HMS *Manchester's* been hit.' Then his voice suddenly rose several octaves. 'High level bombers bearing green 130.'

Feeling the urgency in his voice, I glanced to starboard and nearly missed a heartbeat. About forty high level bombers, having synchronised their approach with the torpedo attack, were closing from supposedly neutral French Algeria, practically unopposed. The Pilot swivelled the bearing indicator towards this dangerous threat. But the four-inch guns had only added two rapid salvoes to a sky pock-marked by shell bursts, before their bombs began to burst in and amongst the convoy with a rippling 'whoomph', 'whoomph', 'whoomph' tossing up columns of black and white water which plunged downwards in a welter of muck and spume.

Another wave of bombers was swooping low towards the destroyer screen and one was flying directly towards HMS *Eridge*. There was no time for the four-inch to shift target but Rayner had spotted the new threat and the measured thud, thud, thud of his pom-pom was quickly joined by the higher pitched rattle of Able Seaman Stone's oerlikon. There was insufficient sea-room for full avoiding action but the helm was put hard over towards the bomber.

The ship was beginning to swing just as the bomber reached its release position. In the same instant the bomber was hit by a pom-pom shell. It lurched violently, causing its bombs to scream harmlessly overhead before exploding half a cable away, shock waves slamming into the hull with a mighty crack.

'There's a destroyer close to starboard,' the Pilot called.

'My God! We're on a collision course. Midships, stop both engines, full astern together,' I ordered sharply.

The ship trembled as the propellers gripped the water in the reverse direction and steadily reduced speed. Three short blasts were sounded but, to anxious onlookers, the speed reduction seemed not nearly fast enough as the destroyer, firing so furiously that our sound signal was probably not heard, shot across our bows barely half a ship's length ahead. As she passed, a seaman on her bridge gave a thumbs up sign.

'Stop both engines, half ahead together, wheel amidships,' I ordered.

The Coxswain repeated the order.

The ship was now picking up headway.

'Port 20, steady on course 090,' I called down the Coxswain's voice pipe.

'Port 20, steady on course 090,' the Coxswain repeated in a casual tone, as if the current events were an every day occurrence.

Gunfire gradually faded as the battle was transferred to the high heavens where vapour trails, the thud of cannon and rattle of machine guns were receding rapidly northwards. Just beyond the screen, a British fighter spiralled slowly downwards and pancaked on the calm sea. Further away, two streams of black smoke plummeted out of the high heavens and struck the sea with shattering explosions.

Meanwhile, the smog-like veil covering the convoy was dispersing. First one, then two, three, four, five, six supply ships steamed steadily into sight. The close anti-aircraft screen apart from HMS *Manchester*, was also intact. But, beyond the convoy, another cloud of black smoke was billowing heavenwards.

Brewer, who was watching it, suddenly exclaimed, 'There's a destroyer amongst that muck.'

At that moment, a current of wind parted the smoke to reveal a slim, grey hull lying low in the water, which was flowing freely through a huge crater where her quarterdeck had been. It was HMS *Fearless*.

The Admiral now ordered a reorganisation following the withdrawal of HMS *Manchester* and HMS *Fearless*. HMS *Hermione* was detached from HMS *Renown's* group to join the anti-aircraft screen in place of HMS *Manchester*, which was ordered to proceed to Gibraltar escorted by HMS *Avonvale*. Another ship could not be spared for the seriously damaged, but less important, HMS *Fearless* so her destruction was ordered. But the transfer of her ship's company with wounded was such a slow process that the damaged ship and her two executioners were mere blobs when a heavy explosion announced the final tragedy. Her resting place was marked by a thin spiral of smoke, like a cenotaph, long after the other two destroyers had rejoined.

Meanwhile, the gun crews had been replenishing the ready use ammunition and sponging out their guns in sombre, thoughtful mood. We had wanted excitement. Now we had tasted it and two fine ships had been hit with the loss of many lives. 'There but for the grace of God goes HMS *Eridge*' must have been the thought in many minds. Never again would we look forward to another operation. Each one, as it arose, would be accepted as a necessary job, to be performed to the best of our ability in the hope that HMS *Eridge* would survive unscathed. In the short period since daylight HMS *Eridge* had grown wise to the reality of war.

The next day was hot and calm. The convoy continued eastward at its best speed. Galita Island rose out of the sea ahead, came abeam and sank below the horizon astern within a span of less than three hours. Reconnaissance aircraft had detected no enemy fleet activity but fighters were in constant action against shadowers or small bombing formations, all of which were driven off. Far to the westward, the crippled HMS *Manchester* and HMS *Avonvale*, lacking fighter cover, were the targets for many attacks.

Algeria gave way to Tunisia which, in turn, fell away to the southward when the convoy reached the approaches to the Sicilian Channel, shortly before sunset. Here, as previously arranged, HMS *Nelson* and several destroyers turned away from the convoy to join the carrier group. As soon as they were steering north-west, HMS *Renown* and HMS *Ark Royal* also started to turn and, in a few minutes were drawing away from the convoy at a relative speed of more than thirty knots. Rear Admiral Syfret now ordered the Malta bound ships to assume their night formation, in which the supply ships were enclosed within a tight rectangle of fighting ships. From now onwards, close to enemy bases, the main assault was expected. Even if no surface ships intervened, there would be bombers from Italy, Sicily and Sardinia and E-boats from Pantallaria in the Skerki Channel.

A fighter patrol remained in company until the sun was below the horizon and then wheeled north-westwards after their carrier.

'That's the last of HMS *Ark Royal's* fighters,' the Pilot announced. 'Four Malta based Beaufighters should be covering us until dark.'

The sun dropped further below the horizon, its pink afterglow fanned brightly across the heavens and then slowly faded as the sun sank even lower. But the western horizon remained starkly outlined by a strip of gold, against which the ships would be clearly silhouetted for the next few minutes. To the east, the horizon had disappeared and dusk was already encroaching. It was too dark for aircraft to remain in sight long enough for controlled fire.

'A medium barrage will be fired,' McCall informed the gun crews. 'If any gun is unable to follow the director, you're to select your own target.'

Leading Seaman Hambrook, gun captain of X gun, grinned at his crew. 'Hear that, lads. If this gun goes into local, I'll expect twenty rounds a minute.'

'Aircraft bearing green 50,' one of his loading numbers called.

Hambrook, staring along the bearing, saw four low flying aircraft emerging from the dusk on the far side of the convoy, flying a reciprocal course.

'Damn,' Hambrook growled. 'The range is foul. We can't engage them.'

The aircraft were also being studied on the compass platform.

'They can't be Beaufighters,' the Pilot stated. 'They should be high above us.'

They had to be hostile and this was immediately confirmed by the opening salvoes from ships on the far side of the convoy coinciding with the aircraft's sharp turn inwards. It was too late to manoeuvre the convoy so each ship had to take individual avoiding action, those to starboard turning towards the attack and those to port in the opposite direction, thereby combing possible torpedo tracks. The two columns were now rapidly opening out, thereby losing the advantage of concentration. So, as soon as the torpedoes were judged to have run their course, the Admiral ordered his force to reform. That was the moment the main assaults were unleashed. The crimson tint had now been replaced by a deep purple staining the high heavens while dusk to the eastward was steadily deepening. Out of this murk, high torpedo bombers, unseen until the last moment, now swooped from all directions: the escorts could only fire a continuous barrage around the merchant ships now swinging back into two columns. The aircraft, too, had little time to select their targets and three groups of torpedo bombers hurriedly released their torpedoes before wheeling back into the gloom within the space of a few seconds.

While the torpedoes were still threatening their targets, a high formation, invisible against the darkening sky, dropped its bombs. As they exploded, the sea heaved vertically upwards and remained poised for a fraction of a second before collapsing with monstrous turbulence. Simultaneously JU 88s were diving in successive waves through the heavy barrage, the deafening detonation of their bombs augmenting the uproar caused by the high level attack. Three of these aircraft had dived on HMS *Edinburgh* and for a long endless moment the flagship disappeared completely amongst the turmoil of their bursting bombs. Between the merchant ships lay a destroyer where no destroyer should have been. As she dropped astern of the columns her safety valves lifted with a roar which could be heard above the gunfire and bomb explosions.

Brewer read her pennant numbers and called out, 'It's HMS *Firedrake*.'

HMS *Firedrake*'s signal lantern was flashing towards HMS *Edinburgh*. Brewer waited until the message was completed and then reported, 'She's had a near miss and temporarily lost power.'

Those toiling at the guns or sweating in the machinery spaces would be unaware of HMS *Firedrake*'s predicament. But, from the compass platform, we watched her with heartfelt sympathy.

'Poor devils,' was the general but silent thought, 'What a place to stop.'

The battle continued as HMS *Firedrake* fell further astern. A light blinked impatiently from the direction in which the flagship had vanished into the dusk. Sometimes it was obscured by bomb bursts or cordite fumes; at others it was dimmed by brilliant gunflashes. Words had to be repeated but the final message was crystal clear.

'HMS *Eridge* stand by HMS *Firedrake* and escort to Gibraltar.'

There was a brief pause; then the lantern added, 'Beware E-boats.'

HMS *Eridge* headed for the damaged ship and slowly circled her before stopping off her port beam. She was listing heavily to starboard but showed no visible signs of damage so Brewer switched on the loud hailer and called, 'What's wrong?'

A metallic voice blaring out of the darkness, barely audible above the roar of escaping steam, more or less repeated the intercepted signal before adding, 'Hope to raise steam for twelve knots. Where are we bound?'

I took over the microphone. 'Gibraltar. We'll patrol around you in case of E-boats. Be as quick as you can.'

HMS *Eridge* commenced a circular patrol. The hiss of steam gradually diminished then died away entirely; the night became uncannily quiet after the fury of the battle which had now moved far to the eastward, where its progress was still marked by the growl of guns and a series of brilliant flashes. It was like a storm which had erupted overhead and then rolled away to the horizon but was still proving its vigour by a distant rumble of thunder and a regular flicker of lightning. It was lonely, too, and we all felt a sharp but unspoken yearning to rejoin the convoy where at least our responsibilities would be shared with other ships.

A light began to flash with monotonous regularity to the southward. The Pilot took its bearing, then dived under the chart table cover and laid it off on the chart.

'That's Cape Bon,' he announced. 'If HMS *Firedrake* raises steam for twelve knots in the next hour or so, at daylight we'll be near the position where HMS *Fearless* was sunk.'

The firing to the east gradually dwindled away. Not so long ago we had pitied HMS *Firedrake*. Now, having joined her, we were also feeling sorry for ourselves as the monotonous, circular patrol continued in a darkness which seemed full of unseen dangers.

A brilliant ball of light burst unexpectedly in the sky, several miles to the eastward, hovered for a few seconds and then began to drift slowly down wind, losing height as it did so. As it hit the water and fizzled out, another flare erupted above it; then a third and fourth, all at two or three minute intervals. An aircraft could now be heard criss-crossing the flare track which was steadily extending towards us. But another threat, sometimes audible, sometimes silent, was also closing from the east – an E-boat stalking the flares, hoping for a target in the pools of light. HMS *Eridge* was slowly manoeuvred to a position from which she could cover HMS *Firedrake* with smoke, her guns trained and ammunition fused for a short-range barrage.

Another flare, alarmingly close, shattered the darkness. The ships would remain beyond the perimeter of light but the next flare would undoubtedly trap us. The guns were loaded and their crews waited expectantly. The flare was still drifting when the E-boat suddenly accelerated, as if attacking. It would have to cross the lighted area and the director was swung towards the sound. But, just as unexpectedly, the E-boat, still short of the illuminated area, swung in a tight semi-circle to starboard and roared off to the north-eastward, closely followed by the flare dropper. We breathed a collective sigh of relief. To have our position accurately fixed so early in the night was the last thing we wanted.

The Pilot's remark had suggested that most of the dangerous waters between Sardinia and Africa could be traversed in darkness after which the passage to 'Gib' would be comparatively safe. Brewer was obviously thinking along the same lines and was muttering something about beer and boiler cleaning leave in Gib when a small, blue lamp began to blink on HMS *Firedrake's* bridge. We kept silent while he was reading the signal, confident that *HMS Firedrake* was reporting that she was ready to proceed. But our optimism was ill-founded. Her brief signal merely stated, 'Regret will be longer than expected. Better take me in tow.... Will be ready in ten minutes. Unable to steer.'

The necessary orders were given for HMS *Eridge's* own preparations. A gun's crew unshackled some cable from an anchor and dragged it to the stern where it was shackled to the towing pendant. HMS *Eridge's* stern was then manoeuvred alongside HMS *Firedrake's* focs'le whence the eye of her long towing hawser was passed over and shackled to the free end of our cable. HMS *Eridge* then crept ahead, her after-gun's crew keeping cable and hawser clear of the propellers. HMS *Firedrake* dropped slowly back into the darkness, remaining stationary until the full 900 feet of her towing hawser was curving in a gentle catenary towards our stern. Then she started to move ahead and her own cable, to which the towing hawser was shackled, was slowly veered until 150 feet were outboard. The cable was then secured and the tow was ready.

HMS *Firedrake* was facing south so our initial course, while working up sufficient speed to achieve steerage way, had to be in that direction. To avoid sudden jerks on the towing hawser, speed could only be increased by a few revolutions at a time. Such caution was agonizingly slow but, even so, our steady penetration into the Gulf of Hammamet was measured by the light on Cape Bon growing broader on the starboard beam.

A listing ship turns more easily towards her least immersed side. That in our case meant to port, so the two ships would have to turn through 270 degrees before reaching a westerly course. Optimistically hoping to shorten the turn, I made several attempts to turn to starboard. But the ship showed not the slightest inclination to obey the helm. Neither did she show much willingness to turn to port and a momentary panic almost persuaded me that we would remain on a southerly course until we hit Tunisia. But, eventually, to my intense relief, HMS *Eridge* began to swing to port, slowly at first but with growing momentum as the listing HMS *Firedrake* tried to drag her faster to port. Only with difficulty was she eventually steadied on a westerly course. It was then 2330 hrs and we were still in the area where HMS *Firedrake* had been crippled four hours earlier. We had just steadied on our course when HMS *Firedrake* reported that her boilers were contaminated with sea water and would not be cleared before daylight. The Pilot returned to the chart, laid off our course and speed and then checked his calculations, hoping vainly to find some mistake. But nothing could alter the ugly fact that, at daylight, we would be at least thirty miles east of Galita and would have to run the gauntlet between Africa and Sardinia without the protective cover of darkness. A long, anxious and, possibly, frightening day lay ahead and the only relaxation we could risk was to light the galley fire to make some tea and to allow the ship's company to get what rest they could at their action stations.

The night dragged slowly away. Eons seemed to drag by before the flashing light on Cape Bon began to drop abaft the beam. By then, the convoy had moved beyond the range of our manoeuvring wave and our wireless was uncannily silent until, sometime during the middle watch, its peace was suddenly shattered by a broadcast on an area frequency, '*City of Brisbane* torpedoed. Dropping astern of convoy.'

Shortly afterwards, HMS *Firedrake's* small lantern confirmed our fears by flashing, 'We seem to be unlucky. No immediate hope of raising steam. Very sorry.'

The first degree of readiness was assumed while the stars were paling in the east and I spoke once more over the broadcasting system, hoping to give a little encouragement without raising any false hopes.

'A lot has happened since I last spoke to you but you don't need to be reminded of that,' I began. 'This is the present situation. HMS

Firedrake cannot raise steam and will have to be towed through waters in which the convoy was attacked yesterday. Now that does not mean that those aircraft will attack us today. For one thing, HMS *Ark Royal* is now bombing the Sardinian airfields in order to weaken the enemy's ability to strike. For another, the enemy is unlikely to waste too much effort on a couple of destroyers so long as the convoy is at sea. Even in these waters, we won't be entirely alone because the destroyer HMS *Encounter* and several empty supply ships, which have broken out of Malta under cover of darkness, will be overtaking us at intervals throughout the day. It's possible, therefore, that the enemy will assume we're covering these ships providing we keep his reconnaissance planes at a distance and thereby conceal that HMS *Firedrake* is being towed. To maintain this deception, it's the responsibility of all of us to keep alert, of the lookouts to sight and report aircraft as quickly as possible, of the gun crews and control parties to open rapid and accurate fire. Submarines may also be operating. Now a periscope should be easy to sight in these calm conditions so keep your eyes skinned. If one is sighted, or if we obtain a submarine contact, we'll have to slip the tow in order to attack before she can fire her torpedoes. That is the only situation in which the tow will be slipped. If we do our job properly, we may experience nothing worse than a long and tiring day. After that, even Gib's beer will be worth drinking. Good luck to you all.'

And it was a long, anxious forenoon that followed. The first enemy aircraft was sighted just as the tip of Galita was rising above the horizon and, for the rest of the forenoon, at least one was always in sight. Mostly they kept out of gun range but sometimes they closed in such a menacing manner that McCall had no hesitation in opening fire. Proof of our alertness was sufficient to drive off the shadowers but that did not mean that the enemy was unaware of HMS *Firedrake's* condition.

Shortly after sunrise, the mighty *Breconshire*, the fastest empty supply ship out of Malta, was sighted astern. A little later Malta reported that the major portion of the convoy was entering Grand Harbour. The damaged *City of Brisbane* and her escorts, under heavy air attack, were still some distance from their destination but struggling grimly towards it. These were now the only ships attracting the enemy's full attention from the scattered ships to the westward. The upper half of Galita was now above the horizon. Reaching it was out first goal. It still looked a long, long way ahead.

The messman clambered to the bridge carrying a plate loaded with sandwiches. The Pilot gazed doubtfully at the slabs of corned beef slapped between slices of bread thick enough to form a formidable obstacle to all but the strongest dentures and exclaimed, 'I thought corned beef was for lunch.'

The messman smiled lugubriously. 'You're not far wrong, sir. Corned beef's on the menu for all meals – breakfast, lunch, tea and supper.'

The *Breconshire*, flying the white ensign, overhauled us, her lantern flashing a laconic, 'Can I give you a tow?' I still felt too depressed to think of a suitable reply.

The whole of the western face of Galita was now visible. The second 'empty' from Malta was chasing us from the east.

Breconshire had passed several miles to the north and, for some minutes, the Pilot watched her proceeding majestically westwards. Then, for about the twentieth time, he crouched over the chart. Having nothing to do except mark the ship's hourly position – and that did not take long – he was occupying his mind by memorising every indentation along the coastline and every sounding along our tack. The vicinity of Galita was now so familiar that he reckoned he could draw an accurate chart with his eyes blindfolded.

'Aircraft closing green 90.'

It was a common enough report but the look-out's voice contained a note of urgency which dragged me upright. Looking north, my heart missed a beat at the sight of an arrowhead of five bombers flying directly towards HMS *Eridge*. McCall's opening salvo was thundering skywards when the aircraft unexpectedly swerved right and hurtled westwards in shallow, high powered dives. The distant *Breconshire* was enveloped by bursting bombs and, seconds later, her wireless indignantly protested that she was being bombed.

Occasionally our ear drums were stunned by the percussion of one of McCall's salvoes. Otherwise the ship was strangely silent except for the gurgle of water alongside and the regular, monotonous high pitched ping of the submarine transmissions. As First Lieutenant, Evans had a roving commission at action stations. He felt concern for the gun crews who were kept fully alert waiting for the next engagement. It was worse for the damage control parties who had nothing to do except crouch or lie on the hot deck, drinking lime juice or munching sandwiches. Few acknowledged Evans' presence, preferring to think of home, wives and girlfriends until the next alarm aroused the prospect of shattered limbs and twisted metal.

Approaching the after four-inch gun, Evans was heartened by a burst of cheerful laughter from a group gathered around the

Gunner on the iron deck. The Gunner was obviously going to be an asset in tense situations. Evans welcomed this but was ashamed to admit that he would have preferred someone else as a messmate, a sentiment which he suspected was shared by the Gunner. As he joined the group, the second 'empty' drew abeam and they sped her on her way with friendly waves and a silent prayer that *Eridge* would survive.

'Destroyer astern,' a look-out shouted.

It was the HMS *Encounter*. She was steaming, as expected, at high speed but, surprisingly was weaving from side to side of her mean course.

'That's a funny...' The Pilot's comment was interrupted by an urgent tinkle from the wireless office.

'Emergency from HMS *Encounter*,' the operator called, 'Two Italian destroyers in sight, am engaging.'

HMS *Eridge* and HMS *Firedrake* were the only two destroyers in view and soon the 'Italians' command of colloquial English was good enough to persuade HMS *Encounter* of her error. But she seemed not to appreciate our gratuitous insults about her ship recognition ability and overhauled us with her bow high in the air, like a haughty dowager showing her disdain for two insolent urchins.

At last, after a seemingly endless wait, Galita slipped slowly down our port side. That wretched rock had been our goal throughout the forenoon and its gradual descent into the sea during the next six hours would be watched with equal fervour. One hundred pairs of eyes stared with loathing at its cliffs and gulleys and at the small boats fishing unconcernedly in its shadow; their crews seemed completely unaware of the war raging around them.

Around the same time, Malta reported that *City of Brisbane* had entered Grand Harbour. The operation had been a complete success although the enemy could still minimise his failure by concentrating his air force against the scattered ships to the westward. That had to be his intention otherwise his constant surveillance of the area would be a waste of time and effort. The ship's company was told about *City of Brisbane* and encouraged to maintain their vigilance which, so far, had been exemplary.

To our surprise, the afternoon followed the pattern of the forenoon – constant surveillance with, perhaps a few more, aggressive approaches. Nevertheless we remained convinced that an attack must eventually follow this activity and, as the moments ticked away, gradually accepted, with some trepidation, that the enemy was reserving his assault for the dangerous period around dusk.

No one on the bridge had time to keep up a running commentary for the benefit of those below so they were usually kept in ignorance of events on deck. The rumble of the main armament might either signify a few long range shots at a single shadower or the beginning of a heavy barrage against a determined attack. The pom-pom overhead merely warned that aircraft, perhaps only one or maybe many, were near the ship and might be diving on her. In such circumstances, those below could only brace themselves against possible explosions and pray that the bombs would miss. To keep himself in the know the Chief had seated himself on the engineer's 'bridge' – the weather screen protecting the engine room hatchways. He had personally experienced the anxiety caused by feeling ignored so, whenever possible, he sat in his 'bridge' where he could keep up a commentary for those in the sweltering compartment below.

From his position the Chief had watched Galita dropping almost imperceptibly astern. He had also seen another 'empty' steadily overhauling us. She was still several miles away when she suddenly altered course to starboard and opened fire. Seconds later, four torpedo bombers skimming just above the sea, flew into sight and swerved under the merchant ship's stern. As they turned eastward the Chief heard four heavy explosions.

'Oh, God! They've got her,' he thought.

The ship had already identified herself as the *Settler*. Having done so, her light had continued to flash, 'I think tanker *Hoegh Hood* has been torpedoed.'

My heart sank at the prospect of more trouble. We could do nothing at the moment but in case we could after nightfall, I told Brewer to ask for the tanker's last known position.

Brewer flashed his message but before *Settler* could reply, she suffered the attack first witnessed by the Chief. From the bridge we watched with helpless frustration as the out of range bombers flew out of sight and our tautened nerves flinched at the sound of the explosions. A dozen pair of eyes anxiously watched the *Settler* which was now swinging back to port. Her lantern began to wink in our direction, persuading us that she was about to call for help. But, to our intense relief, the message was only a continuation of her earlier signal to give *Hoegh Hood's* position. The detonations which had so scared us had, in fact, been caused by the torpedoes exploding in the wake. The ship herself was undamaged.

We now had a problem to exercise our minds and the mental stimulation rekindled my natural impatience, curbed during the long hours of inactivity. HMS *Firedrake* was first asked to report her condition and, while waiting for her reply, I chivvied the Pilot, quite unnecessarily, into working out the times of sunset and moonrise. I then asked him to plot the tanker's and our own estimated position at sunset, between which a return course could be laid off on the chart. The Pilot gave his calculations in a resigned manner and then retired to the back of the bridge, presumably to ponder over the unreasonable behaviour of certain commanding officers. By then Galita's base had dipped below the eastern horizon, its upper bluffs and peaks quite hazy under the shimmering rays of the sun.

HMS *Firedrake* had reported that she did not expect to raise steam until the following morning so, as I had expected, slipping the tow before dark was out of the question. *Hoegh Hood's* last known position would then be no more than 100 miles astern and could be reached before midnight. After a further exchange of signals with HMS *Firedrake* it was agreed that HMS *Eridge* should leave her at 2000 hrs, having first informed the Admiral in sufficient time for him to cancel our intention if other arrangements had been made. *Settler* drew level during this exchange.

As the minutes ticked slowly but inexorably towards late afternoon, *Settler* drew further ahead and eventually dipped below the horizon. Aerial activity was also becoming more intensive. Several shadowers were always in sight and sometimes one would accelerate aggressively towards us, hoping to catch us unprepared. The guns were constantly following the movements and firing rapid salvoes to warn the aggressor to keep out of range. Even so it seemed unlikely that the enemy was unaware by now that HMS *Firedrake* was being towed. But the gun crews were convinced that their alertness was still preventing this discovery. In spite of this confidence, everyone was uneasily aware that our comparative immunity during daylight could easily develop into a frightening ordeal at dusk.

Only the top of Galita, like a pencil pointing out of the sea, was now visible and the rays of the westerly sun were defining it clearly against a blue background of sky. The Pilot, realising that this wretched, loathsome rock might be our last companion for many more hours, focused his binoculars on it prior to taking a final bearing. But another object to the left of Galita caught his eye. He studied it more closely and felt a sudden thrill of relief when he recognised the upper works of a tanker. It was the *Hoegh Hood*.

The ships were so far apart that the exchange of signals was a lengthy business and the sun had set before it was completed.

A golden ribbon glowed briefly along the western horizon and a purple mantle spreading from the west rapidly concealed Galita and the skyline beyond. By then *Hoegh Hood* had finished describing her damage and had reported that she could proceed at slow speed.

The purple mantle and golden ribbon rapidly changed into the usual kaleidoscope of colours following the setting of the sun. Colour and gloom struggled for mastery until light gave up the fight and retreated towards the west. This was the day's most dangerous period and the ship's company, convinced that the enemy had waited deliberately for this moment, closed up automatically at their stations, determined to thwart him. The guns were loaded with barrage and pointed at different bearings; below, supply parties stood by to send up more ammunition and the engine and boiler room crews prepared for demands for speed.

The noise of aircraft grew louder as the now unseen shadowers closed nearer. Suddenly the roar of accelerating engines blotted out all other sounds. This must be the expected attack and tension vanished at the prospect of definite action. A burst of tracer jabbed into the dusk and was reinforced by the four-inch barrage. A large monoplane burst into view, banked steeply to port, as if taken by surprise, and vanished back into the gloom with equal swiftness. We listened for the follow up but could hear nothing but receding engines. It had only been a shadower misjudging its position: the preceeding silence told us that its companions had also departed. Our long, anxious wait was over. The enemy's lack of aggression had been remarkable but our relief was tempered by the knowledge that we were still hampered by the damaged HMS *Firedrake*, in waters where submarines might be patrolling.

The ship now reverted to defence stations and, during a brief confusion, the duty watch changed its action stations while those off duty hurried below for a quick meal and whatever rest they could get. McCall climbed stiffly out of the director and stood unnoticed at the back of the bridge, leaning against the plating and staring at the black water while a cool breeze caressed his aching head. He and his gunnery team had done well but he felt no elation only a deep desire for a long, long sleep, which would certainly elude him that night because he would be back in the director at 2000 hrs. At that moment, the bulky figure of the Gunner loomed out of the darkness and McCall, having no desire for conversation, slipped away to the wardroom.

The night passed without incident and by 0900 hrs next forenoon, HMS *Firedrake* had at last managed to raise steam for slow speed.

A great cheer greeted the slipping of the hawser, that slender line on which so much had depended during the past thirty-six hours. HMS *Eridge* was now free to manoeuvre unhampered by the dead weight astern and our freedom cheered everyone. The sunshine felt more friendly, all of a sudden, and encouraged men to laugh, joke and even sing. Plans for making the best of our boiler cleaning leave once more became paramount.

Later that forenoon, the battle squadron was sighted. As it steamed towards us the flagship, the battlecruiser HMS *Renown*, broke formation and passed close abeam, her company giving each destroyer three cheers in turn. It was very embarrassing but final proof that we had rejoined the fleet. We reached Gibraltar three days later.[3]

Back in Gib, we learned that HMS *Farndale* had been detained in Malta to permit repairs to some action damage and that HMS *Eridge* and HMS *Avonvale*, commanded by Lieutenant Commander Peter Withers, were to proceed to Alexandria without her, taking the long Cape route to avoid the dangerous waters between Crete and North Africa. Accordingly, in mid-August, we sailed for Freetown. Each day's steaming was taking us steadily towards the perimeter of U-boat operations, after which a raider would be the only enemy we could possibly meet until we reached the Red Sea. Consequently, the passage would become more like a peacetime cruise, the ships could revert to cruising stations or one watch in four: fighting boredom would be our main concern.

The ships were approaching the equator on 27 August. At 1600 hrs, a stentorian, 'Ship Ahoy. What ship is this that enters my domain?' heralded the arrival of King Neptune and his retinue for the Crossing the Line Ceremony. His clerk then summoned the ship's company to render homage on the following day. Prudence clearly dictated that such an august assembly should be suitably entertained so I proposed a drink. The offer having been graciously accepted, I watched in silent admiration as the contents of several bottles of whisky, gin and sherry were swiftly vanishing. It must be admitted that the capacious jaws of King Neptune swallowed a considerable percentage of this mixture but he had the grace to excuse his apparent greed by explaining that he was drinking his Queen's share to protect her from the dangers of mortal's firewater. Regrettably, Queen Amphritite's reaction to such solicitude demonstrated a complete absence of gratitude but even this display of temperament could not disguise the fact that her appearance would have been greatly improved had she not so obviously recently entered a beard growing competition.

Next morning, a canvas bath and two thrones were set up abaft the bridge. At 0900 hrs, the police and bears cleared a passage through the assembled initiates for the clerk, scribe, jester, photographer, barber, lather boys, doctor, nurse and chair tipper. These were followed by an unaccompanied monarch of the deep. The empty space beside him caused some speculation about the possibility of a royal scandal until Queen Amphritite was observed hobbling in his wake. Her tight skirt was clearly impeding her movements but her delayed entry presented an opportunity to respond to some gratuitous comments with a solo performance, which was growing increasingly provocative, when a volley of unregal oaths propelled her like a rocket to her sovereign's side. Petty Officer Gibson was looking every inch a monarch. Able Seaman Kidman, on the other hand, could have been a prizewinner as a rag doll in a fancy dress competition; as Queen Amphritite he lacked credibility. Moreover, he was looking even less regal than on the previous evening because the court barber, no doubt encouraged by my alcohol, had shaved off one side of his beard.

Further comment about the Queen's appearance was interrupted by the scribe introducing each of the officers with a verse extolling his peculiarities. The poetmaster was proclaiming his jingles with evident relish when his rhetoric was halted in full flow by an accurately aimed egg.

King Neptune rose in awful majesty.

'Execute that man,' he thundered.

Summary justice having been meted out with a speed which would have delighted the dictator of a banana republic, Neptune then presented each officer with an oceanic order and I found myself attached to a stinking kipper, presumably because it rhymed with skipper. The officers, in turn, were then photographed, lathered, shaved, dosed with some foul physic and finally tossed into the bath for the sport of the bears. I was thankful to be dealt with first because the water was at least clean and I could then enjoy the discomfiture of others with a clear conscience. The officers were followed by the rest of the ship's company, the routine, as the officials wearied, becoming increasingly perfunctory until the bath held more initiates than bears. The clerk, however, kept a careful tally and the police ruthlessly hunted down anyone who tried to avoid the mystic rites of Neptune's realm. Scruffy ran at their heels, barking happily, and the cat slept through it all in my cabin.

The proceedings were drawing to a close when the clerk solemnly announced, 'Your majesty. We have a subject who has not yet paid homage.'

'Who is that?' Neptune demanded.

'A false physician who lances sailors' boils with a marlin spike.'

'Bring me that callous quack,' His Majesty ordered.

Away went the police who located the Doctor in the sickbay from which he was dragged, protesting that he was too busy to play childish games. It was a feeble excuse because everyone knew that he had no patients and his procrastination merely earned him a prolonged ducking in water which, by then, was so filthy that any self respecting practitioner would be reaching for his syringe if any member of his panel had so much as touched it.

The passage to the Cape was made in the teeth of the trade wind and both HMS *Eridge* and HMS *Avondale* developed an uncomfortable corkscrew motion in the heavy seas. After two years of war torn Britain, Capetown and, later, Durban were part of a different world and we gaped like country bumpkins at the bright lights, smart cars and luxurious, well stocked shops. As we experienced life again in a city not torn by war many could not help wondering how long it would be before Britain regained similar conditions. From Durban, we steamed through calm seas up the east coast of Africa to Egypt.

CHAPTER FOUR

Red Tobruk

No one could accuse the Commander in Chief of the Eastern Mediterranean Fleet, Admiral Sir Andrew B Cunningham, of being a pessimist. But, when Withers and I called on the tough, redoubtable ABC, he left us in no doubt that hard, dangerous times lay ahead and that we would be expected to overcome them with minimum air support. At the end of September 1941 his fleet, although lacking a carrier, was a powerful force consisting of three battleships, eight cruisers, thirty destroyers and double that number of ancillary vessels. Its main role, that Autumn, was the traditional task of ensuring the safe and timely arrival of supply ships, maintenance of the besieged fortress of Tobruk – a sustained operation resulting in heavy losses amongst supply ships and their escorts – and support of the Desert Army which was preparing for CRUSADER (an operation intended to relieve Tobruk and then to sweep the Axis out of Cyrenaica).[4] The fleet was constantly at sea but, in spite of the Commander in Chief's warning, opposition, at first, was not particularly heavy and it was difficult to believe that a Mediterranean destroyer's average expectation of life was no more than six months. But, with so much activity, losses were inevitable. HMS *Eridge's* first contact with tragedy occurred when she was detached from a bombarding force to search for the gunboat HMS *Gnat*, reported torpedoed to the east of Tobruk. Her position was well behind the Axis front line so lookouts were scanning the sea and sky with more than their usual vigilance. The damaged ship had just been sighted, lying low in the water, when the stridulous screech of the wireless office buzzer sent an involuntary tremor through our bodies.

'Red Tobruk,' Petty Officer Godfrey yelled up the voice pipe from the wireless office. 'Emergency warning of imminent air attack.'

Being fully prepared, we had nothing to do but wait and ponder if we were about to be attacked by one or many bombers. Five minutes later the warning was repeated. Two red warnings must surely herald a heavy attack and the heavens were watched with even greater concentration. But their blue dome remained unsullied by aircraft. Then the warning was repeated and followed by so many 'reds', with scarcely an 'all clear', that we were beginning to suspect a practical joke when two bombers dived unexpectedly out of the cloud cover. Their bombs exploded close enough to the damaged gunboat to increase her casualties and cause her to wallow deeper in the water. We had learned a lesson – never ignore a 'Red Tobruk'.

HMS *Farndale* rejoined HMS *Eridge* and HMS *Avonvale* in November. On the first night the three ships were together in Alex, Shorty, Withers and I dined at the Union Club. These were exciting times. We were on the eve of Operation CRUSADER, a great land offensive which was confidently expected to drive the Axis out of Cyrenaica. The three 'Hunts' were standing by to escort *Glenroy* to Tobruk, as soon as the fortress had been relieved. *Glenroy* was one of the most valuable supply ships in the Mediterranean and was carrying landing craft. Probably, we were the only officers in the club who knew the exact date of the offensive but everyone knew it was near and the bar and dining room were filled with excited officers, confidently predicting the dates of our entry into Tobruk, Benghazi and even Tripoli. Moreover, news had just been received of a naval victory in the central basin where Force K, a force of Malta based cruisers and destroyers, had totally destroyed a large Italian convoy and its escorts. Their activities almost halved the amount of supplies reaching Rommel's army in North Africa. The Axis seemed to be losing control of the shipping routes to North Africa and one was confident enough to believe that a repetition might force Rommel to withdraw through lack of supplies. Consequently, we were in a gay carefree mood. We also felt some satisfaction in the knowledge that we would be the first ships to enter the fortress during the offensive and that *Glenroy*'s landing craft and crews would be vital for landing seaborne supplies to sustain that offensive.

The offensive commenced that night but immediately ran into unexpectedly heavy resistance in the approaches to Tobruk. In spite of that, we sailed as planned along the Tobruk tramlines, the comparatively narrow strip of water bounded by land to the south and by the limits of fighter cover to the north.

The passage was uneventful until the convoy was off Ishaila rocks to the west of Mersa Matruh. Visibility was poor so the ship was at action stations. No air raid warning had been broadcast when several torpedo bombers swooped low from the direction of the coast, burst through a ragged barrage and immobilised *Glenroy* with one hit. After a brief exchange of signals, HMS *Farndale* immediately embarked her military passengers, whilst her two consorts, under worsening weather conditions and increasing air attacks, stood by the damaged ship until relieved by tugs with local escorts.

HMS *Eridge* then rejoined HMS *Farndale* and the two ships sailed for Tobruk to pick up a returning convoy which was to include *Chakdina*, carrying wounded and prisoners of war. We had just spent several arduous days and nights at sea but every man on board was bitterly disappointed by our failure to protect *Glenroy* and glad to get an opportunity to prove that we could do better. The weather, although improving, was still carrying the aftermath of the storm and, on clearing the breakwaters, both ships began to butt into a short, steep, head sea. Off the Great Pass beacon, that lonely light which was to extend so many friendly welcomes in the months ahead, we passed three inward bound destroyers, the decks of which were crowded with far more than their normal crews. Everyone who could do so grabbed binoculars or a telescope and gazed in shocked silence at the listless groups sheltering from the wind and spray in their motley survivors' rigs, until a shocked voice expressed our unspoken thoughts by muttering, 'God! Something's bought a packet'. Half an hour later, the battle fleet, escorted by cruisers and destroyers, rose out of the sea ahead. But, of the three, squat, powerful battleships which had left Alex to intercept a convoy, only two were now visible. Once more binoculars and telescopes swept the horizon, hoping desperately to find that the third ship was separated only temporarily from her consorts. They searched in vain. By the time the fleet had disappeared astern, it was useless to deny the painful truth: HMS *Barham*[5] had gone forever. Not even reports of another success, in the central basin by the Malta based ships of Force K, could minimise this tragic disaster.

We reached the Cyrenaican coast on an evening of flat calm. Not a breath of wind ruffled the surface of the sea nor a cloud broke the symmetry of the sky. To port, rapidly changing colours were chasing each other across the low lying sandhills as the heavens, now flaming with pink and gold, reflected the many hued rays of the setting sun. Ahead, the masts of Tobruk signal station were silhouetted against the brilliant sky below which the convoy, just visible against the darker background of land, was clearing the harbour.

The destroyers passed on an opposite course; then hauled round to the eastward and took station on either bow of the supply ships *Chakdina* and *Kirkland* while the two trawlers, which had escorted them out of harbour, dropped astern to their quarters. The two ships were making good no more than eight knots so HMS *Farndale* ordered the escorts to zigzag independently at higher speeds.

After daylight had faded, a full moon hung in the sky like a great Chinese lantern beneath which the normally forbidding African coast looked glamorous and romantic. The night was utterly still and the water gurgling merrily alongside *Eridge* was the only sound audible above the submarine detector's transmissions and the hum of engineroom fans. Noise and laughter were unwanted intruders and the watch on deck, having discarded the sea boots, sou'westers and oilskins they'd worn during the past few days, were resting around their weapons. They had no premonition of danger. The ship was in the second degree of readiness and the watch below was mostly asleep. But someone near the transmitting station was playing gramophone records of light music which was rising gently up the bridge voice pipes.

This relaxed attitude was not shared by those on the compass platform. In the bright moonlight we could see the other ships as clearly as if it was daytime and knew that each was a prime target for submarine or torpedo attack. HMS *Eridge's* anti-submarine and aircraft weapons systems were already manned to an extent which would support short term action while full action stations were being assumed. As an extra precaution, she was steaming at twice the speed of the merchant ships and steering a zigzag of short legs and large, frequent, course alterations which needed the full concentration of McCall, the officer of the watch. Consequently, HMS *Eridge*, herself, had reasonable security but were these measures also sufficient to protect the convoy? That question began to dominate my thoughts and made me increasingly anxious.

This feeling of anxiety was demanding that the ship assumed the first degree of readiness but common sense advised otherwise. The ship's company would soon lose confidence, as well as rest, if they were called to action stations each time their Captain had an attack of nerves. Besides, even in moonlight, an aircraft would be sighted so briefly that only one salvo could be fired and the defence watch was quite capable of doing that. So nerves and common sense reached a compromise; the guns were loaded with barrage, the depth charges primed and the gun crews ordered to keep their eyes and ears skinned.

Some clouds were now drifting across the sky, casting deep shadows whenever they crossed the moon. Sometimes all ships were still clearly visible, at others some were hidden in the shadows. This interchange between clarity and obscurity was a little eerie, as if a series of black and white pictures were being projected onto a silent screen. Down below, the unseen record player, anticipating Christmas, was now playing 'Silent Night' which seemed appropriate in such conditions.

HMS *Eridge* reached the end of an outward leg and McCall ordered starboard wheel to swing back towards the convoy. In the same instant, my ears caught the hum of a motor; then it was gone so swiftly that it could have been imagined. I called to the Pilot who was huddled in a corner of the bridge, standing so still that he might have been dozing, 'Did you hear anything?'

His negative was confirmed by the look-outs but I added, a trifle ungraciously, 'Well, stop dreaming and keep alert.'

HMS *Eridge* was now steaming towards the convoy which was temporarily covered by a deep cloud shadow. Checks with the wireless office and after guns had confirmed that no 'Red Tobruk' had been broadcast and that the after look-outs had neither seen nor heard anything. But I was still unconvinced. I strained my ears to catch anything additional to the usual noises of the ship. But there was nothing now except the transmissions, the low hum of fans and the soft strains of 'Silent Night'.

HMS *Eridge*, herself, entered the shadows. She was steaming fast towards the supply ships' track when a gentle thud was audible above the internal noises of the ship. It was an insignificant sound but it was out of the ordinary and my anxiety increased. The look-outs watched their sectors with intense concentration. The duty signalman could see the nearest trawler and one supply ship through his night glasses but nothing else. The space which should have been occupied by the other ship was empty.

'There's only one ship,' he called, his voice conveying uncertainty.

I refused to believe that a ship could vanish so swiftly without a violent explosion and snapped at him, 'Nonsense! Look again.'

Without lowering his glasses, the duty signalman repeated with greater certainty, 'There's only one ship, sir.'

'It's time to alter course,' McCall called. 'Shall I turn?'

'No,' I told him. 'Reduce speed to ten knots and maintain present course. Keep a damn good look out ahead.'

HMS *Eridge* continued towards the convoy's track until the single ship, just visible through night glasses, was broad on her port beam. We dared go no further. At that moment, a flickering light and faint shout coincided with a look-out's urgent, 'Men in the water ahead.'

'Stop both. Full astern together.' The orders followed automatically.

The Pilot, having punched the alarm bell which clanged stridently throughout the ship, took over the watch from McCall who clambered into the director. The watch below, wearing a variety of night clothing, was scrambling onto the upper deck where Evans grabbed some of the damage control party and directed them to lower jumping ladders and scrambling nets over the side. Brewer, clad only in vest and pants, reached the compass platform just as the wireless office called. Jamming his ear into the voice pipe, he repeated, 'From HMS *Farndale*. Trawlers pick up survivors. HMS *Eridge* join *Kirkland* with all despatch.'

HMS *Eridge* had stopped just short of the survivors. We still did not know if they were the victims of a submarine or aircraft but some were already swimming towards the ship from both bows, their cries for help assuming an animal like quality which was horrible to hear. Away in the distance, an unseen voice was maintaining a constant, unnerving howl which rose and fell like a hound baying at the moon; nearer the ship, a little group clinging to the same spar was wailing in unison in a manner resembling a pack of beagles yelping around the carcass of their kill; beyond them, another swimmer was emitting a series of grunts which started as normal cries but dissolved into long, drawn out gasps as if his breath was being punched out of his body. Occasionally, a German prisoner of war's voice mingled with the others.

To obey HMS *Farndale*, we could only move in one direction so the engines were ordered slow astern. In the same moment, there was a sudden roar of accelerating aircraft engines heading directly towards us. While still unseen, the leader banked steeply to starboard and the second to port. In the extending roar of engines, it was impossible to tell if more than two planes were involved but McCall fired a hopeful barrage along the line of attack. At least two torpedoes had been fired but avoiding action was impossible owing to the swimmers. We could only continue our slow move astern and try not to think of the deadly missiles racing towards us.

The survivors suddenly realised that the ship was moving away from them.

'What the hell are you playing at?' An angry voice demanded.

'The yellow bastards are leaving us,' another shouted.

The survivors refused to believe assurances that the trawlers would rescue them but then their angry chorus was temporarily drowned by an agitated shout of, 'Torpedo to port.'

It seemed to be coming straight at us and, as it disappeared under the flare, we held our breath for a long, endless second until it reappeared on the other side. There was another shout of, 'Torpedo crossing ahead.'

Thank God the airman had failed to realise we were moving astern otherwise at least one torpedo might have hit us. But were there any more? Another intolerable few seconds ticked away before we knew that either two only had been fired or the others had passed unseen.

Once clear of the survivors, who were still hurling insults at us, HMS *Eridge* was turned to the eastward and maximum speed ordered to overtake *Kirkland*. We now had time to contemplate the tragedy of the *Chakdina*. Most of her wounded and prisoners would have been below but the ship had gone down so swiftly that few could have escaped. We were appalled that so many lives had been lost while under our protection. As if to mock us, the moon was now benignly shining but we looked at her with loathing. She was an enemy. Moonlight was the ally of submarines and aircraft and we never wanted to see her again until the war ended.

For that matter, neither did we want to hear 'Silent Night' during the forthcoming Christmas festivities.

On reaching Alex, the ship's company received a double shock. The first was news of the Japanese attack on Pearl Harbour although this was quickly tempered by the knowledge that the United States were in the war at last and, with typical British optimism, the prospect of quick victories in the Far East. The second shock was far more personal and outrageous because hopes of satisfying a healthy thirst were promptly shattered by orders to return immediately to Tobruk with HMS *Farndale* to pick up another convoy. As soon as we had refuelled, we left harbour ranting and roaring like true British seamen.

Next day, owing to extremely heavy weather, the convoy's departure from Tobruk was delayed for twenty-four hours so the two 'Hunts' were ordered to take shelter in Mersa Matruh. An hour or so later, we passed between two rocky headlands and entered a shallow outer lagoon through which the channel meandered to the normal anchorage in an inner lagoon. The harbour was flanked by a small town consisting of a few muddy, cratered streets lined by gaunt, shattered buildings with gaping doorways and empty window frames, over which desolation and destruction were brooding like a black cloud. The inner harbour was occupied by coasters and landing craft amongst which we slowly picked our way to buoys in the centre of the lagoon.

Daylight next morning heralded the approach of another foul day. Low clouds carrying a cold, drenching rain, were scudding across the harbour in the teeth of a strong north-westerly gale. The foreshore looked utterly desolate. In the foreground, the wind was whipping up flurries of sand across a wide, barren space which the rain was rapidly churning into a sea of mud. Some lorries, grinding in low gear towards a beached landing craft, skidded to a standstill in the soft ground where their wheels spun uselessly, until a sergeant collected a group of grumbling, cursing men to push them clear. In the harbour itself, several lighters were bumping monotonously against some coasters from which an unwilling team of stevedores was making a half hearted attempt to transfer their cargoes. In short, it was such a miserable, depressing day that even the most cheerful men felt utterly disheartened.

The forenoon dragged slowly away. For about the twentieth time I went on deck to study the weather, thinking that anyone who considered the Mediterranean to be a sea of continuous sunshine needed his head examined. I was staring gloomily to windward when Thomas, my servant, approached, wearing the smug, self satisfied expression of a man with information to impart.

'Heard the news, sir?'

I shook my head. 'No, but it looks cheerful judging by your expression.'

'Oh no, sir,' Thomas grinned. 'HMS *Repulse* and HMS *Prince of Wales* have been sunk.'[6]

The smile froze on my face. 'If that's a messdeck buzz, you'd better forget it.'

'But it's true, sir', he protested in a hurt tone. 'It was on the BBC.'

The HMS *Eridge* was alongside HMS *Farndale* so I went straight to Shorty's cabin. He had obviously heard the news and his face looked pale and drawn while he silently poured a couple of stiff gins. We barely spoke but brooded over the disaster in the Far East while the wind kept howling dismally through the rigging, as if to warn us of further disasters ahead. But, inevitably, our thoughts turned back to the Mediterranean where the loss of two ships in our first two Tobruk convoys had been a bitter disappointment.

'We mustn't get too morbid about the loss of a ship,' Shorty said. 'That's one of the hazards of war and we're bound to see many more sinkings.'

I was still not consoled. Some sixth sense had warned me of the attack on *Chakdina*, but I had failed to close up action stations so my conscience was by no means clear.

'You were at defence stations, I suppose,' Shorty said when I explained this.

'Yes.'

'Guns loaded?'

'Yes.'

Shorty thought for a few moments before replying.

'Look at it like this. Most commanding officers are the best look-outs in their ship because they know what to look and listen for. Likewise, the responsibility of command tunes them up even more than anyone else so, occasionally, they will think that they can hear or see something that doesn't exist. The dividing line between reality and imagination is sometimes very thin. The art is not to allow these borderline alarms to persuade you to assume a higher degree of readiness without corroboration. If you constantly disturb the watch below without good reason you'll soon lose their confidence and their efficiency. In the case of *Chakdina*, we'd received no warning and the aircraft weren't even sighted. But, even if they had been, no more than one salvo could have been fired in the time available and the defence watch was quite capable of doing that. You needn't blame yourself.'

Shorty had more or less repeated my own thoughts just before the attack on *Chakdina* and the knowledge that he agreed with me was some comfort.

We then discussed the two convoys in detail and the action taken by each ship in case any failure or tactical errors had contributed to the enemy's successes. We were quite unsparing in our self-analysis, by the end of which we could honestly claim that we had no reason to blame ourselves. The discussion made us feel better and, when we parted, we consoled ourselves even more with the reflection that the darkest hour always precedes the dawn so this must be the nadir of our fortunes.

For a time, such a condition seemed justified because, on 14 December, four destroyers passing through the Sicilian Channel encountered a force of Italian cruisers and destroyers and sank them all, a success which more than counterbalanced the recent loss of the cruiser HMS *Galatea*. Then fortune decided that she would temporise no longer and swung right against us. On the 19 December, the Malta based surface-force ran into a minefield off Tripoli and, in a few minutes, Force K ceased to be an effective striking force.[7] Consequently, our ability to interrupt Rommel's supplies had largely been neutralised and that, inevitably, would affect the land battle. But even worse was happening further east. On the same night, a special unit of Italian frogmen penetrated the defences of Alexandria Harbour and, in a brilliant attack, severely damaged the battleships HMS *Queen Elizabeth* and HMS *Valiant* with mines. Thus, in less than a month, five of Britain's precious capital ships had been lost or damaged and the Mediterranean Battle Fleet had ceased to exist. Thenceforth, the powerful Italian Fleet would be faced by only a few cruisers, led by Rear Admiral Philip Vian, flying his flag in the HMS *Naiad*, and by four destroyer flotillas which were unlikely to be reinforced in view of the need to reinforce the Far East. Small wonder, therefore, that the ship's company kept asking themselves if a destroyer's expectation of life was to be further curtailed in the grim months ahead.

Curiously enough, HMS *Farndale* and HMS *Eridge* fared not too badly during that dreadful fortnight and several convoys were escorted without loss, if not without incident. We lost count of the 'Red Tobruks'. The trouble was that Tobruk radar covered such a wide area of Cyrenaica and the Eastern Mediterranean that it detected a considerable amount of aerial activity, not all of which was directed against the sea. But, even if the bombers were heading elsewhere, our nerves had to bear the shock of the warning and the suspense of waiting for an attack which might, or might not, develop. We were the target on too many occasions to appreciate sharing the ordeal of others because every 'Red Tobruk' injected a tiny particle of fear which, unnoticed at first, had a slow but cumulative effect on one's nerves. My own reaction was a growing impatience and the poor Pilot, being more or less permanently on the bridge, was the primary target of my ill temper.

In mid-December, HMS *Farndale* sank a submarine. It happened on a night in which heavy rain, high winds, low visibility and stinging hail squalls made conditions more reminiscent of the North Atlantic. Our convoy had become badly scattered and HMS *Eridge* was at least ten miles astern of HMS *Farndale* when some flashes were spotted. We could hear nothing above the sound of seas booming past the ship and the silent flashes flickering through the darkness looked quite uncanny. We were so obsessed by the success of the night attack against *Chakdina* that we feared that torpedo bombers had located the convoy, even in this terrible weather. It was not until we sighted HMS *Farndale* at daybreak that we learned that she had sunk a surfaced Italian submarine. Her success cheered everybody. Compared with the general situation, it was a comparatively minor victory but so raised morale, even in ships not directly involved, that it instilled a feeling of optimism out of all proportion. We now knew that the 'Hunts' could hit back and give as good as they were receiving. For the time being, at least, we could persuade ourselves that life was not so bad, after all, and that it was foolish to worry even though a still, small voice warned me that such good advice would soon be forgotten.

On Christmas Eve 1941, the three 'Hunts', HMS *Avonvale*, HMS *Eridge* and HMS *Farndale*, were together in Alex. As usual Shorty, Withers and I dined ashore together, this time in L'Ecu de France, a restaurant exhibiting the unusual notice, 'any discussion on politics is strictly forbidden' owing to its patronage by both the Free and Vichy French. Even so, an argument, followed by the inevitable fight, did break out and caused a temporary diversion. But, on the whole, we were in a sombre mood. Although the Desert Army was making slow but steady progress, the war situation in the Far East was deteriorating so rapidly that we had little cause to celebrate this festive season. For the past six weeks the three ships had been running at full stretch in exceptionally heavy weather and against persistent opposition. Moreover, we had been constantly keyed up to make immediate decisions which might mean the difference between losing and saving the ship. Any hesitations would be swiftly conveyed to the ship's company whose morale would soon be broken if they suspected indecision on the part of their captain. Nervous tension was also beginning to reveal itself amongst some of the younger ratings and could quickly become aggravated if not handled with tact. We had other worries too. In my own case, imagination had started to play tricks and my brain was such a jumble of thoughts concerning submarines, bombers, sinking ships and drowning men that, in addition to the accepted lack of sleep at sea, I was also sleeping badly in harbour. Fortunately, these fantasies were completely forgotten at sea but I was worried lest they grew worse and needlessly increased my weariness. It was now weariness, no longer lack of self confidence, which was fanning my impatience.

Like all commanding officers, we led lonely lives because we dared not confess our innermost thoughts and fears to anyone onboard. Consequently, we brooded alone, thereby creating an impression that only one's own ship was beset by difficulties and this could be unhealthy if one was worried. In such circumstances, the constant strain of bottling up emotions inevitably had a harmful effect so an occasional chance to let off steam was imperative. This dinner provided that opportunity. All of us eased our pent up feelings, finding, to our surprise, that the others were facing the same problems but, so far as his companions could discern, remained perfectly calm and cheerful.

A trouble shared was half the battle and, for the time being, we could forget our loneliness in the common bond between us. I, for one, was delighted to learn that my nerves seemed normal to Shorty and Withers. Nevertheless, it was not a particularly cheerful evening. The fleet had been seriously weakened by losses and the need to reinforce the Far East. Troops and aircraft were also being transferred from the desert, so it was only a matter of time before the enemy took advantage of our deteriorating circumstances. The end of the war seemed a long, long way ahead and, in that moment of time, its outcome was equally unpredictable.

Returning to our ships after dinner in HMS *Farndale's* boat, we became gradually aware of an uproar in the general direction of the destroyer berths. We sincerely hoped that none of our ships was involved but, as we drew nearer, it became increasingly obvious that the noise was emanating from HMS *Eridge*.

'I'll leave you to sort that out,' Shorty laughed as his boat drew alongside HMS *Eridge's* gangway. 'Have a good Christmas.'

'What the devil's going on?' I asked the Quartermaster on reaching the upper deck.

He grinned. 'Concert party's practising carols, sir.'

No ecclesiastical committee would categorise the current song as a carol. Obviously some libertymen, having anticipated Christmas, were continuing their celebrations onboard. Christmas Eve parties had been expected because, next day, HMS *Eridge* was the emergency destroyer and no leave could be granted. However the volume of noise was loud enough to disturb the whole fleet so the vocalists had to be silenced without heavy handed authority spoiling their fun.

'Give the choir my compliments,' I told the Quartermaster. 'Tell them I'll be glad to see them in my cabin for a drink.'

The message was passed and the noise dwindled away. A few minutes later, a sheepish group, who had obviously wined well, mustered in my cabin. But they soon thawed out and, during the next thirty minutes, were to tell me some interesting tit-bits.

'Your nickname's 'hardover Gregory',' a seaman told me. 'Because the ship's always under full rudder, doing high speed zigzags at meal times.'

'Well,' I laughed. 'It's better to be thrown off a stool occasionally than be torpedoed.'

'The lads believe HMS *Eridge* is a lucky ship,' stoker Maltman, the engineroom vocalist, said. 'Mark my words, sir. Other ships will soon be thinking the same.'

It had never occurred to me that HMS *Eridge* was lucky. In fact, in view of recent events, I had feared the exact opposite. But that simple remark over a drink raised my spirits even more than the discussion with Shorty and Withers. If the ship's company believed they were serving in a lucky ship, it proved they had confidence in her and were satisfied that their lives were not being needlessly risked by stupidity or incompetence. That unconventional party considerably boosted my own morale. Usually such affairs are accepted as an open invitation to air grievances 'off the record' but the nearest approach to criticism had been a jocular remark about the excessive use of helm.

By 0800 hrs on Christmas Day, steam had been raised and Evans walked round the ship checking that everything was ready for an immediate departure in an emergency – slip rope rove, loose gear lashed down, boats hoisted and secured. The galley cooked bacon for the entire crew and we prayed that the dinner would not be spoilt by an emergency on this of all days.

After a short service, in which the singing was noticeably less robust than the 'choir's' effort on the previous evening, the traditional Christmas rounds of the messdecks were carried out. Scruffy, wearing a bow tie, was dragged, protesting vigorously, ahead of the ship's youngest rating wearing the Coxswain's uniform. Then came the Chief Bosun's Mate, wearing some piratical costume, to pipe the officers round the ship. They were followed by the Coxswain, looking most uncomfortable in his usurper's uniform which fitted him like a child's clothing on a bean pole.

The messdecks were a revelation. Streamers, balloons, candles, fancy lights, tinsel, crackers and cards had transformed the austere, overcrowded messdecks into the likeness of a church or village hall. Christmas is a family occasion but these tired men must have worked for half the night to reproduce conditions similar to those in which many families would be celebrating this wartime festival. Their own party would be forced and slightly unreal but, at least, they would be with their families in spirit. It was rather sad because many would be wondering if they would live to enjoy another real family Christmas.

The tables were set for the traditional dinner but space had been found for Leading Cook Hardy's mince pies and cakes, amongst which would be at least one baked with plaster. There was also space for several jugs of rum. Legitimately, the jugs should have contained the day's issue of grog but these were holding at least a week's supply of neat rum.

'Good God! Where did all that booze come from?' I exclaimed.

'Pongos in Matruh. Good old infantry,' exclaimed a seaman in a slurred voice which suggested he had not been backward in sampling the beverage. From the mingled expressions of irritation, embarrassment and feigned innocence, it was obvious that my informant was not familiar with the need to know principle. Only the entrepreneurs would know what had been bartered for this illicit liquor. But Christmas was not an occasion on which to ask awkward questions so I swallowed the proffered glassful and thereby became an accessory to an offence for which the Naval Discipline Act laid down severe penalties.

Similar hospitality at two more messes convinced me that a continuation would be most unwise so, using our emergency status as an excuse, I made my apologies and withdrew. At short intervals after that, the other officers who would be involved in getting the ship swiftly to sea, sensibly dropped out. That left only the Gunner and the Doctor, to withstand the accepted ship's company effort to reduce at least one officer to a state of insobriety. Bowed but undefeated, they returned to the wardroom just in time for dinner.

'Well done', Evans greeted them. 'I didn't expect to see you again today.'

The Doctor gave a feeble grin and muttered, 'We did our best.'

Evans' remark had been made in a jocular manner but the Gunner glared at him and growled, 'At least we tried to be sociable. We didn't chicken out like some people.'

Evans' tongue flicked out ominously but, with a great effort, he held his peace. The Gunner, too, fell silent and ate his dinner with a sullen expression on his face while the Doctor picked reluctantly at his food. The others made a valiant effort to maintain the festive spirit. But naval rum has a depressing effect on those not accustomed to it and their efforts were muted compared to the laughter and singing on the messdecks. It was a relief to finish the meal and to slip away for a post prandial nap.

At daylight on Boxing Day HMS *Heythrop* at last joined us and the four 'Hunts' sailed to escort a large landing craft carrier to Benghazi which had just been recaptured. This ship's craft were just as vital for unloading military supplies as *Glenroy's* had been in Tobruk, so effective fighter cover had been promised. Consequently, the familiar 'Red Tobruks' did not cause too much concern until the force became the target of a succession of bombing attacks without a single friendly fighter.

'Where the hell are the Brylcream boys?' An angry voice demanded at a gun while sponging out the barrels for the fifth time.

'Recovering from a hangover, of course,' a gunlayer, retorted. 'Now stop bellyaching and get a move on.'

The force reached the entrance to the Benghazi swept channel at midnight and the landing craft were lowered to be led shorewards by a minesweeper. We expected this to be the first of many visits but, in fact, we never returned. Demolitions had been so effective, and the weather was to be so bad, that the port was only ready to handle small vessels by mid-January 1942. By then an Indian and an Australian division had been transferred to meet the Japanese thrust in the Far East and the drive into Tripolitania was no longer practical. Rommel's forces then counter-attacked and the Desert Army was forced to fall back to a line covering Tobruk, thereby abandoning Benghazi and, more important to naval operations in the Central Basin, the airfields on the Libyan 'hump'. It was those airfields which should have been providing our fighter cover. Not until later did we learn that heavy storms had made them unusable. The return was similar to the outward passage. The weather was foul with rough seas and driving rain squalls. Air attacks were frequent and, as we were still unaware of the condition of the Libyan airfields, we continued to feel bitter about the absence of fighters. It was during one of these attacks, in the twilight of a bleak, stormy evening, that Rayner almost drowned the noise of gunfire with his thunderous, 'Got the bastard!'

The pom-pom had undoubtedly scored several hits but its target – a torpedo bomber – had been so briefly glimpsed that it was impossible to claim a definite kill. Nevertheless, the incident earned Rayner the reputation of a marksman and was to provide him with ammunition to bore anyone who was foolish enough to listen with stories of the, 'One that didn't get away.'

When the New Year was rung in, I made a silent vow to curb my impatience during the coming year. It lasted exactly five minutes. At five minutes past midnight, the poor Pilot was the target of another verbal blitz which left a glow of satisfaction at the knowledge that the virtue of patience could be conveniently forgotten for another twelve months.

In January 1942, four more 'Hunts' – HMS *Southwold*, HMS *Dulverton*, HMS *Hurworth* and HMS *Beaufort* – joined the Fleet. The eight ships were now formed into the 5th Destroyer Flotilla of two divisions, one containing the four original ships led by Shorty – HMS *Eridge*, HMS *Avonvale*, HMS *Farndale* and HMS *Heythrop* – and the other – the newcomers – under

Commander C.T. Jellicoe in HMS *Southwold*. The partnership of HMS *Farndale* and HMS *Eridge* remained intact and, together with various corvettes and trawlers, escorted several convoys safely to Tobruk- which greatly increased our morale. The last coincided with the evacuation of Benghazi and it was sad to see the motor launches, minesweepers, boom defence vessels and landing craft streaming back to Tobruk after so much effort had been devoted to reopening the port.

At the end of January, HMS *Eridge* had to clean her boilers so HMS *Farndale* sailed with the next Tobruk convoy without her. Having exchanged formal salutes as she passed, some wags on the upper deck sang, 'The bells of hell go ting a ling a ling for you but not for me' and another shouted, 'Don't get into trouble without your lucky ship'. HMS *Farndale's* seamen retorted some appropriate comments as she steamed towards the open boom. Then she turned into the Great Pass channel and headed northward until she vanished over the horizon. Later, we were to regret our facetiousness because we never saw her again. Off Tobruk, she was hit by a bomb and had to return to Port Said for temporary repairs to enable her to make the long passage to the United Kingdom. Her departure was a bitter disappointment. Since leaving the Clyde, we had become 'chummy' ships. More important, we had operated together and become each other's minder. We trusted each other, knowing the other ship would react to any situation with the minimum of signalling. That was now finished and we would have to operate with another ship. Of the other 'Hunts', we knew HMS *Avonvale* best and hoped she would be our new partner.

Shorty, fortunately, was unhurt but the absence of that astute, sympathetic leader was a personal loss to Withers and myself. Shorty had been our guide and a friend to whom we had poured out our doubts and troubles, knowing that we would always receive sensible, practical advice. We doubted if we would ever see his like again and, consequently, felt very lonely.

Not only was the flotilla being reorganised but HMS *Eridge* herself was changing. Every month had seen a constant trickle of ratings, for various reasons such as sickness, advancement and technical courses. A ship's company is a conservative body and we resented the departure of so many familiar faces, fearing their replacements wouldn't fit in. They might be technically competent but each ship had its own individual methods, which took time to assimilate. Our routine did not allow time for training so the newcomers had to learn by bitter experience at action stations. Luckily, our fears turned out to be groundless and, once they were accustomed to the ship, the newcomers were as efficient as their predecessors.

We did not team up with HMS *Avonvale* but with HMS *Beaufort* whose captain, Lieutenant Commander Sir Standish O'Grady Roche was junior to me. We had never met before and were still strangers when the two 'Hunts' and two corvettes sailed for Tobruk escorting three petrol and ammunition carriers – *Bintang*, *Hanne* and *Alysa*. This was the first occasion I was senior officer of the escorts and everyone onboard felt rather proud of our new responsibility.

The first forty-eight hours were uneventful except for a strong head wind which so slowed the convoy that it would never reach the planned rendezvous with fighters at daylight on the third morning. At 0400 hrs, the Pilot calculated our expected position at daylight and had it transmitted to the air base providing fighter cover, as the amended rendezvous. He then went to the charthouse to snatch a short rest. Soon afterwards I followed to my cabin.

The Gunner had the morning watch. As daylight strengthened, he casually searched the heavens, hoping to catch a glimpse of the fighters. Plenty of blue sky was visible above the cloud base but he could neither see nor hear anything. At 0700 hrs Tobruk broadcast a 'red alert'. No indication of the area of aerial activity was given but the Gunner, being fully occupied with handling the ship, called the Pilot.

I had heard the warning in my cabin and went straight to the bridge. The Pilot followed and switched on the fighter control set, grumbling as he did so that there was no rest for the weary. While his set was warming up, Tobruk repeated the warning.

'Looks as if they're trying to scare us,' the Gunner remarked.

The Pilot started to call the fighters but received no reply. He waited a few seconds and then continued to call until convinced he was speaking to an empty void.

'They don't seem to be airborne,' he reported.

The Pilot went on calling, hoping base control would hear him. The wind had now dropped leaving a slight nor' westerly swell into which the three old ships were pitching gently while their escorts were zig-zagging fussily around them. Everything looked very peaceful.

At 0750 hrs Tobruk broadcast a third 'red alert'. The activity could be anywhere in the huge area covered by Tobruk radio. There was still no real cause for concern but the convoy, without fighters, was only partially protected. The watch was due to change in a few minutes but could we afford to remain at defence stations? I looked at the sky. There were enough gaps in the clouds for short bursts of controlled fire which could be provided best by the first degree of readiness. In such circumstances the risk of remaining at defence stations would be unjustifiable even though the higher degree of readiness would deprive the morning watch of both rest and breakfast.

'Sound the alarm,' I told the Pilot.

A second later the alarm bells were clanging round the ship, greeted by a great groan from those who had been looking forward to the end of their watch. A group of grumbling seamen clambered up the ladder and began to muster at A gun while McCall was passing some rapid instructions to the transmitting station.

In the engineroom, Engine Room Artificers Pattinson and Berry – the latter young and newly joined – were starting the forenoon watch. They were constantly operating their manoeuvring valves because HMS *Eridge* was zigzagging at speed but keeping a constant bearing on the convoy, which demanded frequent adjustments of engine revolutions. When action stations were ordered, they were joined by Chief ERA De Gruchy. He was a well built, good looking man but reticent. Without speaking to his colleagues, De Gruchy took up a position from which he could keep an eye on the gauges and auxiliary machinery.

On deck, closing up reports had just been completed when the radar operator suddenly reported, 'Aircraft ahead. Range 15,000 yards, closing.'

His voice sounded quite jubilant about picking up a target on his primitive set.

Ears and eyes were strained towards the lookout bearing, seeing nothing but cloud and hearing nothing, at first, except the sound of water lapping gently. But, soon, the drone of motors grew gradually more audible, steadily closing a gap in the clouds at which McCall instinctively pointed the guns.

A brief hope that our long awaited fighters were at last arriving was soon crushed when we heard the heavy drone which no fighter engine makes. This was a bomber and no friendly bomber would be operating in this area.

'Open fire,' I ordered.

McCall opened fire at the gap even before the aircraft was sighted. The shell bursts were already erupting in the gap like black puff balls when the bomber flew into view. It was already committed to a dive and McCall immediately shifted the guns to fire a barrage ahead of the convoy. The pom-pom and nearest oerlikon kept trained on the diving bomber, firing a continued stream of shells. Just before reaching the barrage zone, the bomber zoomed upwards. As it did so, four harmless looking objects dropped from its underbelly. Fascinated the bridge team watched them fall in a graceful parabola. Even before feeling the shock of their explosion, we were mentally stunned by a great ball of fire and smoke billowing

74

from *Bintang* and, in less than a minute, she was blazing from stem to stern. Two rafts, carrying no more than a handful of survivors, drifted clear of the conflagration only a few seconds before the ship vanished from sight, leaving a black pall of smoke above her watery grave.

The bomber, pursued by high explosive, retreated rapidly northwards leaving a corvette to rescue the survivors without harassment. But, finding no fighters on its trail, it reduced speed and proceeded to shadow the convoy from outside gun range. Angrily, the Pilot continued to repeat the fighters' call sign until, in sheer desperation, he flung down his handset.

'Can you hear the fighters on another frequency?' The Pilot asked the wireless office.

'No, sir', Petty Officer Godfrey replied. 'But the Commander in Chief is raising hell at their absence. Base reports they're airborne but can't find us.'

'What the hell's wrong with 'em?' The Pilot growled. 'They must be blind.'

With such perfect enemy reconnaissance, a reduction in the degree of readiness was out of the question and this was fully appreciated by everyone. Suddenly the fighter direction receiver unexpectedly crackled.

'Have sighted convoy,' a cheerful fighter pilot's voice reported. 'Any instructions?'

'Get 'em on that bloody shadower,' I growled.

The fighters were directed towards the north and, a few seconds later, two naval Hurricanes roared overhead. At the same time, the bomber, as if it had intercepted our signals, turned leisurely towards Crete and dropped below the horizon.

The Hurricanes searched vainly for a few minutes and then returned to the convoy, which had been proceeding doggedly on its way ever since the destruction of the petrol carrier. Another attack seemed highly probable and conditions were ideal for it. A gentle breeze was drifting broken, low-flying clouds across the sky giving sufficient cover for aircraft to make an unseen approach but leaving enough gaps for them to view their target. Moreover, Tobruk was broadcasting a constant stream of warnings.

The rescue corvette, having picked up the survivors, was steaming at full speed to overtake the convoy when HMS *Beaufort* suddenly sounded six short blasts – the torpedo alarm – and our concern about aircraft instantly vanished. HMS *Beaufort* was swinging to port under full rudder and lookouts, searching the sea in her direction, when she sighted three torpedo tracks speeding towards the convoy. Thanks to HMS *Beaufort's* timely warning, the two merchant ships were already turning to comb the tracks. HMS *Beaufort* was now steaming at high speed towards the submarine's estimated position, dropping depth charges at frequent intervals. The corvette, still two miles astern, turned towards her. The torpedoes had harmlessly crossed the convoy's track and the two ships were turning to resume their original course. HMS *Beaufort* reached the submarine's 'furthest on' position and carried out a circular sweep. The corvette was now close to her and HMS *Beaufort* signalled, 'No contact. Am organising search. Water conditions poor.'

HMS *Beaufort* was already four miles away. If she and the corvette continued to search, the convoy would be deprived indefinitely of their gun support. The safety of the convoy was our primary concern. HMS *Beaufort's* action had already prevented the submarine gaining position for another attack. The submarine was no longer a danger – all the portents were pointing to a greater threat from the air. HMS *Beaufort* was needed with the convoy as quickly as possible.

'Make to HMS *Beaufort*,' I told Brewer, the Yeoman of the Signals. 'Negative search. Rejoin with all despatch.'

HMS *Beaufort* acknowledged the signal and a puff of smoke erupted from her funnel as she began to accelerate towards the convoy. Even so, she would be outside effective gun support for at least twenty minutes and the slower corvette for double that time. As if to taunt us, Tobruk broadcast another 'red alert'.

A minute later, Godfrey yelled up his voice pipe, 'Immediate to HMS *Eridge* from Tobruk. Large air formation detected on a southerly course.'

The aircraft could be heading for any target in Cyrenaica. But, in our experience, this was the first occasion in which Tobruk had issued such a definite warning to one of many targets: we were convinced that their radar plot had conclusively confirmed that the aircraft were heading towards our convoy. I ordered the air raid warning to be hoisted and silently begged *Beaufort* to go faster.

The red flag fluttered to the masthead while the Pilot was warning the fighters and stationing them to the northward. Once more anxiety gripped us and lookouts anxiously scanned the heavens. To strained nerves the day seemed evil; the clouds looked darker, carrying a hint of gales, and a watery sun, gazing alike on ships and fighters, appeared to wink sardonically when a small cloud crossed its face. In conformity with this change in nature, the barren land looked even bleaker and more sinister. HMS *Beaufort* was still well astern and appeared to us, so greatly in need of her support, to be loitering.

Six low flying fighters, several miles ahead, suddenly crossed the convoy's track, but not from the direction Tobruk had warned of. My immediate reaction was, 'Thank God! Fighter control has reacted swiftly to the threat'.'

With such powerful reinforcements now available, HMS *Beaufort's* absence was no longer vital. We could relax a little. But McCall, studying

the newcomers through his powerful binoculars, swiftly dragged us back
to grim reality by yelling, 'Those aren't British; they're German!'

The newcomers were now swinging upwards through the clouds
towards our unseen Hurricane patrol. The Pilot's 'Bandits on you
tails; bandits on your tails', was acknowledged by a burst of cannon
fire. Seconds later, the Hurricanes plunged through the clouds, the
Messerschmidts pursuing like a pack of hounds racing for the kill. The
fighters were swerving, climbing, diving to a bedlam of machine gun and
cannon fire. The planes were so inextricably mixed that we dared not fire
the main armament and, as the battle was beyond the range of the close
range weapons, we could only wait in anguish for the inevitable. The two
Hurricanes, outnumbered and outgunned, did not stand a chance and,
within a minute, the Germans were climbing back into the high heavens
leaving two blazing pyres on the surface of the sea.

I gazed sombrely at the Pilot who voiced our common fear. 'That's not
the group reported by Tobruk. Those fighters are from a Libyan airfield,
not the north.'

I nodded. 'The bombers are still to come. Let's hope fighter control has
made the same deduction.'

The second corvette was ordered to search for survivors where the
Hurricanes had crashed. HMS *Eridge* was now the convoy's only
protection. Her speed was reduced and she was manoeuvred as close as
possible ahead of the leading supply ship. HMS *Beaufort*, tossing spray
over bridge and funnel, was still overhauling but, as yet, was too far
astern to give more than partial protection.

The ship was now plodding wearily through a leaden sea, which had lost
much of its playfulness and was recoiling wearily from the bow. Except
for the monotonous anti-submarine transmissions and the gentle hum of
fans, the ship was utterly quiet and men spoke in whispers as if afraid of
breaking such an unnatural silence. Thus our ears were quick to detect a
new sound. Its growth was imperceptible, at first, but steadily expanded
until a roar of motors filled the heavens. Aircraft, still invisible above the
clouds, were converging from all directions just as HMS *Beaufort* drew
level with the stern of the convoy.

'Umbrella barrage above convoy; commence,' McCall shouted to the
transmitting station.

'Here they come,' yelled Brewer pointing at three JU 88s diving out of
the clouds on the port quarter.

The four-inch guns and pom-pom were already pumping out shells
above the convoy but Able Seaman Stone's oerlikon cracked into action
firing at another group on the starboard side. As the bombers screamed
overhead, the ship staggered as if hit by a gigantic sledgehammer and

many below decks feared a bomb had struck her. Astern, bomb bursts blocked our view of the supply ships while shell explosions pitted the sky above them. Now that the bombs were falling, we had time to look around. For a few seconds, we believed that all the bombers were committed to their attack. Then our hearts fluttered with dismay. High in the sky, three more Junkers were approaching in a perfect arrowhead formation, showing an accuracy about their station-keeping which warned us that these were real professionals. McCall swung the guns towards this new threat and opened fire just as the bombers dipped towards the convoy in a controlled, disciplined partnership – like three high divers giving a perfect exhibition of a simultaneous dive. Down, down, down they plunged and we saw the bombs disengage from their underbellies just before the bombers swooped back into the high heavens. We watched the graceful descent of the bombs which seemed to be aimed straight towards HMS *Eridge*, passing so close overhead that we instinctively ducked until our eyes were dragged astern by a devastating explosion. *Hanne* was already engulfed by a blazing, fiery furnace. Rockets and tracer were soaring hundreds of feet into the sky. Then another mighty blast produced a towering column of black smoke, which suddenly lifted to reveal an empty sea beneath it.

Hanne was gone. What had been a solid ship had been reduced in less than a minute to a few pieces of wreckage, to which was clinging one solitary survivor. In the meantime the bombers, having unloaded their bombs, were heading northwards and seemed certain to escape. Then, from the direction of the coast, the high pitched shriek of racing engines grew rapidly louder until ten Spitfires tore across a gap in the clouds.

'You're too late, you bastards; you're too late,' an angry voice yelled.

The Spitfires vanished back into the clouds. A minute later, a familiar cacophony of an aerial battle erupted several miles to the northward. Two JU 88s spiralled slowly through the clouds with smoke curling from their fuselages. Their pilots were clearly losing control; the smoke was rapidly thickening and tongues of flame were beginning to lick wings and cockpits. Tails of smoke reached skywards as the JU 88s' noses dipped into steeper dives then, finally, the dying Junkers hit the sea with mighty splashes. Our Gambut[8] friends had extracted a partial revenge at least, for the day's disasters.

Having witnessed the destruction of the two other supply ships, the emotions of *Alysa's* crew were easy to imagine; the black smoke pouring from her tall funnel testified the determination of her stokers to reach the doubtful security of Tobruk as quickly as possible. The old ship was steaming faster than she had ever steamed in her long life and, thanks to their efforts, we reached Tobruk several hours earlier than expected.

Having passed the familiar green leading light, HMS *Eridge* steamed slowly down the tortuous swept channel, between numerous wrecks, and secured alongside the fuelling jetty opposite the battered Naval Headquarters. We were feeling thoroughly depressed. The fact that we had been running incessantly for ten weeks and had lost only four ships was submerged by the bitter recollection that two of those ships had died in a horrible manner in the first convoy under HMS *Eridge's* control. The officers, reflecting the mood of the ship's company, were shocked and upset. No one wanted companionship, only a stiff drink, a quick dinner and bed. But, shortly after refuelling had commenced, an RAF car arrived with an invitation to dine at Gambut and celebrate the fighters' success. A party was the last thing anyone wanted, especially one celebrating an incident which, from our point of view, had been a near disaster. But now, thanks to the *Alysa's* safe arrival, the invitation could not be refused without causing offence. So, very unwillingly, Evans elected to go and managed to persuade an equally reluctant Gunner and Doctor to accompany him.

Next morning, we were to sail at daylight. The weather portents of the previous day had proved accurate and my servant Thomas called me to the strident shriek of a nor' westerly. Feeling as depressed as on the previous evening, I dressed slowly, praying for a quiet passage and listening sombrely to the preparations for departure. But, instead of Evans, the Pilot reported the ship ready for sea.

'Where's Evans?' I casually asked. 'Is he ill?'

The Pilot looked embarrassed and hesitated.

'Come on, man,' I snapped. 'Is he ill or not?'

'He looked even more flustered. 'He – he's under arrest.'

I gaped at him. 'What the hell are you talking about?'

The Pilot gulped two or three times before mumbling, 'He had a fight with the Gunner last night and placed himself under arrest.'

'Tell him to report to me as soon as the ship reaches the open sea,' I snorted.

HMS *Eridge* cleared harbour and was bumping heavily into a rough, tumbling sea when a sheepish looking Evans arrived on the bridge. He was completely unmarked and, even though my temper was not improved, my worries were eased. The fight could not have been serious if Evans was showing no signs of damage after fighting a man who was bigger and stronger.

'I'll investigate later,' I growled. 'But no officer is to skulk in his cabin while the ship is at sea. Return to duty at once.'

Evans mumbled a shamefaced apology and left the bridge. After his departure forming the convoy and disposing the escorts demanded my full attention so, knowing the Gunner had the forenoon watch, I decided to postpone giving him a piece of my mind until he took over at 0800 hrs. But the watch changed without any sign of the Gunner. Thirty minutes later, he had still not reached the bridge and McCall, while doing his best to keep out of my way, was obviously prepared to keep the forenoon. That convinced me that he was covering up for the Gunner who, presumably, had drunk too much at Gambut and was unfit for duty.

Irritated by this effort to conceal the truth, I spoke sharply. 'Tell the Gunner I wish to see him.'

McCall's obvious discomfort, while instructing the messenger, confirmed my opinion. I was now thoroughly angry and, using McCall as a scapegoat, vented my wrath on him while the minutes were ticking steadily away. That made him flustered and me angrier until, about 0900 hrs, a sound like an arthritic man climbing a steep ladder became gradually audible. The watchkeepers turned towards the hatch in time to see a cap poking slowly above the combing. Then came a pair of black eyes followed by a swollen, distorted nose and thick, cracked lips: the Gunner was only recognisable by the stripe on his sleeves. I was appalled. He looked more like a victim of a beating than the loser of a harmless fight. The situation was clearly far too serious to keep concealed.

Quite apart from this, the weather was foul and a miserable passage followed. It was bad enough having to listen to the officers clucking about the incident like a lot of broody hens. But, unfortunately, the fight had been witnessed by the Quartermaster who, not unnaturally, was regaling his messmates with a very lurid account. Tradition always maintained that such behaviour amongst the officers would have a disastrous effect on discipline. During the three day passage to Alex there was a noticeable change, though not in the manner I feared. If anything Evans' authority seemed to be enhanced, as if he was respected for inflicting so much damage on a bigger and heavier opponent. Nevertheless, I was angry with myself for having allowed Evans to accept the RAF dinner invitation. No one had wanted to go. The officers were not only exhausted but deeply shocked by the events of the previous twenty-four hours and had only controlled their feelings at an unwelcome party out of respect for their hosts. Back onboard, with no such restraint, a trivial argument between Evans and the Gunner had caused their mutual dislike to erupt into violence. There could be no excuse for such stupid behaviour, which was now known by every man onboard and could no longer be treated as a simple internal disciplinary matter. How I yearned for Shorty's advice. But Shorty was beyond reach and I was feeling very lonely, especially as reporting the incident might add a court martial to our other troubles. But back in Alex, Rear Admiral

Glennie, commanding the destroyer flotillas, took a surprisingly lenient attitude.

'Obviously they can't remain in the same ship,' was all he said. 'Who's to leave?'

That rightly threw the ball straight to me but it was not a pleasant choice. I liked them both. The Gunner, apart from bouts of truculence, was a capable officer and had been a tower of strength on many occasions. But so had Evans and, whereas the Gunner had only limited responsibility, all the threads concerning organisation, welfare, discipline and administration passed through First Lieutenant Evans' hands. He would be far more difficult to replace and the decision needed no more than a moment's reflection.

'You're right,' the Admiral said. 'I can transfer your Gunner to another ship without any reflection on his character.'

After that, we discussed HMS *Eridge* and he was astonished to learn that the ship had only four seaman officers. He then enquired about their routine at sea: on learning that, for the past twelve months, they had been working a daily average of fifteen to sixteen hours, decided that we were undermanned and promised to do his best to obtain some additional officers.

The Gunner was immediately transferred to a cruiser. His relief, a newly promoted officer, had served under me as a Petty Officer in HMS *Jaguar* and I was glad to have him. But the Admiral was as good as his word and two extra officers also joined. The more senior was a Portsmouth solicitor named Cox, a Royal Navy Volunteer Reserve Lieutenant. He was to be a great asset because he had just completed a course in anti-submarine warfare for which he now assumed responsibility, thereby allowing the overworked Pilot to concentrate on navigation and fighter direction. His companion was a midshipman, always called 'the snotty', who had been loaned by a cruiser to gain experience in destroyers. Although not qualified, he could undertake a number of duties as part of his training and thereby reduce the load of other officers. On a less serious note, the newcomers formed a handsome trio and HMS *Eridge* rose several places in the Adonis league.

Having just lost two supply ships, we needed a quiet Tobruk convoy, if there was such a thing, not only to restore our composure but to acclimatise the new officers. Instead, HMS *Eridge* was one of the seven 'Hunts' detailed for a Malta convoy. Several supply ships had reached Malta while the Libyan airfields had been held by the RAF but these had been lost when the Desert Army retreated. Moreover, the Navy, like the Army, had been compelled to transfer many ships to Australia and the Indian Ocean. So only a weak force could be mustered to escort *Clan Chattan, Clan Campbell* and *Rowallan Castle*. In such straitened circumstances only the island's desperate needs could justify the risk of despatching an inadequate force into the Mediterranean Central Basin without fighter cover.

That convoy was another unpleasant experience. Off Tobruk, *Clan Campbell* was damaged by a bomb and had to turn back. On the following forenoon, her sister ship, *Clan Chattan*, was set on fire and subsequently sunk by a destroyer. Then, as the convoy penetrated into the Central Basin beyond the range of fighters, Tobruk kept broadcasting a stream of 'red alerts', depressing warnings of heavier and more frequent air attacks. In one of them, a bomb exploded uncomfortably close to HMS *Eridge* and Ordinary Seaman Rowson, a loading member at X gun, was hit by a splinter. It was not nearly so serious as he later boasted and the Doctor soon had him back at his action station.

In the early evening, a convoy of empty ships, including *Breconshire*, which had left Malta the previous night, was sighted. *Rowallan Castle*, with less than two hours to live, and the group from Malta, maintained their course while their escorts exchanged convoys. For the next thirty minutes cruisers and destroyers were criss crossing each other's tracks, or making drastic alterations of course, while steaming to their new screening positions. The sea was choppy and a stiff breeze was driving low clouds across the sky. Aircraft, either singly or on small groups, were frequently crossing breaks in the clouds and the guns were in almost continuous action. By the time our shells exploded both bursts and bombers were hidden once more by clouds. The gap in the clouds also allowed the bombers only brief glimpses of their targets. But bombs have to fall somewhere and several ships were shaken by near misses. Only darkness could bring some respite but, to the toiling gunners, the transition from daylight to dusk seemed to take an unconscionable time. The dangerous period of dusk was equally agonising and the guns were firing one barrage after another in the direction of unseen aircraft. But visibility gradually closed down until it became difficult to see nearby ships: the men, at last, could look forward to some relaxation in the ship's degree of readiness.

'Look out astern,' Brewer suddenly yelled.

His warning was cut short by the roar of accelerating engines and a low flying JU 88, looking like some monstrous bird of prey, flew along the entire length of the ship, the snarl of its engines mingling with the shriek of falling bombs. A compact group exploded simultaneously, just off the bow, and tossed up a gigantic mushroom of blackened water. HMS *Eridge* staggered as if she had collided with a stone jetty, teetered on the edge of the crater, then tumbled in: tons of water crashed onto the upper deck, pouring down hatchways and ammunition chutes. The ship struggled in the maelstrom before rising, with water gushing over the sides, as if she was a dog shaking itself after an unexpected immersion.

The main engines and steering gear appeared to be undamaged but most compartments had been plunged into complete or partial darkness. The repair parties immediately began to assess the damage and to replace smashed bulbs and blown fuses. In the engineroom, steam was leaking from a number of joints. The Chief, meanwhile, was carrying out a rapid inspection of the machinery spaces. Reaching Number Two boiler room, he could barely distinguish stoker Petty Officer Grantham in the eerie semi darkness through which shafts of light from the fire box were flickering on the bulkhead.

'Any problems?' he asked.

Grantham shook his head but drew the Chief beneath a fan's down draught.

'Case of nerves behind you,' he said in a stage whisper.

The Chief looked round and saw a pale faced young stoker staring at the bulkhead with unseeing eyes. Going to him, he placed a fatherly arm on the young man's shoulder.

'Take it easy,' he said in a quiet voice. 'Go on deck for a breath of fresh air.'

In the store beyond the stokers' messdeck the Shipwright busied himself patching a hole in the side-plating that was leaking water into the ship. Elsewhere the ship was steadily returning to near normal and the convoy reached Alex without further incident. A few days later, the cruisers and Fleet destroyers carried out a westerly sweep, during the course of which the cruiser HMS *Naiad*, flagship of Rear Admiral Vian, was torpedoed and sunk. The Admiral then transferred his flag to the newly arrived HMS *Cleopatra* and promptly replaced many of her officers with HMS *Naiad's* survivors. The displaced officers felt some resentment but the rest of the fleet had little sympathy for them. Recent Malta convoys had provided ample warning of the dangers of such operations and we reckoned that a tough, resolute commander would stand the best chance, not only of achieving success but also of preserving our lives. Rear Admiral Vian was the seagoing commander and everyone had faith in his leadership. If he wanted officers whom he knew could stand up to his brusque manners and carry out their duties with the efficiency he demanded, that was considered fair enough by the rest of the fleet.

Having reached Alex, HMS *Eridge* was towed to the dockyard and placed alongside a Free French destroyer for action damage repairs. It was nine months since I had last spent a night ashore and I needed a change. So I booked a room at the Union Club and then joined O'Grady Roche and another Hunt commander, Lieutenant Commander Bill Petch, of HMS *Dulverton*, for a round of golf. It was not a game at which any of us excelled and our performance drew some exceedingly caustic criticism from our caddies. Nevertheless, we enjoyed ourselves. We then went to Monseigneur where we drank large quantities of beer amongst a crowd of soldiers and airmen from the Western Desert. After that, we went round the night clubs where O'Grady Roche, who was a handsome man, danced with a succession of seedy looking hostesses while Petch and I watched in silent disapproval. Anyway, the run ashore did us good.

Chapter Five

The Battle of Sirte

I n March 1942 HMS *Eridge* took part in an exercise with most of the fleet. It was unusual for so many ships to be available for such a purpose but it soon became obvious that Rear Admiral Vian was practising some special tactics. This suggested he was testing his intentions for a forthcoming Malta convoy in case it was intercepted by a surface force. A day or two later the operation orders were issued for such a convoy with the unglamorous title of MW10.

MW10 sailed in three groups spread over thirty-six hours. The seven 'Hunts', under the command of Commander Jellicoe in HMS *Southwold* sailed first, to carry out an anti-submarine sweep along the convoy's planned track. Onboard HMS *Eridge* were two fighter pilots bound for Tobruk where the flotilla was to fuel before joining the convoy.

The 'Hunts' reached a position north of Sollum and reversed course to the eastward. While on this course, the supply ships *Breconshire*, *Clan Campbell*, *Pampas* and *Talabot*, escorted by the anti-aircraft cruiser HMS *Carlisle* and destroyers, left Alex, heading for a position north of Tobruk where the three groups were to concentrate thirty hours later.

The 'Hunts' continued their easterly sweep to the meridian of Mersa Matruh and then altered course to the westward for the final leg of their sweep. It was then daylight on Friday, 20 March 1942, a cold, blustery morning with an overcast sky and choppy sea. Conditions were at their very worst for submarine detection. Petty Officer Davey and his team, listening to the monotonous transmissions of their detector, knew by experience that they were being deflected by a water layer of variable temperatures: that a submarine could lurk beneath the layer in almost complete immunity. Nevertheless, they kept pinging away, trying not to let their concentration wander, until late afternoon when HMS *Southwold* ordered a new disposition and course for Tobruk.

'When will we arrive?' McCall asked from the director.

'About 1900 hrs.'

'And depart?'

A shattering explosion drowned the Pilot's answer and all other noises in the ship. About a mile away, HMS *Heythrop's* quarterdeck had vanished into a mass of mangled, twisted metal. Black smoke was rapidly enveloping the ship with a dark pall, through which a vertical column of white steam was erupting with a doleful shriek. HMS *Southwold* immediately cancelled her flag signal and ordered a submarine search around its suspected position. But time was critical. Any delay in fuelling could jeopardize the entire operation so, after two or three abortive sweeps, Jellicoe ordered HMS *Avonvale*, HMS *Hurworth* and HMS *Eridge* to stand by the damaged ship while the other three 'Hunts' headed for Tobruk. As a parting shot, HMS *Southwold's* signal lantern ordered HMS *Eridge* to take HMS *Heythrop* in tow.

By now, most of the smoke had been dispersed by the wind. HMS *Heythrop* was lying broadside to the sea, down by the stern and listing heavily to starboard. Seas were breaking against her hull like waves against a semi-submerged rock. Her motor boat and whaler were already ferrying wounded and surplus crew to her consorts so, while the tow was being passed, our own boats were lowered to help.

HMS *Eridge* was moving slowly ahead, to take the strain on the towing hawser, when Petty Officer Davey heard a whisper of sound in his head phones. He swung his transmitter back across the bearing and, this time, an echo cracked sharply in the receiver.

'Submarine contact 250 degrees, range 2,000 yards,' he yelled.

The submarine had obviously risen above the temperature layer and was in an attacking position. But HMS *Eridge*, held by HMS *Heythrop's* dead weight astern, was helpless. Brewer hoisted the 'submarine starboard' flag signal and the telegraphist transmitted its range and bearing over the manoeuvring wave. HMS *Avonvale*, off HMS *Heythrop's* starboard bow, immediately accelerated towards the submarine's position and HMS *Hurworth* crossed ahead to join her. Heavy depth charging by both ships obviously forced the submarine to dive deep but had she been allowed time to fire torpedoes?

'Aircraft off the port bow,' a look-out suddenly shouted.

The bridge team had been searching apprehensively for torpedo tracks but one look-out had resisted that temptation. His warning was heard by McCall who immediately trained the director, followed by the four-inch guns, towards the look-out bearing where he sighted a formation of torpedo bombers flying along the horizon, obviously assessing the situation. They would now know that one ship was towing another but they would be unaware that the other two were hunting a submarine? The important thing, as far as they were concerned, was that the tow was masking the gunfire of those two ships so they were in the ideal position for an attack. The bombers swung towards us in a compact group and their swift approach so outpaced McCall's methodical control orders that I struggled not to shout, 'Get a move on, man.'

But I kept my mouth firmly shut and was glad I had done so when McCall's opening salvoes burst immediately in front of the leading aircraft which jerked violently to one side. The others broke formation and, for a few seconds, threatened simultaneous attacks from different directions. But McCall shifted to barrage fire and a wall of shell bursts clearly weakened their determination, persuading them to fire their torpedoes at long range. As soon as they had fired, they swung in a semi-circle towards the horizon and disappeared without even waiting to see the result of their attack.

Nevertheless, one torpedo, at least, might have been accurately aimed and look-outs anxiously scanned the heaving sea, trying not to think of the deadly missiles beneath it. Avoiding action was impossible and, as the seconds ticked remorselessly away, tension steadily mounted until the Pilot looked up from a stop watch and muttered, 'They should be crossing our track now.'

His audience became even more absorbed with the white horses breaking against the hull but the airmens' aim had been no better than their courage and we saw nothing.

Our progress was painfully slow because the towing hawser was sloping at such an awkward angle to HMS *Heythrop's* tilted bow that we dared not risk a sudden strain. A long, slow tow lay ahead; several hours would elapse before we could turn over the tow to a minesweeper which was proceeding from Tobruk to relieve us. Knowing this, the Pilot was calculating our possible time of arrival in Tobruk when, without warning, HMS *Heythrop's* stump slipped below the surface and her bows rose even higher. She was so obviously doomed that we slipped the tow even before her lamp started to signal, 'Am abandoning ship.'

Seeing this the senior officer in the group, Withers, very conscious of the need to fuel, ordered HMS *Avonvale* and HMS *Hurworth* to proceed to Tobruk, his aldis lamp paraphrasing a popular song 'We hate to leave you but I think we ought to go'.

And we did feel lonely, knowing that we had to pick up HMS *Heythrop's* crew with a submarine lurking nearby – the same submarine which, a few days later was to sink the HMS *Jaguar*.[9] HMS *Eridge* was kept moving while the survivors were encouraged to concentrate in groups so that her stops could be reduced to a minimum. Lieutenant Commander Stafford, HMS *Heythrop's* captain, remained to confirm that his ship had been abandoned. While so engaged, the slope of her hull grew steadily steeper showing more and more of her bright red keel; Stafford barely had time to leap overboard before she slid slowly downward until about twenty feet of her bows were visible. Thus she remained poised, like a blunt pinnacle of rock, until a few rounds of pom-pom released the air which was giving her buoyancy.

HMS *Heythrop* disappeared forever with a gentle gurgle and, feeling intense relief, we headed for Tobruk at twenty-five knots. Although one of the original four 'Hunts', which had been at the Clyde in May 1941, HMS *Heythrop* had always been the odd ship out and her three consorts had found so few opportunities to get to know her. We in HMS *Eridge* now felt we had attended the funeral of an acquaintance who had deserved more consideration in her lifetime. Now, all we could do was to make her survivors as comfortable as possible and when Stafford embarked, barely recognisable under a coating of oil, I could mutter nothing more comforting than a few meaningless platitudes.

In spite of the Doctor's effort, a badly wounded seaman died when still sixty miles from Tobruk. The current situation in that base was unknown so Stafford agreed to conduct a burial at sea during the period of dusk, when a stationary ship would provide a less easy target. The Chief Bosun's Mate sewed the body in a weighted canvas shroud as the cheerless day imperceptibly slipped into an equally cheerless twilight. The shroud, now covered with an ensign, was gently placed on a plank surrounded by a group of shivering survivors. In the background, HMS *Eridge's* gun crews, masking their true feeling behind blank expressions, stared impassively at this final homage to the stranger within their midst. Perhaps the more imaginative were wondering what the spirit which had once lived in that poor, motionless body would be thinking of this sombre ending to its earthly existence. On the horizon the darkened outline of the Libyan coast looked grim and forbidding while, all around us, the restless sea was waiting to claim its victim.

It was a simple, melancholy scene. Stafford read the burial service with some difficulty in the gathering gloom, his voice whisked away by the wind. Then, at a pre-arranged place in the service, Stafford raised a hand. The Pilot immediately ordered, 'Stop engines.'

Stafford was faintly heard pronouncing, 'We therefore commit his body to the deep.'

The plank was upended, the ensign whipped off it and the body slid gently into the sea. Almost before it had hit the water, the Pilot was ordering revolutions for twenty knots. Stafford continued with the collect, which was suddenly drowned by the high pitched whine of accelerating turbines.

Having reached Tobruk, we had just sufficient time to land the survivors, re-fuel and top up with ammunition before sailing with the rest of the

dshipman Gregory-Smith, Chatham 1928.

Lieutenant Gregory-Smith in full dress uniform for the Coronation Review, 1937.

Lieutenant Commander
Gregory-Smith.

MS *Eridge*.

Newlyweds Jean and Frank. Dundee,
14 October 1940.

Flag and Signal staff, HMS *Eridge*. Yeoman
the Signals Brewer front centre.

A rare run ashore.

Sailers from HMS *Eridge* posing
for a postcard home.

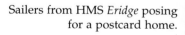

IS *Barham* re-oiling HMS *Eridge*.

gun crew, HMS *Eridge*.

Thinking of home, HMS *Eridg*

Searching the skies, HMS *Eridge*.

Crew with an unknown dog, HMS *Eridge*.

HMS *Eridge* in floating docks,
Alexandria 1941.

HMS *Eridge* in floating docks, Alexandria 1941.

HMS *Heythrop*, mortally wounded, before the Battle of Sirte, March 1942.

Scruffy the dog and friend.

geon Lieutenant Lee Abbott and
egory-Smith, HMS *Eridge*.

U568.

Joachim Preuss,
commanding officer U568.

Crew of U568 at base in Italy.

Crew member relaxing,
HMS *Eridge*.

Dropping depth charges,
HMS *Eridge*.

HMS *Eridge*, Alexandria, after being torpedoed.

Stoker Blizzard, HMS *Eridge*, killed
when the ship was torpedoed.

HMS *Eridge*, Alexandria, after being torpedoed of El Daba.

CREW SHOOK HANDS BUT X BEAT AXIS BOMBS

THIS is the story of the destroyer X, which has just figured in one of the most heroic naval episodes of the war.

The story starts after the bombardment of Rommel's shore positions near El Daba. X had taken her due share in that successful operation.

Then, under a full moon, her ordeal began.

The look-out suddenly shouted: "E-boat." The E-boat fired its torpedo. We saw the thin white wake it left behind it as it darted through the water (writes a correspondent who was on board the X).

The torpedo struck. There was a terrific gust of wind.

Then pom-poms and heavy guns opened up and the E-boat vanished into the sea.

Dawn came, then men rushed to action stations as a wave of dive-bombers, escorted by Messerschmitts, poured in on us.

For many hours after that the bombs came in at high level and low level, and more torpedoes came in, too.

Plane after plane dived down on the destroyer, and hour after hour our gunners, stripped to the waist, fired at them, never faltering no matter how near the bombs fell.

The gunners had no time to eat, no time to rest.

"This Is the End"

Once, when thirteen dive-bombers attacked at the same time, men in other ships said: "This is the end."

On destroyer X, some men shook hands, just in case. . . .

But the destroyer survived. Bombs plopped into the water all round. The number of near-misses could not be counted.

Nine times in a few hours the dive-bombers came back, and nine times X nosed its way through the spray and came out triumphant.

One of the planes was definitely shot down and another probably.

But there was still no rest. Shore-based bombers took up the attack. And, to make things worse, field guns on shore loosed off at the ship. They missed.

"Nice Work"

Finally the destroyer made port, and with surprisingly few casualties.

She had survived the most murderous air attacks ever directed against a ship.

As we steamed into port the captain said: "We're lucky to be here. We gave it to them last night, but we certainly got it today."

And then Rear-Admiral Harwood came along in his launch. Waving a hand to the crew, he shouted: "Nice work, boys. Nice work."

Larry Allen's report after HMS *Eridge* was torpedoed.

Torpedo damage, HMS *Eridge*, Alexandria.

Captain Gregory-Smith and the Marchioness of Abergavenny, HMS *Eridge* reunion, Eridge village
October 1980.

flotilla during the middle watch. Having cleared the harbour, the compass platform seemed more crowded than usual and I was astonished to find one of the fighter pilots standing next to me.

'Good heavens,' I exclaimed. 'Haven't you landed?'

He giggled sheepishly. 'We've still got a few more days leave so we decided to see more of the Navy in action. We hope you don't mind?'

'Glad to have you with us,' I grunted. 'At least we'll enjoy some decent aircraft recognition for a change.'

At daylight, we were faced by an empty sea; then a forest of masts began to poke above the horizon and swiftly extend into the hulls of the supply ships and their escorts. Having joined the convoy, the 'Hunts' took up prearranged positions on the anti-aircraft screen gathered closely around the supply ships. While doing this, the cruiser squadron and its destroyer screen were sighted astern, overhauling the convoy at high speed; these were ships with bones in their teeth, faithfully reflecting the cavalier spirit of our pugnacious Rear Admiral Vian. The cruisers, having broken formation, proceeded to reinforce the anti-aircraft screen while the destroyers joined the anti-submarine screen. The cruiser HMS *Penelope* and destroyer HMS *Legion* from Malta were still to join on the following forenoon. Even so, the force would contain no more than four light cruisers, one anti-aircraft cruiser, eleven fleet destroyers and six 'Hunts'. When concentrated, the force looked impressive but, in reality, it was dangerously weak because of the possible opposition from both sea and air. The powerful Italian surface fleet, operating with air superiority, could be confident of turning back or even destroying our convoy.

It was an unpleasant day and weather forecasts were predicting that worse was to follow. Visibility was poor; low clouds were scudding across an overcast sky and all ships were labouring uncomfortably in a moderate sea running out of the south-east.

Such conditions were poor for reconnaissance and not even a 'Red Tobruk' disturbed us. The afternoon, in fact, was so quiet that Lieutenant Cox, the officer of the watch, told the duty telegraphist to tune into Radio Tripoli on one of his spare sets and was rewarded by a rendering of 'Lily Marlene' – sung, against a background of rumbling tanks and revving engines, as Rommel's Africa Corps prepared to advance from their base. The German soldier's sad farewell to his girlfriend must surely rank amongst the best of wartime songs.

Our hope that poor weather would enable us to pass undetected between Crete and North Africa was dashed. Either a submarine or aircraft must have spotted us because, sometime during the middle watch, a British submarine patrolling the Gulf of Taranto reported that an unknown number of Italian surface ships had passed in a southerly direction. The

Pilot rubbed the sleep from his eyes, plotted her position on the chart and measured its distance to our track. He then stared to windward where massive black clouds, piling up along the southern horizon, warned of gale force winds. Already ships were rolling and pitching heavily in a rough, tumbling sea, which would be dead against the Italians in their 300 mile dash to the point of interception.

'They'll have a rough passage,' the Pilot eventually stated. 'But they could reach our track sometime during the afternoon.'

Night gave way to a black, stormy dawn when HMS *Penelope* and HMS *Legion* joined from Malta. As soon as they were in station, Rear Admiral Vian signalled that a superior enemy surface force was expected to make contact during the late afternoon. No intelligence about its composition was to be expected because Malta was being so heavily bombed that its aerial reconnaissance was unreliable. But all ships were to understand that, whatever the opposition, the convoy was to be fought through to Grand Harbour. There would be no turning back.

I then spoke briefly to the ship's company over the address system, telling them the gist of the Admiral's signal. I then added, 'The 'Hunts' and HMS *Carlisle* will remain with the convoy so we'll probably get a belly full of bombing. Rear Admiral Vian knows exactly how he intends to fight an action – in fact we were practising his tactics last week. You all know what to do. Keep cool and shoot straight and, tomorrow evening, we'll be comparing Maltese beer with Egyptian. Good luck to you all.'

The forenoon started quietly enough and the first shadower was not sighted until about 1000 hrs. After that, the number of aircraft steadily increased until at least six were circling the convoy, well outside range. By then, the radar reporting lantern in the flagship was never still and Brewer's eyes grew red with the strain of reading reports of single planes or of small formations. The nature of the reports gradually changed and, by midday, radar contacts were concentrated on three large formations waiting, in a circle, about thirty miles from the convoy. Their actions were so deliberate that they were clearly waiting to synchronise their attacks with the surface force's, which must be making faster progress than anticipated.

Tension was now mounting. Our small force, hampered by an important convoy, was about to make contact with a fleet of unknown strength operating under an umbrella of complete air superiority. The afternoon and evening would hold many dangers and fear of the unknown gripped most hearts during those final minutes of anxious waiting.

To occupy minds, men concentrated on trivialities or invented jobs. The gun captains checked and rechecked ready-use ammunition and then chivvied their loading numbers into rearranging its stowage. In shell rooms, the leading hands ordered surface ammunition to be moved to more accessible positions; then decided it interfered with the movement of anti-aircraft shells and moved it back again. Stoker Petty Officers in the boiler rooms adjusted and readjusted their fuel jets and earnestly studied the flames, as though trying to influence their intensity. In the engineroom, the artificers concentrated on the ever changing revolution telegraph, almost anticipating its movements; auxiliary watchkeepers staggered around the heaving platforms, feeling moving machinery and topping up lubricating boxes with quite unnecessary oil. Meanwhile, in the galley, Leading Cook Hardy and his sandwich cutters relieved some of their pent up nerves by hacking at loaves as though they bore them a personal grudge.

A flag signal fluttered to HMS *Euralysus'* yardarm and Brewer, glancing briefly at it, called excitedly, 'Enemy in sight bearing nor' nor' east.'

McCall immediately trained the director to the bearing. Away in the distance, clearly silhouetted against a rare patch of blue sky, spiralled a thin wisp of smoke, below which the masts of three ships were poking out of the sea. All of a sudden, we felt curiously relaxed. All our previous doubts and uncertainties were swept away by a combination of excitement and curiosity, which remained unaffected even when a second hoist reported that the enemy force consisted of three battleships. There, on the horizon, lay the goal to which the training of every gunnery officer had been devoted – the enemy Battle Fleet! The bridge's reaction was shared by every man onboard. The tension suddenly lifted and was replaced by an exhilaration which refused to recognise that three battleships were impossible odds. We felt invincible.

The battle plan was immediately put into effect. All ships started to make smoke with the intention of concealing the convoy behind a great barrier of smoke. This would be effective so long as we retained the windward position, which we now held – the wind's direction, in the coming engagement, would as vital to us as it had been in the battles of the sailing ship era. At the same time, the cruisers and fleet destroyers disengaged from the convoy, the cruisers concentrated in one group and the destroyers formed into five independent divisions as they headed for the enemy.

Captain Hutcheson, the convoy's commodore in *Breconshire*, immediately turned the convoy to the southward. Five 'Hunts' promptly took station ahead and on either beam of the supply ships, steaming in two columns, while HMS *Carlisle* and HMS *Avonvale* covered their stern.

The cruisers and fleets destroyers were quickly hidden by the smoke which, apart from concealing the convoy, would provide them with cover from which they could launch a sudden attack whenever the opportunity was offered. HMS *Euralyus*, steaming hard to catch HMS *Cleopatra*, caught another brief but closer glimpse of the enemy and promptly amended her original sighting report of battleships to cruisers. So high were our spirits that many felt a twinge of disappointment that the enemy should be so downgraded.

A series of flashes in the smoke followed by a dull, rumbling boom announced the opening of the surface engagement. As if this was a signal, a formation of torpedo bombers flew into sight, skimming just above the sea. Simultaneously, an even larger group of high level bombers were briefly glimpsed through the smoke and clouds on the opposite side of the convoy. Escorts to port and astern of the convoy immediately engaged the high formation, leaving the torpedo bombers to HMS *Southwold*, HMS *Dulverton* and HMS *Eridge*. The ship shuddered under the opening salvoes and high explosive started to burst around the low flying aircraft. Their crews, obviously surprised by such a heavy concentration from so few ships, promptly split into smaller groups and tried to penetrate the screen on a broader front. Even then gunfire continued to harass them, forcing them into individual units which dropped their torpedoes haphazardly and at such long range that all ships had time to turn towards their tracks, just as bombs from the high formation exploded in a compact mass well astern of the supply ships.

Meanwhile, the two surface forces, exchanging rapid fire as they rolled, twisted and plunged through the heavy seas, were closing at a relative speed of fifty knots. The British were already partially hidden by smoke, which the Italians would have to penetrate if they were to get within range of the supply ships. Just before reaching effective gun range, the Italian Admiral swung his ships to port. To prevent him stealing the weather gauge, the British followed his movements and stretched at high speed eastwards. On this course, British smoke drifted rapidly to leeward and, when its outer fringes reached the Italians, their Admiral, fearing a torpedo attack, edged his ships further to port. But the smoke still thickened around his ships, harassing them until the Italian Admiral suddenly lost his nerve and swung his cruisers, followed by a division of destroyers which had unexpectedly appeared astern, in a broad sweep to the northward. Rear Admiral Vian held on until satisfied that the enemy was definitely retiring and then turned towards the convoy, some twenty miles to the south-westward.

During this opening phase, the convoy had headed in a general south westerly direction under heavy air attack. Every few minutes, a fresh formation of ten or twelve bombers kept flying into the gunnery zone. Since low cloud was hindering controlled fire, the escorts countered each attack with a continuous barrage. This expended an enormous amount of ammunition but forced most aircraft to drop their bombs haphazardly from a moderate height. Those which dived through this barrier of steel were then engaged by so heavy a concentration from the close range weapons that they too, had no time for careful aim. Nevertheless, the attacks were so frequent that it seemed only a matter of time before a hit was obtained.

At each attack, the director was aimed at the approaching bombers. To hold the target, the sights were constantly moving – up, down, left, right – sometimes violently to counter the ship's erratic pitch and roll. Every movement of the director was transmitted to the guns, where the layers and trainers were sweating and cursing as they tried to keep their heaving mountings aligned with the director. The director layer's hand was permanently clenched around the firing trigger so each gun fired the instant its breech block had closed. As soon as the recoil had ejected the spent cartridge case, the loading numbers, struggling to maintain a foothold on the slippery deck, slammed home another round. Often their gun was so elevated that considerable strength was needed to load the twenty pound cartridge case, not to mention nimbleness to avoid the recoiling barrel.

HMS *Eridge* was zigzagging at fifteen knots across the mean line of advance, sometimes being only a few hundred yards from the nearest supply ship; sometimes as much as 3,000 yards. But, whatever her position, the hull was constantly shuddering from bursting bombs, although it was often difficult to distinguish misses at the convoy from those which had been deliberately aimed. Conditions onboard were growing quite intolerable. Each time speed was increased, the bows plunged deeply into the short, steep seas and flung solid green water across the focs'le and bridge, drenching everyone in exposed positions. At each alteration of course, the ship heeled sharply and cross-seas swept hungrily along the low waist, turning it into a seething cauldron of turbulent water. Funnel smoke and cordite fumes were sweeping the upper deck, leaving the gun crews coughing and gasping for breath. It kept seeping into magazines and shell rooms and was sucked through the engine and boiler room fans. On the whole, the greater volume was drawn into the boiler rooms where it was quickly dispersed by the high pressure fans. But water was apt to linger in the engineroom, which was now gloomier than a London power station on a foggy day. Conditions were not too bad under the air streams but on the heaving control platform the Chief was keeping one eye on the pressure gauges and the other on the artificers, who were swinging the heavy manoeuvring valves in response to the constant demands from the bridge. But the fumes were clinging to the wings of the compartment where stokers Edwards and Maltman, staggering around the plunging steel gangways to tend the auxiliary machinery, were retching repeatedly in the foul atmosphere.

A stick of bombs from a briefly glimpsed JU 88 straddled the ship. The hull was still shuddering from the concussion when a strange alarm, with a more piercing note than normal, unexpectedly blared on the compass platform.

'What the hell's that?' A startled chorus demanded.

'Damn,' swore the Pilot. 'It's the gyro. The repeater's wandering all over the place.'

I glanced briefly at the errant repeater and then at the magnetic compass before calling to the Coxswain, 'Steer by magnetic until further orders. Steady on sou' sou' west.'

The Coxswain repeated the order while the Pilot was trying to locate the electrical artificer by telephone. Having reached him, he gave the necessary instructions and then added, 'First stop that blasted alarm before it drives me crazy.'

The battle had been raging for a long two hours when the cruiser HMS *Cleopatra* was briefly glimpsed to the north eastwards. The covering force was holding off deliberately, waiting for the enemy to reappear, but we were thankful to intercept a signal ordering HMS *Sikh's* division of fleet destroyers to re-force the hard pressed convoy escorts.

The alarm abruptly ceased. But the moment of blessed silence was swiftly shattered by the scream of a JU 88 diving at the ship. It was too close for avoiding action but, instinctively, I ordered, 'Full ahead.'

As it reached its release position, the six four-inch guns fired simultaneously and a huge ball of fire erupted in the sky. Seconds later, some small objects fluttered over the ship followed by a heavier splash some distance away. There was not even time to congratulate McCall before the pom-pom and oerlikon were jabbing away at another diving plane.

The electrical artificer materialised on the compass platform. He was obviously dressed for working in hot, confined spaces, not appreciating the wind and spray on deck.

'The gyro's had a nasty jolt,' he reported. 'It will eventually settle down but will need regular checking.'

HMS *Sikh's* division of four fleet destroyers was sighted astern, rapidly overhauling the convoy, when, without the slightest warning, some bright flashes were sighted to the north-west. The Italian capital ships were firing their main armament at the supply ships. Seconds later, tall columns of water from large calibre shell bursts were rearing skywards, just short of the smoke. Even before the next salvo had fallen, the four destroyers were turning towards the flashes, HMS *Sikh's* signal lantern impatiently warning *Breconshire* to, 'Steer south; steer south.'

Breconshire was leading round the supply ships when the manoeuvring wave began to chatter, bringing news of a more powerful Italian presence.

'Enemy report from HMS *Sikh*,' the wireless operator called out. 'One battleship escorted by destroyers bearing north-west.'

A minute later, he was shouting to make himself heard above the wind, 'Emergency from HMS *Dido*; unknown number of cruisers bearing nor' nor' west.'

HMS *Eridge*, having turned with the convoy into the wind, was butting uncomfortably into the heavy seas. Our view to leeward was restricted by the great bank of smoke but, every half minute, the gloom was torn apart by a series of brilliant flashes, followed, after an interminable wait, by a group of gigantic splashes always creeping closer and closer to their target. But we had no time to worry about the battleship because another formation of torpedo bombers was streaking towards the convoy. Once again, the heavy barrage forced most planes to fire at long range but two bombers continued to press courageously towards the convoy, heading for the gap between HMS *Dulverton* and HMS *Eridge*.

Leading Seaman Rayner, drenched to the skin by heavy spray, had been having an impossible task to control his pom-pom on its plunging, reeling platform. Whatever the ship's heading, he kept his weapon pointing in a westerly direction, hoping for a snap shot at bombers diving from that bearing. He was now struggling to steady his sights when the leading aircraft flew into his line of vision, straight towards his centre head. He squeezed the trigger and a stream of shells flowed towards the target, blowing off large chunks of fuselage. HMS *Dulverton* also hit her and soon the damaged torpedo bomber glided gently towards the sea, bounced two or three times and then vanished beneath the waves. The second aircraft pushed through the same gap and headed for the convoy. The guns of the nearest supply ship immediately opened fire and some of the tracers streaked across the bridge, forcing us to duck for cover. Suddenly there was a shattering explosion then a ball of dirty, black smoke erupted from the bomber, which flew on like a flaming torch before plunging into the sea to a chorus of grim cheers.

Meanwhile, the covering force, using the huge area of smoke to conceal its movements, was fencing skilfully with the powerful, modern Italian battleship, *Vittorio Veneto*. The battleship was trying to reach the convoy by working round the western edge of the smoke. From time to time, the Italian cruisers were briefly glimpsed in her wake but they suddenly vanished and did not reappear. Rear Admiral Vian, fearing they were trying to seize the weather gauge by doubling back to the eastward, promptly led his cruisers at high speed in that direction. But the Italians had not doubled back and ten minutes later, the whole Italian force – battleships, cruisers and destroyers – was sighted only eight miles from HMS *Sikh's* division. These four destroyers were now the only ships between the enemy and our convoy and, for the next fifteen minutes, they skirmished skilfully with their heavier opponents, darting in and out of the smoke, persuading them that many more ships were hidden by the screen. Once again the Italians were deterred by the smoke and wasted valuable time trying to get round it. Meanwhile, our cruisers had turned back and were pounding across the stern of the convoy, their hulls barely visible amongst turbulent green seas and flying spray. Their broadsides were already rumbling like thunder but, before they could influence the duel, HMS *Havock* was hit by a heavy shell. For several long, anxious minutes the damaged destroyer lay motionless in the no man's land between the two forces, surrounded by shell bursts and covered only by her consorts' smoke. Then the cruisers vanished into the murk and the grumble of gun fire moved rapidly westward. HMS *Cleopatra*, emerging briefly from the smoke, fired her torpedoes at the *Vittorio Veneto*, thus allowing HMS *Havock*, in the ensuing confusion, to limp out of the battle and follow in the wake of the convoy.

The *Vittorio Veneto* had countered the torpedo attack by turning westward. This engagement gave the British ships a brief respite but the battleship increased speed and tried to work round the smoke by steaming in a sou' westerly direction. She nearly succeeded and, when she reappeared, her salvoes searched for the supply ships with increasing accuracy. Once again, only a few destroyers were in a position to intercept. HMS *Sikh* had deliberately fought a delaying action but this new engagement had to be more like a charge and Captain Poland, in HMS *Jervis*, led his division at full speed towards their target. His destroyers hurtled through a barrier of shell bursts to within 6,000 yards of the enemy and then turned to fire torpedoes. At that moment HMS *Kingston* was hit by a fifteen-inch shell. The destroyer was still struggling towards the sanctuary of smoke when the manoeuvring wave began to chatter.

'From HMS *Jervis*,' the wireless operator sang out. 'Have attacked *Vittorio Veneto* with torpedoes. Believe one hit.'

This attack was followed by a heavy gun dual between the cruisers and the whole Italian fleet, during which HMS *Cleopatra* received a direct hit and suffered many casualties. But, after ten minutes, the Italians hauled round to the northward and appeared to be breaking off the action because the noise of gunfire was receding rapidly astern.

During these surface engagements, the convoy escorts had engaged a succession of bombing attacks. The earlier euphoria had steadily given way to a dogged determination to preserve their charges and everyone was proud that we had, so far, succeeded. It was now dusk. The gun crews were gathered round their mountings in weird looking groups, their faces, oilskins and duffel coats blotched grey by cordite dust, waiting for the final assault.

'It'll soon be dark,' Petty Officer Gibson, gun captain of Y gun, told his crew. 'Give 'em hell when they come.'

'We've only six rounds of ammo,' a loading number told him.

'Nonsense,' Gibson exploded. He stormed from his position at the gun and hastily inspected the ready use lockers, most of which were empty.

'Get off your backsides,' he bawled down the ammunition chute. 'Send up more ammo.'

'You've got it all,' an indignant voice yelled back. 'We're empty.'

'God Almighty,' Gibson muttered.

The Gunner's Mate had overheard the exchange.

'Not to worry, Gibbo,' he said. 'I'll get some from the other guns.'

He lurched away into the darkness, leaving an anxious gun's crew. But the ammunition never arrived and neither, in the end, did the bombers. The enemy had obviously coordinated their main assault with the surface battle and had nothing left for this dangerous period, having lost at least ten of the 200 bombers which had attacked the convoy. A notable victory had been won. A superior surface force had been held at bay for several hours and the convoy had been preserved with only minor damage, despite bombers operating in conditions of complete air superiority. But no one felt any elation, only an intense desire for sleep, which would be unlikely in the night ahead, and a hot drink to warm their wet, chilled bodies.

The cruisers and undamaged fleet destroyers pursued the retreating Italians, who had suffered some damage, until they were no longer a threat to the convoy. Then, with depleted bunkers, they turned eastward, away from the convoy, to clear the Central Basin before dawn. It would be unfair to compare Rear Admiral Vian's fighting withdrawal to Kipling's 'captains and kings' (who left others to clear up the sorry aftermath of battle), besides a dangerous situation had still to be overcome before the convoy and three damaged destroyers – HMS *Kingston*, HMS *Havock* and HMS *Avonvale* – reached Malta's Grand Harbour. No one could be certain that all enemy forces had withdrawn so a brief signal from the flagship, now some thirty miles to the eastward, ordered the convoy to disperse and proceed at their best individual speeds. *Breconshire*, the most important ship, headed north-west with HMS *Carlisle* and three 'Hunts', the others were escorted by one 'Hunt' each while HMS *Penelope* and HMS *Legion* acted as an independent covering force. The Italian Fleet had achieved one partial success by forcing the convoy to take evasive action. This had carried it so far south of the direct course to Malta that not even the fastest ship could reach Grand Harbour by daylight. The bombers had been given a second chance to attack.

HMS *Eridge* was escorting *Clan Campbell*, the slowest of the four ships. After parting company, I remained on the bridge to get the feel of the ship on her new course. The wind and sea were now directly astern and both ships were yawing and rolling dizzily in the heavy, following sea: drifting funnel smoke was also adding to the discomfort. During an exchange of signals, *Clan Campbell* reported that she had been near missed and doubted if she could steam at more than ten knots. This, indeed, soon proved to be the case and we knew that we were falling well astern of the other ships. Moreover, her rudder had also been damaged and she was finding such difficulty in steering that Grand Harbour would still be many, many miles away at daylight.

Having digested this disagreeable information, I climbed wearily down the bridge ladder, hoping to find some dry clothes in my cabin. Normally this was a cheerful, cosy compartment but, as a precaution against blast and rough weather, its pictures and ornaments had been stowed away and was now looking little better than an empty steel shell. Angry seas were pounding against its bulkheads and the wooden furniture was creaking in sympathy with the violent motion of the ship. Water, seeping through a deadlight, was sloshing wearily from side to side, churning into a soggy mess the contents of a drawer which had been jolted onto the deck. At that moment, I could not imagine anything more inhospitable.

I picked up a mirror and gazed at a pair of red rimmed eyes set in a dirty, grey face which I scarcely recognised as my own. I was feeling utterly drained of energy and so wet and desperately cold that I switched on the radiator. I was crouching over it, hoping to get some warmth into my chilled body, when I was unexpectedly aroused by an angry, sarcastic jeer from the messdeck below.

Meanwhile, Evans was clawing his way around the ship. Having left the bridge, he waited under the break of the focs'le while a succession of heavy seas were sweeping across the low waist. Then, choosing a brief lull, he dashed to the after superstructure where he felt, rather than saw, someone was standing there in the pitch darkness.

'Who's that?' Evans shouted above the wind.

'Gunner's Mate, sir,' a voice yelled back.

'Good. I wanted to find you. Targets will be ships tonight but aircraft tomorrow. Put surface ammunition in the ready use lockers but change to high explosive at daylight.'

'Bad news, I'm afraid,' the Gunner's Mate continued with his mouth close to Evans' ear. 'There's only twenty rounds of high explosive in the whole ship.'

Evans whistled tunelessly. He had guessed ammunition would be low but this was far worse than he feared.

'What about the pom-pom and oerlikons?' He asked.

'They've still got a few belts.'

Evans thought for a moment. 'Fill the lockers at daylight with starshell, blank, smoke and practice,' he eventually instructed with as much confidence as he could muster. 'They'll make a noise, if nothing else.'

Choosing his time and holding onto lifelines, Evans visited the guns, warning their crews that enemy ships might still be in the vicinity so they would have to remain at action stations but could rest and shelter in the lee of their weapons. They were about to face an unpleasant night but they accepted it philosophically.

'I'm sorry lads,' he apologised. 'We can't take any chances.'

Evans then went to the forward messdeck where conditions were not much better than on the upper deck. Gushers of water were spitting down the ammunition chutes and surging angrily from side to side. Lockers and crockery had been torn from the bulkheads, and broken plates, cups and saucers were piled into a mobile mass amongst a heap of sodden clothing. The compartment stunk of vomit and funnel fumes. The supply and damage control parties, sitting or lying in duffel coats and oilskins, were coughing and retching in the foul air. Leading Cook Hardy's assistants were handing round cordite covered sandwiches which were not being received with any degree of enthusiasm.

'Is this all you've got?' A disgusted voice demanded.

'You can have ship's biscuits if you want.'

'What about a hot drink?' A seaman shouted.

Hardy looked at Evans who nodded, 'OK, light the galley fire but put it out by daylight.'

Evans then struggled through wind and spray to my cabin and reported what he had done. The heavy expenditure of ammunition was alarming but it had not been wasted so lamenting our shortage was pointless. I merely said, 'You've done everything possible. We must just hope for bad visibility in the morning.'

Then I remembered the jeer and asked, 'What was the messdeck bellyaching earlier about?'

'The BBC news.'

'Why? Did it mention the battle?'

Evans snorted. 'Not a word about the Navy but the RAF claim to have done pretty well over the Central Basin.'

'Perhaps they have without our knowing.'

Evans snorted even more indignantly. 'There's not a man onboard who'll believe that. Damn it all. We haven't sighted a single fighter since leaving Tobruk.'

'There's more to air support than fighter cover, you know,' I retorted.

That was true and no doubt the air crews had done their best to help us. But their efforts had been far too weak to influence the scale of opposition and one had some excuse for feeling irritated by this RAF habit of trying to hog the inter-service limelight. But, before I could say anything, the bridge bell crackled harshly and I plunged into the black, heaving night.

'Is that the Captain?' Cox, the officer of the watch, called as I reached the bridge. '*Clan Campbell's* broached to.'

I picked up some night glasses and stared at the supply ship which was now lying broadside to the wind and sea, almost rolling her gunwales under. The seas looked massive enough to hold her there forever but, endless minutes later, her bows began to swing ever so slowly towards the north and, after a long, hard struggle, she was yawing and wallowing in our wake once more, like some great, ungainly sea monster.

I did not leave the bridge again but swallowed some tepid tea and stale sandwiches and alternated between trying to doze on a wet chair and watching *Clan Campbell* rolling and pitching uncomfortably astern of us. The weather was growing steadily worse and, sometime during the night, two Italian destroyers capsized and sank while withdrawing to their base. *Clan Campbell's* steering was quite unreliable and, twice more, she broached to. Moreover, she was not maintaining her modest ten knots and we were painfully aware that Grand Harbour would still be a very distant goal at daylight.

Cox returned for the morning watch and he and I watched the long night turning into a cold, cheerless dawn. It had been a filthy night but the coming day, without the cover of darkness, promised to be even more unpleasant. The wind was shrieking eerily through the rigging and an endless succession of steep, breaking seas were surging out of the south-east and sweeping past the ship with a sullen boom. *Clan Campbell* was plunging astern, sometimes perching perilously on the crest of the seas, sometimes disappearing entirely in their trough. The sky was completely overcast by low, scudding clouds and frequent rain squalls reduced visibility to less than a mile. That was the only factor in our favour.

At daylight, Evans slithered along the heaving, slippery decks to check the quarters. Below, the supply and repair parties were still suffering in the smoky atmosphere and the weary, unshaven faces of the gun crews, trying to shelter in the lee of their mountings, warned him that despair was beginning to set in.

'Cheer up, lads,' Evans chided them, trying to instil some confidence. 'We've not far to go and visibility's bad. We'll soon be drinking Maltese beer.'

On the bridge, the Pilot was crouching over the chart table, measuring bearings and distances on the damp, soggy chart.

'I've not had a fix since Tobruk. *Clan Campbell's* steering is all over the place and our gyro's still unreliable,' the Pilot said almost apologetically. 'But by dead reckoning, we're here.'

He pointed to a mark on the chart and measured its distance from the end of the swept channel.

'Fifteen miles,' he added. 'That's assuming we averaged ten knots during the night which I doubt.'

'I'm damn sure we didn't,' I retorted a trifle impatiently. 'I reckon we're another ten miles to seaward. Then there's ten miles of swept channel. I doubt if we'll sight Grand Harbour before midday.'

The Pilot was about to say something but was interrupted by a look-out's urgent, 'Aircraft on the starboard bow.'

'Bearing, man, bearing,' Cox snapped.

'Can't say, sir. Can only hear it.'

By then, everyone could hear the aircraft and the ship was edged to port to bring all guns to bear. As we were turning a JU 88 burst out of the clouds, flying straight at us.

If precious ammunition was to be used only in an emergency, this surely was the occasion and McCall fired without hesitation. The shells burst around the target, forcing it to bank steeply back into the clouds but not close enough to cause serious damage. We had expended all our ammunition for nothing.

The radar bell shrilled. Even before the operator could report, another JU 88 had slipped into sight and, thenceforth, an unknown number of aircraft, but certainly more than two, kept dodging in and out of the clouds as if playing hide and seek with each other. Sometimes, they broke cover in such a menacing manner that we fired a mixture of our useless ammunition to warn them that we were ready. Sometimes, they came so close in the bad visibility that the close range weapons had the chance to fire brief bursts. Sometimes, they were visible on the radar, sometimes only their engines were audible. Occasionally, they were neither seen nor heard but we knew they were never far away.

In these trying circumstances, the two ships rolled and pitched northwards for two hours without sighting anything but these wretched shadowers, which continued to harass us without the slightest hindrance. Another thirty minutes slowly ticked away but, towards the end of it, we could faintly hear the distant rumble of heavy gunfire from Malta's anti-aircraft defences. That gave us something else to worry about – minefields. We were obviously closing the island but from an uncertain position. If we failed to hit the entrance to the swept channel, we could easily blunder into one of the minefields covering the approaches to Grand Harbour.

Many miles ahead of us, *Breconshire*, *Pampas* and *Talabot* and their escorts, all short of ammunition, had been under heavy air attack since daylight. By 0900 hrs, the three separate groups were within a dozen miles of Grand Harbour, steaming at full speed and racing like Victorian tea clippers to be the first to reach harbour. By 1000 hrs, *Pampas* and *Talabot* had entered Grand Harbour. The mighty *Breconshire* had been less fortunate and was lying disabled eight miles from her destination. Although immobile, she was still a prime target, especially with HMS *Penelope* trying to tow her. But with fewer ships at sea more bombers could be diverted to attack the *Clan Campbell* whose position, after more than three hours of constant surveillance, must have been known more accurately by the enemy than by ourselves.

The attack came without any warning. A formation of low flying JU 88s, in single file, burst suddenly out of the clouds and headed at full speed for *Clan Campbell*. Our four-inch guns fired their useless ammunition while bomb bursts were straddling the supply ship. Perhaps our make believe did distract the bomb aimers because the ship appeared to be undamaged until the last bomber attacked. Its bombs fell short but bounced along the sea, like badly hit cricket balls. The first twisted into *Clan Campbell's* wake but the second plunged into her hull. There was no audible explosion and, for a few hopeful seconds, we silently prayed that she was not seriously damaged. Then she yawed slowly to port until she was lying broadside to the wind and, to our dismay, began to settle by the stern. Lifeboats were already being swung outboard and rafts lowered over the side, grim preparations for abandoning ship which we could only watch in helpless frustration.

I grabbed the Pilot's shoulder. 'Break wireless silence. Send an emergency report; then ask for bearings and get an accurate fix.'

A light began to flash on the wing of the dying ship's bridge, spelling out slowly and distinctly and without the least sign of panic, 'PLEASE COME ALONGSIDE AND TAKE.'

As each letter was transmitted, the ship's list became more and more pronounced and seas surged higher up her superstructure until water was lapping around the bridge, giving an impression that the light was flashing from the surface of the sea. Then it ceased abruptly, its message incomplete. The Master's last thoughts had been for the safety of his crew and passengers and a brave signalman had been overwhelmed at his post, trying to transmit his plea for help.

Clan Campbell's focs'le reared sharply upwards, remained poised for a few seconds and then slid gently into the sea. She had vanished in less than ten minutes, sinking so swiftly and at such an awkward angle that only two partially filled lifeboats had been lowered. These and some floats carried the majority of the survivors but many others were clinging to pieces of wreckage or floating forlornly in their life jackets. Already the fierce wind was beginning to disperse them.

Our task now was to ignore the shadowers and to rescue as many survivors as possible. That could best be achieved by going first to the larger concentrations.

'We'll go first to the lifeboats and then the rafts', I told Evans. 'After that, first come, first served. The pom-pom and oerlikons have been warned to keep an eye on those aircraft and to open fire without orders.'

'I've got those bearings,' the Pilot called. 'We're in a minefield.'

The first aid and repair parties, having forgotten the discomfort of the previous night in their determination to help, were lowering nets and jumping ladders over the sides or preparing lines and life buoys while the ship was being conned to windward of the nearest lifeboat. The rescue of the lifeboat's crew was comparatively simple because the boat held enough active men to tend the lines, clear away any wreckage and to help each other out of the boat. While manoeuvring alongside the second boat, the wireless office bell rang briefly and Godfrey called up the voice pipe, 'Immediate from Flag Officer, Malta to HMS *Legion*. Proceed with despatch to the assistance of HMS *Eridge*.'

It was good to know that help was coming because the recovery of survivors in the second boat was proving far more difficult. This boat contained a number of lascars who seemed so apathetic about their fate that Evans, Petty Officer Wilcox and other volunteers had to go over the side and literally drag them out of the boat. By the time it was empty the floats and other flotsam had been dispersed over an even wider area.

I sent for Evans and told him, 'Your chaps are doing splendidly. But its only fair to warn them that, if we're attacked, the ship will go full ahead. Anyone over the side won't stand much chance.'

Evans was drenched to the skin and blood was dripping from an ugly gash on his head. But his tongue slithered over his lips and his jaw jutted out pugnaciously. 'We know that, sir. We'll have to trust to providence.'

Evans was still on the bridge when the wireless office again called. 'Immediate from HMS *Legion*. Have been hit by bomb. Am returning.'

We were on our own and it was not a cheerful prospect. The survivors had now been dispersed over such a wide area that, in the poor visibility, the furthest away were barely visible. The original plan had already been abandoned because it would have been inhuman to pass a half drowned man in order to reach a larger group. Under the constant watch of shadowers, the ship had to be manoeuvred to windward of each group, whether it contained one or ten men. Then, after a pause which must have been agonizing to those waiting their turn, and not much better for their rescuers momentarily expecting a bomb or mine explosion, the ship would drift alongside only to find that the shipwrecked men were either too weak from exposure to move or that wreckage pounding alongside was preventing them from doing so. Evans and his volunteers then went over the side and secured lines to the helpless bodies so that they could be hauled onboard and then led or carried to the forward messdeck where, among the shambles, a first aid post had been established.[10] Here the Doctor and Morgan, his sick berth attendant, were treating injuries while the ammunition parties were stripping off wet, oil soaked clothes and wrapping blankets around shivering bodies. There was no sign of the ship's Master but one oil covered figure, when cleaned, proved to be the Chief Officer.

HMS *Eridge* continued her lone rescue work whilst racing engines and thudding cannon above the clouds confirmed that unseen fighters were waging a persistent battle. It was comforting to be under fighter cover, at last, even though we sighted only our shadowers, sometimes approaching close enough for the close range weapons to open fire.

'Why the hell don't they attack us?' I wondered. 'Is chivalry deterring them?'

Whatever the reason, they continued their maddening circuits throughout the protracted operation, which lasted three long, nerve-wracking hours. One of the last to be rescued was clinging to some half submerged wreckage but was far too weak to help himself. Two seamen climbed down a scrambling net and hauled him clear of the water. Eager hands on deck grabbed his arms and dragged him upwards. His clothing was so sodden with oil that it was impossible to tell his service. The whites of his eyes stared fixedly out of a filthy, gaunt face. Above it was a bedraggled beret from which proudly rose a white hackle, unbelievably, almost unmarked. The first aid men grabbed his arms but the man shrugged them off, swayed to attention and saluted smartly before collapsing onto the deck. He was a Major in the Fusiliers, half drowned and exhausted but determined to observe an inter-service courtesy. On the Snotty, at least, such conduct made an impression which would last forever.

All the living had been rescued. The restless sea was now covered with empty floats and boats amongst which a few pathetic, lifeless bodies were floating in their now useless life jackets. We were still looking for signs of life amongst this human flotsam when a JU 88 dived unexpectedly out of the clouds.

'Full ahead together. Hard a port,' I yelled.

HMS *Eridge* surged ahead, bombs were shrieking over the bridge and detonating close alongside with a sickening thud. *Clan Campbell's* lascars, fearing a direct hit, piled out of the messdeck just as the ship heeled under the influence of her rudder and pounding propellers. They were engulfed immediately by a succession of seas sweeping hungrily across the low waist. For several grim seconds a tangle of human bodies was jammed against the guardrail but, fortunately, easing the rudder righted the ship and the counter surge of the receding waters swept them back to safety.

We had spent several worrying hours in a minefield and would still be in it, whichever course we took. The most sensible choice was the shortest to our destination and we were soon heading at full speed towards the sanctuary of Grand Harbour. Eventually the loom of the land cast its shadow along the horizon and our aerial escort departed. Soon afterwards, we sighted the disabled *Breconshire*; the cruiser HMS *Penelope* had failed, owing to heavy weather, to manoeuvre her between the breakwaters and she was now lying at anchor, guarded by HMS *Southwold* and HMS *Hurworth*.[11]

Then the battlements and turrets of Grand Harbour, ringed by a background of low hills with the mighty Cathedral of Medina on their crest, came into view. A surge of relief swept through the ship. This island, in spite of its hammering, was the goal which the cold, wet, weary ship's company was optimistically regarding as a refuge from stormy seas and the hazards of battle.

After passing the breakwaters, HMS *Eridge* steamed past St. Angelo. This had been the main bastion during the first siege and was bearing up remarkably well under the battering of its modern counterpart. It was deceptively calm and peaceful. The creeks were sheltered from the wind, which no longer howled through the rigging, and the ship moved on an even keel for the first time in many days. Some of the seamen, lounging on the deck of a submarine, reminded one more of a peacetime make and mend than of the storm which was raging over Malta. Dghaisas cut across our bows; children, waving union jacks, cheered shrilly from the battlements while their parents, on hearing the noise, hurried from their shattered homes to join in the welcome.

I felt a lump rising in my throat and saw a mental picture of the sleek, grey ships of the peacetime Mediterranean Fleet entering harbour after a cruise to the French Riviera or the Greek Islands, while sweethearts and wives watched from the Barraka and children like these cheered their return. I had witnessed that scene many times but, now, I was feeling tired and weary and these people's homes were broken shells; they were cheering a filthy weather beaten ship, manned by an exhausted crew still closed up at action stations, because we reminded them that Malta was not forgotten.

Meanwhile, HMS *Eridge* had turned in the main harbour where, hard against the shore, *Pampas* and *Talabot* were already discharging into dozens of lighters. These would unload several hundred tons of vital stores before nightfall. *Eridge* then backed into the dockyard creek and secured to buoys just ahead of HMS *Beaufort*. The ship had only just secured when ammunition and fuel lighters were towed alongside and the Chief Bosun's Mate was piping 'prepare to ammunition ship' around the messdecks.

'So much for the skipper's Maltese beer,' grumbled a seaman in a resigned voice.

But the ship had to be made operational as quickly as possible and the weary ship's company understood that. A few men were detailed to restore order on the messdecks while the remainder continued to embark ammunition until 2200 hrs when the lighters were withdrawn to a safer place. The exhausted men were then sent to their hammocks for the first time for six nights. The hours that followed were filled with the grumble of guns and the crump of bursting bombs but nothing less than a direct hit would have disturbed their well earned rest.

Ammunitioning recommenced at daylight. I got up later, revelled in the luxury of my first bath for several days and dressed slowly while the ship shuddered gently under the impact of the heavy shell cases. I had a lazy breakfast while reading a month old Times. I was still drowsy, but feeling completely relaxed and contented as if this was the start of a holiday instead of another day on a beleaguered island. This blissful moment was short lived. A curt signal, reporting that HMS *Southwold* had been mined and sunk, soon jerked me back to grim reality.

That forenoon the heavy massed raids, which had been temporarily suspended to provide striking forces against the approaching convoy, re-commenced with fury: the island's fighters, now reduced to about thirty Spitfires and Hurricanes, could barely cope.[12] The air raid sirens were constantly sounding their dismal warning, which stopped work in the dockyard, halted unloading and drove people to their caves and shelters. An unnatural silence followed until the bombers, escorted by fighters weaving vapour trails high above them, droned steadily into sight. A few ragged, long range probing salvoes would be joined by more and more guns until the whole island was trembling under a heavy barrage, concentrated around the vital supply ships. As the bombers dived over the harbour, pom-pom and oerlikon augmented the unholy babel until smothered by the crunch of bombs and the crash of falling masonry. Then the bombers would race back towards Sicily, sometimes being intercepted by our own fighters but always leaving another deep silence out of which columns of smoke and dust spiralled heavenwards to form one gigantic pall above the harbour. Eventually the 'all clear' would set life in motion again and people would reluctantly leave their shelters, as if anxious to postpone the inevitable encounter with yet more death and destruction. Malta, by any standards was a grim place during its second siege.

That evening, O'Grady Roche and I hired a dghaisa to take us sightseeing around the harbour. At the western end *Pampas* and *Talabot* had survived the raids and were still discharging. Every hour these two ships remained afloat meant so many more tons of vital supplies for the defence of Malta. We were then rowed up French Creek, passing HMS *Penelope*, soon to be known as 'HMS Pepperpot' because of the innumerable holes in her hull and superstructure caused by near misses. All these ships were resounding to the clang of metal against metal as riveters, fitters, blacksmiths, plumbers, welders and platers – British and Maltese – worked against time to patch the ships up sufficiently. We needed to escape from a trap which was daily drawing tighter around the dockyard.

Having seen HMS *Avonvale's* damage, we knew at once that she would never be repaired in time to return to Alex with the flotilla. She was one of the original 'Hunts' and we had been through so much together that I could not leave without saying farewell to Withers. Unfortunately, he had gone to Naval Headquarters and, as we left his ship, I had a premonition that we had seen each other for the last time.

The dry docks were occupied by the wrecks of two destroyers and by the cruiser HMS *Aurora*, damaged in a minefield off Tripoli. Repair work had now been accelerated to get her away from a berth which was becoming more and more precarious. Already, near misses had so strained the caissons that pumps could hardly keep pace with the seepage and workmen were fighting a desperate battle to replace some hull plating before rising water reached her open side. Happily their efforts were to be successful and HMS *Aurora*, HMS *Penelope* and HMS *Avonvale* were all to reach Gibraltar.

Leave to Valetta could not be granted but everyone was still so tired that this caused little disappointment. A few hardened drinkers tried the makeshift dockyard canteen. To reach it, they had to pass through a silent, uninhabited world which had once echoed to the hum of dynamos, the clatter of forges and the whir of lathes and presses. Now, it was a wilderness of rubble amongst which stood the skeleton of a power station and the shells of workshops and storage sheds, grim reminders that the dockyard was a primary target. The ruined slopes of Vittoriosa towered above them while, overhead, a haze of smoke from the day's raids was still rising into the evening sky. Desolation and decay brooded over the whole area and they were feeling thoroughly depressed by the time they had returned to the ship.

The gale began to moderate that evening and Flag Officer, Malta organised an attempt to tow *Breconshire* into Marsaxlott Bay, the weather still being too severe to get her into Grand Harbour. A little later, HMS *Eridge* and HMS *Beaufort* were warned to sail at daylight to provide gun support, in case the disabled ship was still outside the gunnery zone which the army was establishing around her intended anchorage. This order drove everyone to their bunks and hammocks, devoutly hoping that the supply ship would be safely berthed long before daylight.

We passed between the breakwaters just as the sky was paling in the east. The elements were still carrying the aftermath of storm and the wind began to moan dismally through the rigging the moment our bows began to butt into the heavy swell. The look-outs, vainly trying to shelter from the flying spray, strained their eyes into the gloom, hoping to find that *Breconshire* had reached her anchorage. But, as the light strengthened, she gradually took shape, labouring painfully in the wake of two small tugs. Delimara Point, marking the entrance to Marsaxlott, was still three miles ahead and several hours of full daylight would obviously elapse before she could reach it.

To add to the discomfort, I was suffering from an attack of dysentery which propelled me up and down the bridge ladder like an express lift. I was thus occupied when a sudden roar of motors developed into the high pitched whine of a power dive; the alarm was still sounding when a violent explosion close alongside knocked me down. I struggled back to the bridge in time to see tracers chasing the tails of two fighter bombers heading into the cloud wrack. As they vanished, two more dived on us from the opposite side. Ahead, bombs were exploding around *Breconshire* and the tugs.

We joined the little group of ships now heading towards Delimara Point. The leading tug was trying to pull *Breconshire* to starboard but, each time she started to turn, the wind caught her and pushed her back again. To help her, the other tug had taken a hawser from *Breconshire's* port quarter and was pulling her stern in that direction. But, with only one small tug towing, the heavy ship quickly became unmanageable and began to wallow helplessly in the trough of the swell. All efforts to swing her great, inert mass were unavailing.

The roar of aircraft above the clouds was a constant reminder of enemy activity: fighter bombers kept diving through the murk and dropping their bombs before zooming back into cover. Sometimes the clamour would be augmented by machine gun and cannon fire when British fighters intercepted but we knew that these tip and run raids might be replaced at any moment, by heavy, deliberate attacks. The same view was obviously held by HMS *Penelope's* captain, who was conducting the operation from the leading tug, because he pointed a megaphone in our direction and shouted, 'Take a hawser from *Breconshire* and pull her to starboard. Make it snappy. We've got to berth her before heavy raids commence.'

'Christ!' An indignant voice floated up the wheelhouse voicepipe. 'First HMS *Firedrake*, then HMS *Heythrop* now *Breconshire*. We're becoming a bloody tug.'

Every man onboard was thinking the same while the ship was being manoeuvred close to *Breconshire's* plunging bow. It was a delicate operation and we had had enough experience of towing to know that a warship, with its towing slip right aft, was a most unhandy tug. Moreover, in the short distance to Delimara, we had no chance of working up sufficient speed to gain steerage way. Our only hope of helping was to use a shortened tow and to steer to starboard of *Breconshire's* present heading and hopefully, thereby, swing her towards the bay. Bombing attacks were becoming more frequent but those concentrating on the tow tried to ignore them, trusting McCall to make best use of our guns.

The operation started quite well. HMS *Eridge* went ahead slowly to work up some speed. The engines were then stopped, allowing the hawser to slacken enough for the ship to be turned a few degrees to starboard. Speed was then increased to prevent *Breconshire* overrunning our quarterdeck. This manoeuvre was repeated two or three times and the disabled ship was beginning to turn quite freely. Seeing this, the after tug began to pull her stern to port while the leader edged over to starboard, converging slowly but surely across our bows. I tried to conform by turning further to starboard but the ship's head did not budge by so much as one degree. The engines were stopped to reduce the tension on the hawser. At the same moment, the wind caught HMS *Eridge*, still firmly held by her stern, and pushed her to port with increasing momentum. The engines were immediately worked in opposite directions in an effort to hold her. The swing never faltered.

The revolutions were increased until both engines were moving at half speed. The relentless swing still continued! With a sudden shock I realised the ship was out of control. We were helplessly trapped between the 15,000 ton *Breconshire*, moving relentlessly towards us, and the leading tug's towing hawser, which was about to hit us. I stopped engines and waited resignedly for the crash. For one ghastly moment, I had a grim vision of the three ships hopelessly entangled while the Luftwaffe blew them to pieces. As if to confirm these fears another fighter bomber attack was adding to the confusion. Then sanity flowed back and I realised that the leading tug master, having seen our predicament, had stopped engines to slacken his hawser.

'Slip the tow.' I ordered.

The Gunner's Mate, standing by with a sledgehammer, delivered a well aimed blow and the hawser leaped back with a vicious swish. The tug slowly crossed our bow and, even more slowly, dropped down our starboard bow. Simultaneously, the bight of her slackened wire dipped below the surface and scraped along our keel. By now *Breconshire's* bow was only a few feet away from our quarterdeck, which would be ripped open like a can if even touched by the flukes of one of *Breconshire's* heavy anchors. But we could not move because of the hawser beneath our keel.

'Dear God,' I prayed. 'Don't let it foul the screws.'

The next few seconds seemed like a lifetime but, to our immense relief, the hawser eventually leaped clear of the stern, cascading water in all directions. Half speed ahead was promptly ordered and the ship jerked forward just before *Breconshire's* bow crashed down on the spot where our stern had been. Fortunately she was continuing the swing started by our initial pull and the tugs were able to maintain her momentum until she was pointing towards the bay. Then, in spite of repeated air attacks, she was towed to a buoy to which she was quickly secured. The third ship had reached her destination forty-eight hours late.

HMS *Eridge* and HMS *Beaufort* immediately headed for the deceptive safety of Grand Harbour. As we were rounding Delimara Point, more fighter bombers dived through the clouds and our last view of *Breconshire* was partially obscured by bursting bombs. Half an hour later, we were turning in Grand Harbour when wailing sirens drove the islanders once more to their shelters. Immediately afterwards, a score of JU 88s swooped across the harbour in a ragged file to aim their missiles at the supply ships, *Pampas* and *Talabot*. Their sticks of bombs exploded in rapid succession tossing up a screen of smoke and blackened water around their targets. We watched anxiously while the turbulence was subsiding and then breathed a collective sigh of relief. Both ships were still afloat. A little later, the sirens warned of another raid and our guns were trained onto a formation advancing relentlessly beneath the vapour trails of its fighter escort. Something looked different about these bombers and McCall, watching through the director's binoculars, felt his heart sinking. There could be no mistake. They were Stukas. They had returned after several months absence on the Eastern Front and their presence confirmed Hitler's intention to crush Malta. McCall waited anxiously for the moment to open fire. But, while still outside the gunnery zone, the Stukas swerved unexpectedly to the southward and peeled off into vertical dives above *Breconshire*. The anti-aircraft guns, now sited around her, were pitting the sky with shell bursts as plane after plane dived through the barrage into another hail of fire from the gallant ship. Then Spitfires and Hurricanes were racing into action and the sky resounded with the harsh clamour of an aerial battle which receded rapidly northwards. Two vapour trails suddenly blackened into oily smoke and spiralled downwards in an increasing angle until they dropped vertically into the sea. This was followed by a bloodthirsty roar of approval.

Three supply ships were now being unloaded and the task of the 'Hunts' was completed. At dusk, just as the sirens were wailing for the first of the night's raids, the four survivors headed seawards with the HMS *Carlisle* to return to Alex. Our Air Force passengers were reconciled to disembarking there but, off Cyrenaica, HMS *Carlisle* diverted HMS *Dulverton* and HMS *Eridge* into Tobruk to escort an Alex bound convoy. We had accepted that we would have to spend another twenty-four hours at sea, followed by the possibility of a few hours ashore, but this new task would treble that period and that was asking too much of tired men. As we turned away from HMS *Carlisle*, the language would have shocked those old time British seamen who were notorious for ranting and raving across the salty seas. The cruiser was still in sight when a 'Red Tobruk' was broadcast and, a few minutes later, her anti-aircraft guns opened fire just before her hull was temporarily hidden by a series of bomb explosions.

'Serves you bloody well right,' we yelled.

Such an act of justice partially restored our spirits. But it was not the last laugh because, on reaching Tobruk, we became involved in the heaviest attack on the fortress for many months. We had experienced many raids on Tobruk but this one was significant because it was carried out by Stukas, thereby proving that the dive bombers had returned in sufficient strength to operate simultaneously over Cyrenaica and Malta. That was a grim augury for the future.

Before leaving Tobruk, we bade farewell to our two volunteer passengers. The presence of those young pilots had done so much to improve inter-service understanding; we had soon decided there could be nothing wrong with a service which could produce young men, themselves involved in dangerous fighter operations, who were willing to forego a well earned leave in order to gain first hand experience of their sister service in a hazardous Malta bound convoy. The men providing the air cover must be alright. Its inadequacy was not their fault; it was the fault of those deciding priorities. Of course, we would still grumble about the lack of air support and refer to the RAF as the 'Brylcream boys'. But our moans would now be good natured banter without any of the venom which had previously coloured our criticisms.

Before reaching Alex, we had learned that the three supply ships had succumbed to the remorseless bombing. Of the vital stores which had left Egypt, less than one quarter had been unloaded, not enough to replenish Malta's depleted stocks. Consequently, the just rewards of a notable naval victory had been denied because of our inability to protect the supply ships in and around Malta. The 'Hunts' had been so closely involved that their destruction was a personal loss. We felt sadness, and even a little bitterness, at the knowledge that these brave ships had endured so much for so little.

But brooding over the past was soon replaced by the need to concentrate on our own activities. This was a vital period. Both the Desert and Axis armies were preparing for an offensive and the first to build up sufficient supplies would gain the initiative. Consequently, HMS *Eridge* and HMS *Beaufort* were engaged, almost continuously, in escorting convoys to and from Tobruk and our time in harbour was reduced to the bare minimum required for embarking fuel, stores and ammunition.

At the end of April 1942, HMS *Eridge* was taken in hand for a fourteen day refit. She had now been in commission for fifteen months without a real break and her need of an overhaul was only exceeded by her company's need of a rest. We were all very conscious of the fact that, of the seven 'Hunts' which had sailed for Malta, only four had returned and that HMS *Eridge*, herself, was the sole survivor of the original four Hunts that had been in the Clyde in May 1941. After her recent ordeals, it was difficult to agree with the ship's company that this was further proof of *Eridge's* luck. Indeed, their own doubts were confirmed by a noticeable increase in leave breaking, drunkenness and venereal disease which, added together, were danger signals of men seeking temporary relief for their overstretched nerves.

Few of the officers were enjoying the best of health. The Chief was looking positively ill and poor Evans collapsed unexpectedly with a severe attack of dysentery and had to be sent to hospital. My own attack had cleared up but I was still feeling unwell. Months of lack of sleep at sea and irregular meals had meant many of us had not even laid down, never mind slept, twelve nights out of fourteen. But I was sleeping badly in harbour and, sometimes, would lie awake for hours while my thoughts were running riot amongst a medley of such realistic maritime disasters that it was often difficult to realise that they were only figments of a too vivid imagination. Even asleep, dreams were mostly an extension of those troubled thoughts and I got no real rest. Fortunately, at sea, I could thrust these fantasies aside but the constant strain was increasing my impatience and breeding a hearty dislike of danger which was shared by most of those onboard. HMS *Eridge* had already exceeded a Mediterranean destroyer's average span of life but the more attacks she survived, the more we craved an unattainable dream – the chance to live a quiet, normal life. Consequently, the prospect of fourteen days without having to be constantly keyed up to deal with a sudden attack by submarine or aircraft seemed the most wonderful reward.

If one had to fight a war overseas, Alexandria was one of the best places on which to be based. It possessed clubs, bars, restaurants, cinemas and excellent facilities for sport. For those so inclined, there were establishments of a more sordid nature. The place catered for every taste from the exotic to the erotic. Altogether, it was a fascinating city possessing a definite character of its own. It was the junction between the Eastern and Western worlds. People of every nationality jostled each other on its crowded pavements; the mysticism of the ancient east with its veiled women, muezzins, smells and beggars mingled with the cinemas, trams, cocktails and plumbing of the modern West. War and peace stalked each other side by side. Allied troops, airmen from the desert and seamen from the convoy routes rubbed shoulders with wealthy, well dressed women to whom the war was utterly remote. Bomber squadrons, forming up for a blitz, flew above – happy, carefree racegoers, few of whom spared a thought for those who might never return. In the harbour, ancient feluccas sailed past modern fighting ships while trim yachts glided amongst men of war and rust stained merchant ships, some still bearing the scars of some bitter convoy battle. In a city of such contrasts, it seemed quite natural to find the flag of Lorraine flying above the defeated, discredited and disarmed ships of Vichy France.

As much leave as possible was granted. Those with friends ashore were encouraged to stay with them. Others went in groups for a few days to a rest camp which had once been an infants' school. Most of its furnishings still seemed to be designed more for infants than for adults. Moreover, the temporary residents were treated as if they belonged to the same age group as the earlier occupants so they were not sorry to return to the flesh pots of Alex.

The Pilot and I spent a few days with friends in Sidi Bisr. Some afternoons we played tennis with Cox and the Snotty although Cox, being on christian name terms with most of the Women's Royal Naval Service contingent in Alex, had few free periods in his social calendar. This game provided great entertainment because the courts, being alongside the swimming pool, offered sex starved mariners a ringside view of scanty bathing costumes and the female figures inside them. Tennis was automatically followed by tea on the balcony, where members used to foregather for their evening gossip. The young and slim wore as little as decency permitted to display their vital statistics to the best advantage. One girl, in particular, had the most beautiful figure which fascinated her stern, nautical critics who watched with concern while she wandered from table to table chatting to her numerous friends. Not that we objected to her friends but we did disapprove of her willing acceptance of their offers of extremely sticky and fattening cakes. But, if unmindful of her body's future shape and size, she was well aware of its present attractions. She flaunted this to full advantage by leaning provocatively over each table, thereby exposing long, slender legs terminating in the briefest of brief shorts which barely concealed the sexiest bottom in the Middle East. Little did she realise how sorely she was tempting some licentious sailor to take a swipe at it.

CHAPTER SIX

The Hunt for U568

In May 1942, the great Admiral Andrew B Cunningham, 'ABC', that tough, determined, indomitable fighting leader, who had inspired the Fleet with his own courage and confidence during its grimmest ordeals, was relieved. To those who knew him only as the Commander in Chief and not personally, he seemed a formidable character but he was universally trusted and respected. He had been in command for so long that he had become an institution and his departure left a great, yawning gap which the Fleet feared would never be adequately filled. His relief was Admiral Sir Henry Hardwood, the victor of the Battle of the River Plate. His was a more gentle personality and one of his tasks, so it was rumoured, was to placate the RAF who were upset by his predecessor's constant criticism of the lack of maritime air support.

Since February, the British Desert Army and Rommel's forces had been more or less static on a line to the west of Tobruk, rebuilding their strength for a summer offensive, each hoping to strike the first blow. Thanks to the Axis blitz on Malta, the submarine and air offensive from that island had almost ceased so Rommel's supplies were reaching him with little interference. Our only hope of winning the race for the offensive was to ensure that the tonnage carried by the Tobruk convoys exceeded that carried by Axis shipping. The enemy, of course, appreciated this and had steadily increased his own air and submarine offensive along the Tobruk tramlines. In spite of that HMS *Eridge* and HMS *Beaufort* lost only one ship out of the fifty or so escorted during April and May. In the third week of May, our convoy was attacked by fifteen Stuka dive bombers in the approaches to Tobruk. During the minute the attack lasted, the two destroyers fired more than one hundred four-inch shells. Thanks to that barrage, no ship was hit but those sixty seconds were amongst the most unpleasant in HMS *Eridge's* career.

Our next convoy, in a bid to win the build-up battle, was one of the largest to sail for Tobruk. The ten supply ships, escorted by six corvettes and trawlers, reinforced by the destroyers HMS *Hero*, HMS *Eridge* and HMS *Hurworth* had a quiet passage for forty-eight hours. But, on the third morning, when approaching the coast of Cyrenaica, Tobruk began to broadcast a stream of red warnings. HMS *Eridge* was at action stations, everyone remembering the Stuka attack on our previous convoy and waiting tensely for a repetition.

Cox, the officer of the watch, was like everyone else, beginning to feel the strain of constant 'Red Tobruks'. During his three months onboard, the ship must have received at least 100 alerts. Each one, even those not concerned with activity over the sea, had raised a niggle of anxiety which remained dormant until aroused and augmented by the next alert. This effect was cumulative and Cox was beginning to realise that his nerves were not quite so strong as they once had been. He would have felt happier without the general warnings, which added nothing to the state of readiness of a ship experienced enough to be constantly prepared for air attack.

The wireless office call bell tinkled briefly and a voice called up the voice pipe, 'There's a signal in the carrier.'

Brewer hauled up the carrier, glanced briefly at the signal and handed it to me.

'Oh God, another bloody warning, I suppose,' Cox groaned.

'Not this time,' I told him. 'It's an aircraft reporting a submarine.'

The Pilot plotted the position and measured its distance and bearing. 'Its ten miles to the north-east,' he announced. 'No danger to the convoy.'

A few minutes later, the signal lamp on the bridge of the escort commander's corvette began to flash towards HMS *Hurworth*. Both ships were zigzagging so the light was sometimes invisible from our compass platform but Brewer got the gist of the message.

'He's telling HMS *Hurworth* and HMS *Hero* to go after that submarine,' he announced.

We were surprised and angry. The safety of the convoy was our main responsibility. The frequent 'Red Tobruks' warned that an air assault might be launched at any moment; yet the escort commander had denuded the convoy of nearly half its air defence to chase a non-existent threat. It seemed unnecessarily foolhardy. In fact, it was not so rash as we feared. The commander had been informed that Rommel had started his offensive and had correctly deduced that the aerial activity was supporting the land battle. Unfortunately, he had failed to share his knowledge and was thereby causing us much unnecessary anxiety.

Petty Officer Davey turned over the submarine detector to one of his operators and left the bridge. He was bitterly disappointed at being left out of the hunt. The Mediterranean was notoriously difficult for detecting submarines and his previous encounters had occurred at times when the water layers were at their worst. That had not prevented

Davey's messmates from airing their views about the unreliability of his equipment so he had been waiting anxiously for an opportunity to prove that the ship possessed other effective weapons beside guns. That chance had now been snatched away so he retired gloomily to his mess while the lucky ships were steaming north-eastwards.

The convoy plodded steadily towards Tobruk as the forenoon slowly gave way to the afternoon. The air raid warning was being repeated even more frequently and look-outs were anxiously scanning the skies hoping to spot the bombers in time to engage them with controlled fire. Davey was still brooding about his ill luck and the Gunner's Mate, making one of his inspections of the gunnery quarters, did not improve his temper by boasting that the convoy needed his guns more than Davey's temperamental gadgets.

Argument was pointless so Davey ignored his sally and maintained a gloomy silence until the action cooks brought the inevitable tea and sandwiches for the fire and repair parties. He took a cup of tea and was having a drink when the ship heeled unexpectedly to port and cups and plates slithered across the table.

'Petty Officer Davey,' a voice called down the hatch. 'Wanted on the bridge.'

The increased vibration warned Davey that the ship was steaming at high speed. Looking aft, he could see the white wake stretching astern in a hard, straight line towards the convoy, now steaming in the opposite direction. A keen wind caught him as he reached the bridge where Cox greeted him with a broad grin.

'We're joining HMS *Hero* and HMS *Hurworth*,' Cox told him. 'They're in contact with a U-boat but running short of charges.'

Davey's disappointment vanished instantly and he grinned back. 'Good! We'll show 'em this time.'

Davey remained on the bridge watching the bows cleaving through the clear, blue sea and the sunlight sparkling on spray sweeping past the hull. Soon the masts and upperworks of the two destroyers rose above the horizon and grew steadily more distinct.

Speed was reduced when we were about two miles away and HMS *Eridge* crossed their sterns at slow speed. Their masts were bare of flags indicating that they had lost contact.

'You're the senior officer', Brewer reminded me.

It would have been stupid to take command without knowing the situation so we waited until HMS *Hurworth* had made a report. The gist of this was that conditions were excellent but so many attacks had been made that each ship had only five charges remaining. Cox and I had discussed the submarine's intentions and decided that she would attempt to reach deeper water. So, at the end of HMS *Hurworth's* signal, a square search, starting in a northerly direction was ordered.

The three ships forged ahead and were approaching the end of the first leg when HMS *Hero* hoisted the submarine contact flag. HMS *Hurworth* then crossed under her stern and also regained contact. HMS *Hero* promptly steamed ahead and dropped her last pattern of charges which reached their depth, exploded and threw up a great upheaval of water. The destroyer continued until well beyond the explosions, turned round and regained contact as soon as the turbulence had subsided. HMS *Hurworth* then steamed towards the U-boat's position and released her five charges. HMS *Eridge* was now the only ship with depth charges and, while the rumble of explosions was dying away, she steamed slowly towards her consorts who continued to pass ranges and bearings to allow the Pilot to get an accurate fix of the U-boat. She was exactly one mile ahead of us.

Cox, on learning this, gave Davey an arc through which to sweep while the ship was advancing along the bearing. Everyone was excited now that offensive action had replaced our normal defensive role and Davey, although more affected than anyone, was determined to show the Gunner's Mate that he could win a far greater prize than a mere bomber. He quickly realised that conditions were perfect. His transmissions were flowing out loud and clear and one, near the centre of his arc, cracked back sharply in his ear phones. His heart gave an exultant leap as he made another transmission which echoed just as loudly.

'Echo bearing due south,' he sang out. 'Range 1,800 yards.'

'Confirm it quickly,' Cox snapped.

Davey made several more transmissions. For the first time, there could be no shadow of doubt that he was in contact with a submarine. I grinned at his confident report. A hunted U-boat would naturally dive deep so I told Cox we would attack at once with depth charges set at their maximum depth. Then a quick order to the Coxswain and the ship began to forge ahead.

'Range 1,000; target moving left,' Cox called out.

'Range 800; steady.'

'400; moving right.'

'300; steady.'

'100; stand by.'

'Fire one; fire two; fire three.'

At each command, Brewer and bridge messenger pulled the heavy firing levers. Five charges were either dropped or fired and, a few seconds later, five deep explosions barely rippled the surface of the sea. HMS *Eridge* ran on for nearly a mile and repeated the attack. A few dead fish were visible but there was no positive evidence of any damage to the U-boat.

Attacks at great depth were inaccurate because a submarine had time to manoeuvre between the firing of the charges and their detonation. Nevertheless, HMS *Eridge* carried out a series which followed each other quickly and smoothly. But time was always winning. The sun set; darkness steadily engulfed us and, eventually, a full moon rose serenely out of the sea – the perfect background for a torpedo attack from the darker sector. By then, HMS *Eridge*, herself, had only five charges left. Each pattern of five weighed more than a ton and Petty Officer Paine and his team had loaded ten of these with blocks and tackles while the Gunner placed ejector charges in the throwers, screwed in the detonators and set the ordered depth on the charges. Now, at last, the team could relax, secure in the knowledge that no attack had been delayed through lack of loaded charges.

The submarine would have to surface, probably within the next twelve hours, to recharge her batteries. Until then, tracking would present no problems providing conditions remained unchanged. But this was the fickle Mediterranean and the U-boat might enter an area where conditions could be reversed in a matter of minutes. That possibility would be a constant worry because a quick 'kill', with only five depth charges, was too improbable to contemplate. More charges could be obtained in Tobruk if one destroyer was detached for several hours. That would not help the short term situation but, if the hunt was prolonged, extra depth charges might prove decisive. For that reason HMS *Hero*, the fastest ship, was ordered to proceed to Tobruk and reload.

After HMS *Hero's* departure, the hours followed each other in monotonous succession while the two destroyers slowly tracked their quarry's northerly withdrawal. I was standing at the compass, keeping the U-boat fine on the bow. Cox was sitting alongside Davey in the cabinet, where he could pass ranges and bearings to the Pilot in the charthouse. The signalman and telegraphist were occupied with their own affairs and the Doctor, hoping for excitement, was jammed in a corner of the bridge. We seldom spoke but, occasionally, someone made an entirely superfluous remark merely to stay awake. It was far more difficult for Davey seated in the cabinet, illuminated only faintly by his gyro repeater. The high pitched transmissions, drumming continuously in his ears, had a soporific effect and his senses were reeling with weariness. At times, he feared the echo was only a figment of his imagination; at others, if he swung off the target, he sometimes made three of four transmissions before realising he had lost contact. He gritted his teeth with determination to concentrate.

Gradually a new noise impinged on his ears. It was repeated at short intervals and sounded like the sigh of air escaping from a blacksmith's bellows. It was a new experience and he was about to ask Cox to listen through the spare ear phones when its significance dawned on him.

'She's blowing her tanks,' Davey called.

This report warned that the submarine might be rising to a depth at which she could fight and weariness instantly vanished. The submarine's range and bearing were passed to the director and I glanced quickly around the horizon, noting that she would clearly see the destroyers silhouetted against the moon in the southern sky. It was just midnight.

The Doctor, who had just decided that, except for those directly involved, submarine hunting was intensely boring, was about to leave the bridge when Davey's report persuaded him to remain. He was staring into the night when the look-out beside him reported, almost casually, 'There she is; green 30.'

The Doctor had a brief glimpse of a shapeless smudge as the ship surged ahead and rapid orders were given behind him. Then the searchlight shutter opened and the smudge instantly hardened into a submarine rolling gently in the swell. We had barely absorbed the fascinating sight before the ship shuddered as the four-inch opened fire. For a brief instant, a vivid orange flash turned night into day, followed by a blackness which was blacker than the pit of hell. The second salvo, if possible, made the night even blacker. The Doctor was not the only one to be blinded. So was the whole bridge team and, cursing silently, I rang the cease fire bell. Our night vision took an unconscionable time to return to normal but, when it had, the searchlight was searching an empty sea. At the same time, Davey reported having lost contact.

'Damn and blast,' I swore again. 'Close the shutter; stop engines; anyone see her?'

The searchlight flickered out and a brief silence was broken by two hesitant voices, one reporting, 'She went ahead, I think,' and the other 'No, she dived.'

Two contradictory reports, each requiring a different course of action, did not help. But a quick decision was imperative because the submarine could be increasing her distance in any direction or even exchanging the role of hunted for hunter.

'Look-outs watch your sectors; radar search ahead,' I ordered. 'Davey, carry out an all round search and listen for her propellers.'

At that moment, HMS *Hurworth* reported that she, too, had lost contact.

'Keep calm,' I told myself. 'Don't panic but think.'

'Her surfacing position is 1,000 yards to the south-east,' the Pilot reported.

That was on our starboard quarter so we could have passed her while temporarily blinded by gunfire. Of prime importance was the state of the U-boat's batteries; they must be nearly exhausted after being so long submerged so her captain would be reluctant to dive before recharging. While doing this, he would want to head towards the darker northern horizon against which the small silhouette of his U-boat would be difficult to spot. But, first, she would have to pass close to two destroyers and then through the arcs covered by their radars. Neither radar nor look-outs had detected her so our brief acceleration to counter such a move appeared to have been successful. Neither was she on the surface astern, otherwise she would have been sighted against the lighter horizon. She must have dived so why had the detector missed her in such excellent conditions? Perhaps they had changed as we had always feared. But, even so, she would be astern where, perhaps, the brief turbulence from our propellers might still be acting as a screen.

'She's submerged astern,' I told Cox.

He nodded tersely. 'I agree.'

We reversed course and commenced a southerly search. Then followed a long, anxious thirty minutes. Having forced a U-boat to the surface and then allowed her to escape would not endear us to the Commander in Chief nor, for that matter, to anyone else. But, as the minutes dragged slowly away, the likelihood of having to explain her escape steadily grew more probable. If I had decided wrongly, it was already too late to search in any other direction. Our only hope was to continue southwards, although every minute without regaining contact seemed to emphasise that we were heading in the wrong direction.

Davey, having lost all trace of his earlier lethargy, carried out his search with intense concentration, straining his ears to catch the slightest whisper of an echo. He, too, was angry at losing contact. Transmissions were flowing freely and he knew that conditions were still good. But, at the end of thirty, long, endless minutes, he was still searching an empty sea. He was almost reconciled to the conclusion that the ship was searching in the wrong direction when he heard a wisp of a sound off the port bow. Scarcely daring to breathe, he checked the bearing and made another transmission. Its note echoed, faintly but distinctly, and his heart thumped with excitement.

'Echo bearing Red two zero at extreme range,' he called exultantly.

The report revived our waning hopes. Speed was reduced, to lessen the risk of water noises interfering with the transmissions, and course altered towards the hidden contact. As the range closed, the echoes became louder and clearer until there could be no further doubt. Davey's prayer had been answered and, shortly afterwards, HMS *Hurworth* also confirmed the contact.

The U-boat steered south for another hour. Then, in a desperate effort to throw us off, she suddenly doubled on her tracks and started to zig-zag in a northerly direction. But it was useless and the prospect of a kill steadily mounted. Nevertheless, many times during that long middle watch, HMS *Hero's* return with more depth charges was urgently awaited. But, unknown to us, a report of a seaborne force, which later proved to be false, had diverted her to the west of Tobruk and she was now completely out of the hunt.

At 0400 hrs , U568 surfaced for the last time. She came up gently, silently and without any fuss. One moment, the sea ahead was empty; the next, she was rolling sluggishly in the slight swell. A second later, she was held firmly in the searchlight's beam which revealed her gun crew tumbling out of the conning tower and running towards their gun, as if intending to fight.

Having learnt our lesson, the engagement was left to the close range weapons and depth charges. As we moved ahead, the pom-pom and oerlikon opened fire and tracers flowed towards the target, creating fantastic patterns as they ricocheted off her hull. Still raking her decks, HMS *Eridge* surged alongside and the final pattern of charges, set shallow, detonated with a mighty crack, drenching her decks with a great gush of water. Her gun's crew began to fling themselves into the sea, followed, in a long, straggling line, by others of her ship's company.

Evans and the Gunner's Mate, looking like Elizabethan pirates wearing pistols and cutlasses, ran onto the bridge.

'A boarding party's ready,' Evans breathlessly reported. 'Can we board her?'

A captured U-boat would be a wonderful prize but the black shape, now so harmless, was rolling with the sluggishness of a stricken ship and settling deeper in the water. She could only remain afloat for a matter of minutes and risking our own men could never be justified.

'It's too late, I'm afraid', I said. 'But lower the whaler and pick up survivors.'

We had won the battle but, with victory, the U-boat's crew had changed from enemies to stricken seamen crying for help. The searchlight was depressed to aid rescue work. HMS *Hurworth* was following our motions and the edges of the two searchlight beams were holding the U-boat, picking out the rear guard of her crew huddled together on the casing, as if reluctant to leave. The water was rapidly rising and, one by one, they slipped into the sea and struck away from their stricken ship. Then the hull disappeared with a dismal gurgle and the Captain, standing on the conning tower, had to make a desperate leap to get clear. A moment later, his command had disappeared forever.[13]

The whaler was now amongst the main group of survivors. Some were already swimming towards the ship so scrambling nets and jumping ladders were lowered over the side. By these means the rescue work was quickly completed. Evans, his face split by a broad grin, returned to the bridge.

'We've picked up everyone we could see,' he reported. 'Do you want to see the Captain?'

Elation at our success had slowly ebbed away, leaving a feeling of utter weariness. I had no desire to gloat over my luckless rival or mumble platitudes about the fortunes of war.

'No thanks,' I replied. 'I suppose you've given him some dry clothes and a hot drink?'

The Captain was the only man recognisable as an officer by his uniform. His crew were wearing such a motley collection of clothing that ranks and ratings could not be distinguished. Consequently, all were herded into the tiller flat where they could be sorted out while discarding their wet clothing. A large, blonde man climbed down the ladder, protesting vigorously.

'What's his belly ache?' Evans asked.

'He's your opposite number', the Snotty, who could speak German, told him. 'He's complaining that he's only been given a blanket and that he's in the same compartment as his ratings.'

'He should be thankful that he was picked up,' Evans grunted. 'He wouldn't have helped a merchant ship's crew.'

The Snotty, scenting a chance to practice his German, hopefully asked, 'Can I speak to them?'

'No,' Evans forcefully retorted. 'Better wait for the official interrogators.'

Seeing the Snotty's disappointment, he added. 'But keep your ears open. You may learn something useful if they don't know you can speak their language.'

Meanwhile, Davey, having turned over to a relief, had left the cabinet, exhausted but proud. He climbed slowly down the bridge ladder at the bottom of which he bumped into the Gunner's Mate. The Gunner's Mate gave him a friendly grin and patted his shoulder.

'Well done, Davey,' he said. 'You got her with the aid of my guns. You'll have a decent weapon in a few years time.'

Davey grinned back. 'Your guns can't shoot straight. They didn't cause a single casualty. They frighten us more than the enemy.'

The ship reached Tobruk in the forenoon watch. The rumble of guns, marking the extent of Rommel's advance, could be clearly heard. Captain

Smith, the naval officer in charge, was always optimistic but no one in Tobruk Naval Headquarters seemed worried. A conviction prevailed that Rommel was outstripping his supplies so rapidly that British armour would soon have an opportunity to counter attack.

As soon as the luckless HMS *Hero* returned, we divided the prisoners between the three ships and then sailed for Alex. While we were clearing the harbour, the wail of sirens just preceded a swarm of Stukas which dived out of the clouds, attacking ships, jetties and anti-aircraft batteries. The rumble of bursting bombs, mingling with the crack of guns, followed in our wake. Smoke and dust, spiralling heavenwards, slowly drew a dark veil over this battered fortress for which we had fought so many convoy battles. It was to be our last sight of Tobruk. Incredibly, we had escorted our last convoy and, three weeks later, on 21 June 1942, this vital base was to be overrun by Rommel's armour.

Any hope that our success would be rewarded by a respite was quickly dispelled. Within forty-eight hours, HMS *Eridge* was at sea. But, instead of another Tobruk convoy, she had been ordered to carry out an anti-submarine patrol between Alex and Port Said, in waters seldom troubled by enemy aircraft. Consequently, the patrol was quite enjoyable and the ship's company, freed from the strain imposed by Tobruk's 'red alerts', was able to relax to some extent. It was an interesting experience also. At intervals, the ship passed the cruisers HMS *Birmingham*, HMS *Newcastle* and HMS *Arethusa*, as well as several British and Australian destroyers, all newcomers to the Mediterranean.

One forenoon, those on the bridge and upper deck were enjoying the warm sunshine when Godfrey called up the voice pipe from the wireless office, 'Just intercepted an aircraft report in plain language. HMS *Duke of York* in sight.'

'A damn silly signal to send uncoded,' Cox muttered. 'It's told the enemy that a battleship's back in the Med.'

Shortly afterwards, the ship concerned was sighted. At a distance she certainly looked like one of our most modern battleships. But as she drew closer, she seemed to lack the massive solidarity expected in that class of ship and those who had served in the pre-war Home Fleet gradually recognised something familiar about her.

'It's old HMS *Centurion*,' the Gunner's Mate laughed.

HMS *Centurion*, a First World War battleship, was disguised as a modern battleship and the enemy had been deliberately informed of her presence. We reckoned that the enemy would be suspicious of such a gift. Surely, we argued, it would have been wiser to remain silent and to allow enemy intelligence or reconnaissance aircraft to spot her during their normal activities and be deceived, perhaps, by her false role. However, one thing was crystal clear. Such powerful reinforcements could only mean that another Malta convoy was in the offing. HMS *Eridge* would be one of the escorts. We would have felt offended if she had been omitted but that did not prevent some grumbling, echoed no doubt by every destroyer in the fleet, that she seemed to be getting more than her fair share of tough operations. This would be her fourth Malta convoy in twelve months. Also, being the oldest 'Hunt' on the station, *Eridge* had carried out many Tobruk runs so her continued survival without serious damage did support the contention that she was a lucky ship. But, no matter how much one tried to believe that, each operation was demanding a price which steadily mounted until every passage, and there was no such thing as a quiet one, developed into a constant battle for the mastery of one's nerves. Only the individual could gauge the extent to which his own were being racked and the effort needed to control his feelings. I could only judge my own mental strain but guessed it was shared by every man onboard, probably more so by those working in cramped conditions below deck.

Thinking along those lines was making me even more impatient than usual and I kept nagging the Pilot over trivialities. Months of tension had not lessened my impatience and its main targets were the Pilot and Brewer, whose duties kept them constantly on the bridge. Brewer was tough enough to ignore it but the Pilot was more sensitive and often upset. Nevertheless, by absorbing these outbursts, these two were shielding the bulk of the ship's company, who seemed to believe that their Captain was always cool, calm and collected. This was good for the morale and well being of the ship but offered little comfort to the Pilot, whose life, at times, must have been very difficult.

Back in Alex, the harbour, with a reinforced fleet, presented an animated scene. The 'Hunts', too, had been joined by five more ships. HMS *Grove* was to be sunk almost immediately but that still left a flotilla of eight. Since the departure of Commanders Shorty and Jellicoe, Lieutenant Commander Petch of HMS *Dulverton* had acted as senior officer. Although administration had been transferred elsewhere, it was a heavy responsibility for a comparatively junior officer. It was to him that we brought our problems and poured out our hearts. Naturally, he lacked the experience of his predecessors but he listened sympathetically and did his best to help. He always looked cheerful, showing no sign of being weighed down by the responsibility, and it was only when ill health forced his early retirement that his friends realised how great the strain had been.

In the short period between the sinking of U568 and the forthcoming Malta convoy, HMS *Eridge* experienced a series of blows. First, Evans suffered a relapse of dysentery and was removed to hospital. Then, both Cox and the Snotty left without relief. They had been pleasant, cheerful messmates and we were sorry to lose them. We had expected the Snotty's departure because he had been on temporary loan from a cruiser. But, in addition to his training, he had undertaken numerous tasks which would have fallen on the shoulders of the other officers so we had hoped that he would be replaced by another Midshipman. The loss of Cox, of course, was far more serious. He was qualified to keep a watch at sea and his training in anti-submarine warfare had been invaluable; his removal, so soon after helping to sink a U-boat, seemed a churlish reward. A protest extracted a promise of a relief for Evans but a shortage of officers prevented replacements for the others. Consequently, we were about to face another Malta convoy with a new First Lieutenant and insufficient seaman officers.

A few days later, Charles Edward Thornycroft, whose good looks would certainly retain the wardroom's standard, joined as First Lieutenant. On that day, HMS *Eridge* and HMS *Beaufort* were at four hours notice for sea so O'Grady Roche and I, guessing that this would be our last chance to get ashore for the next ten days or so, landed for lunch and tennis. Having feasted our eyes on the bathing belles, neither of us felt in the mood to face the monastic life of our ships so we decided to dine at Monseigneur. Unfortunately, our meal was somewhat disorganised by an itinerant conjuror who, without asking permission, transferred O'Grady Roche's signet ring to the centre of a walking stick and then changed all his silver into coppers. While still under shock, he produced an enormous snake from one of his pockets. We both loathed reptiles and, to the alarm of some young soldiers who were wining well but unwisely, nearly yelled the place down. Having persuaded our tormentor to return the ring and silver, less, of course, a hefty percentage, we returned to the dockyard before he could try any more tricks. The weather had deteriorated since coming ashore but O'Grady Roche, somehow or other, had acquired a motor dinghy and offered me a passage. He then started the engine while I lit the navigation lamp – or at least we tried. That wretched engine refused to start and, while O'Grady Roche was cursing it, I kept striking match after match (which merely scorched my fingers without burning long enough to light the lamp). To get some shelter from the wind, I crouched below the gunwale whereupon my wallet fell into the bilge water, ruining my favourite snapshot of my wife. Consequently, we were both in a foul temper when the dinghy eventually left the Yacht Club and butted into a rough sea which broke over the bows, drenching us to the skin.

We bumped on and on without sighting the familiar hull and, eventually, I snapped, 'Where the hell are you going?'

'To HMS *Eridge*, of course,' O'Grady Roche retorted, not unreasonably. 'She's lying between HMS *Zulu* and the breakwater. That should be easy enough to find.'

'I know exactly where she's supposed to be,' O'Grady Roche snapped back. 'We've passed HMS *Zulu* and can see the breakwater but not HMS *Eridge*. To paraphrase an old nursery rhyme, 'when we got there, the buoy was bare'.'

Like Queen Victoria, I was not amused and O'Grady Roche, guessing this, hastily added, 'I expect she's shifted berth. We'll go to HMS *Beaufort* and check.'

He steered towards his own ship where, in due course, we were to learn that, in response to a submarine alarm, HMS *Eridge* had been ordered to patrol the swept channel. I was dismayed to think that, in all probability, the ship had gone to sea under the command of an officer who had never handled her before.

'How the hell did we miss the recall?' I demanded. 'I bet it was that bloody conjurer's fault.'

'Well, you can't do anything about it,' O'Grady Roche retorted. 'You can have the chart house bunk.'

That was a miserable night. Men who missed their ship on sailing were not popular and leave breaking, in such circumstances, could lead to serious charges. Consequently, the Captain, like Caesar's wife, had to be beyond reproach and, by that standard, I had miserably failed.

'How can I possibly face future leave-breakers with a clear conscience?' I asked myself as I tossed restlessly from side to side.

My only consolation was that I had always been prepared to be lenient with men who had missed the ship by accident rather than design. With experience, it was not difficult to differentiate between the two, no matter how plausible the excuses sounded. But would the ship's company be willing to remember such tolerance if the Captain himself was at fault?

HMS *Eridge* returned shortly after sunrise and I was relieved to note that she looked unharmed. As soon as she was secured, I returned in HMS *Beaufort's* boat, feeling far too conspicuous in my weatherbeaten, dishevelled uniform. I looked like a reveller returning from a night long debauch hoping to slip onboard unnoticed while the hands were at breakfast. What a hope! It was soon obvious that the side was manned by what appeared to be the entire ship's company, amongst whom the regular leave breakers were prominent near the gangway. As the boat stopped alongside, a sea of faces looked down with disapproving frowns and several heads were shaking more in sorrow than in anger. This was no time for humility so I ran up the gangway and grinned defiantly at the spectators. Faces stared back without expression. Then, like a ray of sunshine, answering grins rippled unexpectedly along the line and erupted into friendly laughter. The prodigal had returned and been forgiven.

The incident ended happily, at least, for me. The Naval Provost Marshall admitted that the correct procedure for recalling officers had not been carried out and accepted full responsibility. So he got the blame while I, quite unjustifiably, earned a reputation as a bit of a character.

CHAPTER SEVEN

Operation Vigorous

Germany and Italy were determined to eliminate Malta. We were equally determined to hold a base from which we could harass enemy shipping lanes to North Africa and support future offensive operations. But, after months of incessant aerial bombardment, Malta was desperately short of everything – fuel, food, ammunition, spare parts, medical supplies – and replenishment was vital before even the first of these objectives could be achieved.

The June 1942 plan was to escort two convoys to Malta, one from the west containing six supply ships, codename HARPOON, and the other of eleven ships from the east, codename VIGOROUS. Both convoys would obviously arouse fierce resistance. Unfortunately, our increased commitments worldwide prevented the allocation of properly balanced naval forces to beat off determined surface attacks. Only one cruiser, the HMS *Liverpool*, was available to cover HARPOON through the dangerous Sicilian Channel, compared with the four covering SUBSTANCE eleven months earlier. The Mediterranean Fleet could, and did, receive reinforcements from the Eastern Fleet but it still lacked a battleship and an aircraft carrier. These deficiencies could have been made good by powerful land based air support. But the bombers, long range fighters and reconnaissance planes were just not available in sufficient numbers.

On 11 June, four supply ships escorted by the anti-aircraft cruiser HMS *Coventry* and all the 'Hunts' sailed from the Canal Zone as a diversionary convoy. Their purpose was to entice the enemy battlefleet into a premature sortie to intercept. HMS *Eridge's* ship's company, faced with an operation which promised to be even more hazardous than its predecessors, sailed in a mood of gloomy resignation. Laughter and jesting were replaced by mutual irritation and impatience. The Gunner's Mate chivvied the gun crews with less than his usual jocularity. The captains of the guns grumbled at their crews and supply parties and swore at their lookouts. The Shipwright ordered his wooden shores to be stowed in different positions and chided the damage control parties for not foreseeing his wishes. Below, in engine and boiler rooms, men performed their tasks in silence, trying to rid their minds of the fear of being trapped in their dangerous compartments. These were early symptoms of battle weariness and, in such circumstances, it was more important than ever that my own feelings were kept under strict control.

The diversionary convoy steamed westwards for thirty-six hours. Then, when HARPOON had already passed through the Straits of Gibraltar, it reversed course without having provoked any noticeable enemy reaction. On 13 June, it joined the main convoy. When all units had concentrated, this convoy provided a magnificent spectacle. Fifty ships, including minesweepers and rescue ships covered an area of some twelve square miles. At the core were the HMS *Centurion* and eleven supply ships steaming in four columns. Encircling them was an anti-aircraft screen formed by all the cruisers and 'Hunts'. Further away were seventeen destroyers stationed on the anti-submarine screen. The cruisers and 'Hunts' could muster more than 150 heavy anti-aircraft guns and several hundred close range weapons, so hostile aircraft would meet fierce opposition.

Daylight slowly faded into a warm, dark, moonless night. HMS *Eridge*, although surrounded by darkened ships seemed to have the sea to herself and only an occasional wisp of white from a bow wave indicated that she was not alone. It was very peaceful and war seemed remote until Tobruk unexpectedly broadcast a stream of 'red alerts'. We were hoping these involved the land battle, still raging to the west of Tobruk, when a ball of light suddenly erupted in the sky, some miles to the southward. Other flares began to fall but, as the convoy would be difficult to locate in the dark, moonless wastes, Rear Admiral Vian immediately ordered a policy of evasion by which ships were forbidden to open fire. This tactic was generally successful but a few flares fell close enough to drift over the convoy, starkly illuminating any ship within its circle of light. Then a bomber would glide out of the darkness and a stick of bombs would explode somewhere amongst the convoy. One flare drifted over HMS *Eridge* and we felt horribly naked and exposed while waiting for the bombs to follow.

At daybreak, the Dutch steamer *Aagtekirk* began to drop astern with engine trouble. To avoid forcing the other ships to reduce speed she was ordered to proceed to Tobruk alone. A few minutes later, a discordant racket of racing engines, machine guns and cannon fire erupted to the southward where long range fighters had intercepted a formation of bombers. The formation was barred from the convoy and forced to disperse. But the defeated bombers unfortunately spotted the luckless Dutchman, now well clear of the gunnery zone, and seized their opportunity to claim a successful sortie. McCall, watching the attack through binoculars, felt utterly helpless as the supply ship was battered into a doomed hulk.

Far to the west, HARPOON was under heavy air attack. One supply ship had been sunk but even more serious was the disablement of the HMS *Liverpool*, which meant that the convoy would have to face the dangerous passage through the Sicilian narrows without heavy gun support. To VIGOROUS, Tobruk was still signalling 'red alerts'. At first, the radar guard ship was reporting that these referred only to single aircraft but, off the Libyan 'hump', the nature of her reports changed rapidly to large formations. Every man in VIGOROUS was only to well aware that the assault was about to be unleashed. McCall trained his guns into the sun and waited in an atmosphere of mounting tension, which was suddenly snapped by HMS *Dido's* opening salvo. As it burst in the sky, McCall spotted a seemingly endless procession of tiny, black specks. First ten, then twenty, thirty, forty, fifty Stukas took shape, advancing remorselessly towards the convoy. Fire was opened immediately and the deep boom of heavy gunfire mingled with the continuous smack of shell bursts. Smoke and fumes slowly drew a dark screen across the sky through which the rays of the sun, penetrating with difficulty, twitched eerie, dancing shadows across the sea. Two bombers, reeling drunkenly away from their companions, spiralled lazily seawards in a series of huge loops; the rest of the air fleet advanced steadily towards their diving positions, accompanied by an extending line of shell bursts. At a signal, the bombers peeled out of formation and dived onto the convoy. The sharp snap, snap of close range weapons immediately joined the bedlam of the heavier guns and accelerating aero engines. Then the bombs began to burst in and around the supply ships, blotting them from view as wave after wave dived to the attack.

A frightening pillar of flame followed by a heavy detonation suddenly flared up amongst this upheaval. An agonizing few seconds was ended when the supply ship *Bhutan*, turning helplessly in a wide semi circle with her hull rent by internal explosions, drifted into sight.

Leaving a rescue ship to pick up survivors, the convoy pressed steadily westwards under constant air attack which continued throughout the forenoon and afternoon. The enemy was obviously using every available aircraft in a determined effort to claim as many victims as possible before nightfall restricted aerial activity. But, in spite of the number of bombers engaged, they obtained no more hits. As the day slowly advanced, weary, cursing, sweating gunners, firing as fast as their ammunition could be loaded, cast many an apprehensive glance at the sun. They dreaded the coming twilight but hoped that the following darkness would bring them a little respite. As a blood red sun sank into the sea, a flotilla of E-boats was sighted ten miles north of the convoy. Destroyers on the outer screen immediately turned towards them at high speed, hoping to fire a few salvoes before the faster craft slipped out of range. That, to everyone's relief, was the only twilight activity.

Once HMS *Eridge* had become actively engaged, the earlier reluctance to face another Malta run was replaced by a determination to defend the convoy. Now that men had time to think again, their main emotion was a mixture of thankfulness and optimism. The convoy had endured a night and day of heavy bombing but had lost only one ship within the gunnery zone. Malta lay two nights and a day ahead but, so long as our resolute defence was maintained, most of the supply ships should reach their destination.

As darkness closed down, the flare droppers returned, trying to illuminate targets not only for bombers but also for E-boats. These craft kept probing the anti-submarine screen, trying to find a weak link. The destroyers involved were obliged to open fire, first with starshell to locate the attackers and then with high explosive. This gunfire allowed the flare droppers to estimate the convoy's position with greater accuracy, with the result that some part of the convoy was always illuminated. The bombing was becoming more accurate and so frequent that the Rear Admiral Vian cancelled his evasive tactics and allowed the ships to open fire. The night was becoming utterly unreal. Flares and starshell were hovering in the sky: gun flashes seemed to be darting hither and thither amongst the close screen and flickering around the outer screen; the thud and crack of heavy and light guns mingled with the crump of bombs. It was like a scene from Dante's *Inferno*.

At 2300 hrs the flare droppers mercifully withdrew. Fifteen minutes later, it became known that Italy's two powerful modern battleships, *Littorio* and *Vittorio Veneto*, accompanied by cruisers and destroyers, were at sea.

The Pilot plotted their position relative to the convoy's track and announced, 'Assuming twenty-five knots, they could be in range by 0800 hrs.'

'I'm going to fire this gun at a battleship, if it's the last thing I do,' Leading Seaman Hambrook announced to his X gun crew.

In the calm windless conditions, there would be no chance of repeating the Sirte tactics and holding off such a powerful force during twelve hours of daylight. So the Commander in Chief, from the Joint Headquarters in Alex, ordered the convoy to continue westward towards Malta for as long as was prudent and then to reverse course. Such a move would obviously prolong the convoy's exposure to air attack.

At 0200 hrs, the Rear Admiral ordered a 180 degree turn in succession. Turning fifty darkened ships on a pitch black night was a difficult, lengthy manoeuvre and look-outs kept their eyes glued to their binoculars, trying to watch the movements of adjacent ships. Destroyers on the outer screen turned first and, except for the occasional patch of phosphorescence, passed HMS *Eridge* unseen. The dark mass of a supply ship or cruiser then crossed our bows and our own course reversed and speed reduced to drop astern of the convoy. Thirty minutes later, all ships were heading east more or less in their correct station.

I spoke briefly on the public address system. 'Your Captain's voice is the last thing you want to hear in the middle watch. By now you all know that the Italian Battle Fleet is at sea. To intercept, the Italians will have to pass through a barrier of our submarines and air attacks from Egypt and Malta have been planned for dawn. We are now marking time to await the results of those attacks. Upon them will depend our future movements. I don't expect anything to happen before dawn so get as much rest as you can at your action stations.'

As if to throw the words back in my face, the silence of the night was suddenly shattered by a dull boom. A minute later, the wireless office bell shrilled.

'HMS *Newcastle* torpedoed by an E-boat,' Godfrey yelled up the voice pipe.

The news about the cruiser had barely filtered round the ship before a ball of fire erupted far away on our starboard quarter, expanded viciously and then subsided into a steady glow. This was followed by an anxious wait until Godfrey announced from the wireless office that HMS *Hasty* had been torpedoed and was abandoning ship. He paused and added, 'HMS *Newcastle's* just reported she can steam at twenty knots.'

The E-boats had obviously penetrated the outer screen during the disorganisation caused by the reversal of course. Some of these vicious craft could still be lurking around so the unfortunate gun crews had no hope of getting any rest. But, somehow, the long eventful night gave way to a beautiful dawn of ever changing colours. No aircraft were in sight; the radar screens were blank. Tobruk was silent. It was quite uncanny.

At 0730 hrs, the Commander in Chief in Alexandria ordered the convoy to reverse course again and head for Malta. Another difficult turn was completed without incident and speed, which had been reduced during the westerly withdrawal, was increased to maximum. It was a hot, windless day and VIGOROUS plodded peacefully westwards through calm seas beneath a cloudless sky.

These peaceful conditions were not being repeated in the Sicilian Channel where HARPOON's situation was growing increasingly dangerous. At daylight, Italian cruisers had intercepted the convoy. In a running battle to head them away, the fleet destroyers HMS *Bedouin* and HMS *Partridge* had been disabled. To replace them, other escorts had to be thrown into the surface engagement, leaving the supply ships virtually without anti-aircraft gun support. This was the moment when the enemy unleashed his bomber squadrons and one more supply ship was sunk and another damaged.

Few in VIGOROUS were aware of these events several hundred miles to the westward. In HMS *Eridge*, the resumption of a course for Malta had aroused a great upsurge of confidence because men believed the Commander in Chief would have ordered such a move only if he was convinced that the enemy fleet had been seriously damaged by our dawn bomber attack. They were debating our unusual immunity from air attack and convincing themselves that the enemy forces had shot their bolt.

'What do you make of it?' Petty Officer Gibson asked the Gunner's Mate.

'The Eyeties have obviously suffered losses,' the Gunner's Mate replied. 'The Commander in Chief must believe we can handle the survivors otherwise we wouldn't be heading west.'

'Do you thing they'll fight?'

'No, if they've been deceived by HMS *Centurion*. Yes, if they know she's a dummy.'

'Then we might have a fleet action?' Hambrook hopefully asked.

'HMS *Eridge* won't,' the Gunner's Mate told him. 'Our job is to protect the convoy against air attack. Don't kid yourself that we've seen the last of the bombers. They'll be back.'

In spite of the Gunner's Mate's sombre caution, the ship's company remained in confident mood. True, marking time had prolonged the passage by another ten hours of daylight. But, what did that matter if we were opposed only by a battered Italian Fleet and a weakened air force? Malta suddenly seemed quite close and, in such an atmosphere of optimism, even Hardy's sandwiches tasted quite palatable.

A flag signal fluttered slowly to HMS *Cleopatra's* yardarm. Brewer, studied it through a telescope, blinked and rubbed the lens. Then he looked again.

'Alter course in succession 180 degrees to starboard,' he sang out. 'Executive to follow.'

'Turn away from Malta again? I don't believe it,' I snorted irritably at him. 'You've made a mistake. Look again.'

Brewer shook his head. 'It's true, I'm afraid, sir.'

The news spread like a shock wave to the guns, shell rooms, engine and boiler rooms creating a feeling of anger and disbelief.

'What the hell are those bastards in Alex playing at?' An angry voice demanded at A gun. 'They don't know what they're doing.'

Unfortunately, they were only too well aware of what they were doing. A reconnaissance plane had regained contact with the enemy fleet and established that the successes claimed by the bombers after their dawn attack had been far too optimistic. Only one cruiser, later to be sunk by a submarine, had been hit and the Italian Battle Fleet, otherwise undamaged, had been closing at a relative speed of more than thirty knots.

The flag hoist jerked downwards. The leading ships started their turn and, within a few minutes, the convoy was reduced to a state of organised confusion. Ships were passing close to each other on reciprocal courses; others were in the act of turning. Destroyers on the outer screen were steaming at high speed to regain station ahead. That was the moment the bombers hit us. They were still invisible to the naked eye when a cruiser on the close screen opened fire: the beginning of another furious onslaught was heralded by a blazing Stuka plunging vertically into the sea. The remainder pressed on resolutely through heavy gunfire and dived steeply over the swinging ships. The terrifying scream of engines racing at full throttle rose in crescendo until it was suddenly submerged by the concussion of bursting bombs. A giant's hand seemed to be agitating the sea which suddenly boiled skywards, completely hiding HMS *Birmingham* and HMS *Centurion*. Cordite fumes, drifting from the muzzles of a hundred guns, hung over the convoy like a shroud, beneath which sweating gunners were ramming home round after round as soon as their guns recoiled. Another Junkers dropped like a plummet. The barrage continued but the attack was over. The bombers, flying at different altitudes, fled in a southerly direction pursued by a ripple of shell bursts. Two Stukas were falling steadily astern of their companions; one of these suddenly banked steeply to port and spiralled gently downwards until it hit the sea in a shallow dive, bounced once and then plunged beneath the surface. Then an uneasy silence replaced the fiendish din. Brewer, his face unnaturally pale, studied the supply ships and escorts.

'No apparent damage,' he reported.

One more chance remained of stopping the Italian Battle Fleet. A squadron of American Liberators based in Egypt had been ordered to attack and they now flew high above the convoy in a westerly direction. Their arrival was greeted by a deafening cheer from men who were beginning to despair of ever seeing friendly aircraft again. Thirty minutes later the Italian Fleet, below the horizon, opened fire and the continuous rumble of their guns emphasised their closeness to VIGOROUS. This was our first direct evidence of an attack by Allied air forces and the noise sounded like music to the men who had endured a surfeit of similar raids. The enemy, at last, were getting a taste of their own medicine and, with luck, would get such a hammering that they would be forced to retire and open the way to Malta. The distant rumble ceased and, after an anxious wait, the bombers reappeared over the convoy, the sun glinting on their fuselages as if signalling a message of encouragement.

Away to the west HARPOON was still in a very dangerous situation. Only two undamaged ships remained in convoy; others, in various degrees of disablement, were scattered over a wide area. Falling astern of the convoy was the recently bombed supply ship *Burdwan*. Miles to the westward, another supply ship, *Kentucky* was under tow. South of Pantellaria, the destroyer HMS *Partridge*, although damaged, had managed to take the destroyer HMS *Bedouin* in tow. The escort force was quite insufficient to provide protection for all these groups so its commander took the difficult decision to sink *Kentucky* and *Burdwan* and concentrate around the two surviving supply ships. HMS *Bedouin* was sunk by the Italian cruisers but, somehow, HMS *Partridge* survived and eventually reached Gibraltar.

The results of the Liberator attack were eagerly awaited. The preliminary reports were so optimistic that the Commander in Chief immediately ordered, 'Resume course for Malta.'

Then, as the claims were analysed, they aroused more than a suspicion of gross exaggeration, causing the Commander in Chief to send another signal giving Rear Admiral Vian discretion to hold on or retire. That second signal was not received for ninety minutes so, throughout that period, every man in VIGOROUS, from the Rear Admiral Vian downwards, knew they were heading east when they had been ordered to steer west. But the Rear Admiral was too experienced to place too much reliance on optimistic aircraft reports made in the heat of battle. He was determined not to commit his force to a course which could swiftly develop into a surface engagement until the state of the Italian Battle Fleet had been confirmed. Unfortunately, a shortage of aircraft meant we had only sporadic surveillance and at least an hour elapsed before a reconnaissance plane regained contact. The Italian Battle Feet, apparently undamaged, was still in hot pursuit.

The convoy could only continue at slow speed, hoping that the Italians would retire and give us a chance to follow in their wake. The air attack was heavy, determined and continuous, as if to mock our facile assumption that the enemy had shot his bolt. All long range fighters being out of action, the force was now entirely dependent on its own gunfire. It was unbearably hot. A brilliant sun burned in a cloudless sky and the hull and superstructure radiated heat like an oven. The morning's optimism had given way to a mood of bitter frustration. The gun crews and supply parties, by serving their weapons with great aggression, were able to work off some of that frustration. But men doing routine jobs in the stifling heat of the machinery spaces had no such safety valve.

Hidden in the bowels of the ship, few of them knew much about events on deck except for scraps of information shouted down the hatchways in the few brief lulls. Usually, the thunder of guns and concussion of bombs were their first warnings of attacks in which any number from one to fifty bombers might be involved. The Chief, moving from one hot compartment to another, recognised the signs of stress and fussed over the auxiliary machinery, grumbled about steam pressure and invented jobs to occupy his stokers' minds. No such subterfuge was needed on the engine-room control platform where the artificers, standing in pools of sweat, were perpetually revolving their heavy manoeuvring valves in response to constant commands from the bridge. The Chief Artificer, De Gruchy, prowled between them, keeping one eye on the pressure gauges and the other on the dynamo and pumps. But the repair parties had a much grimmer time. They would only be needed in the event of damage so they had nothing to keep their minds off the morbid thought that many might be trapped if the ship was hit. They could only crouch in their steel compartments, smoking innumerable cigarettes and praying that this was not to be their unlucky day. For them, time barely moved.

During these attacks, Rear Admiral Vian kept signalling his intentions in the event of a surface engagement. Enemy gunfire was now even more audible as the Italian ships fired at our shadowers or repelled light air attacks but, at their present speed, they could not reach gun range before nightfall. No one seriously believed they would seek a night action but Rear Admiral Vian was obviously hoping that they would get close enough for him to counter attack under cover of darkness. The knowledge that our Admiral, and he was our Admiral sharing our dangers, was planning offensively was a tremendous morale booster. Especially during an aerial bombardment in which the noise alone was frightening enough to dampen one's mental processes.

More air formations appeared on the radar screens. HMS *Eridge* was now stationed astern of a centre column with the cruisers HMS *Birmingham* and HMS *Newcastle* on either beam. Both were zigzagging independently at fairly high speeds so it was our responsibility not to impede the movements of these heavier ships. We were the meat in the sandwich. The Coxswain, through a wheelhouse scuttle, could see HMS *Birmingham* closing rapidly from wide on our port quarter. A bow wave was snarling angrily around her forefoot and the Coxswain was waiting instinctively for a course alteration when he noticed the damaged HMS *Newcastle* closing on our starboard beam.

'God Almighty!' He muttered.

'Stop both engines,' the bridge curtly commanded.

The telegraphs were swung to stop. The Coxswain waited for the engineroom's acknowledgement that both engines had been stopped. As he did so, a mass of bombers dived out of the sun and the noise of heavy guns, pom-poms and screaming motors built up another deafening cacophony which tore at our nerves. Bomb explosions began to erupt amongst the supply ships but our eyes were riveted on a Stuka diving almost vertically over HMS *Birmingham*, now perilously close despite our reduction of speed. The bomber dropped through the murderous barrage, released its load and soared skywards. I braced myself for the explosion, ready for any orders and, for one dreadful moment, thought, 'My god! she's bought it', when a ball of black smoke bubbled out of the roof of one of the cruiser's turrets. I closed my eyes, trying to shut out the ugly sight, before jerking them open and ordering, 'Half ahead together'. Unwillingly, I glanced again at HMS *Birmingham*. A wisp of smoke was still rising from the turret but, to our relief, the cruiser was turning at high speed to port, her rudder and main engines apparently undamaged.

Further away, the destroyer HMS *Airedale*, thick, black smoke billowing from her hull, was swinging away from the close screen like a groggy boxer reeling round the ring. The fleet was already engaging another formation of dive bombers and the damaged ship was quickly hidden behind bomb bursts and cordite fumes. By the end of the attack, she had turned a complete circle and stopped about 3,000 yards astern of the convoy.

A light flashed on HMS *Cleopatra's* flag deck, 'HMS *Eridge* stand by HMS *Airedale*.'

We hated this sort of task. A single ship outside the gunnery zone was a hostage to fortune so it was some consolation to see two other 'Hunts', HMS *Hurworth* and HMS *Aldenham*, also closing the stricken ship.

'You're the senior officer,' the Pilot reminded me.

'Not another towing job, for God's sake,' a plaintiff voice grumbled in the wheelhouse.

A circular patrol was ordered to keep the ships moving while HMS *Airedale's* damage was being assessed. She looked stable but scorched paintwork and a fresh cloud of black smoke were grim reminders of internal fires. During those painful minutes of waiting for her report, we suffered the troubled emotions of spectators at a fatal accident, guessing it would be a kindness to put the victim out of his misery but lacking the courage to express such thoughts.

A signal lamp flashed from HMS *Airedale's* bridge, 'Unable to steam. Ready to be towed in ten minutes.'

First Lieutenant Thornycroft had reached the bridge when Brewer reported this signal.

'Who's to be the tug?' He asked, in a tone which suggested that he hoped sincerely that it would not be HMS *Eridge*.

'No one,' I grimly retorted. 'There'll be no towing without a direct order from the flagship.'

We were already four miles astern of the convoy. Not only was a Italian Battle Fleet somewhere below the western horizon but too many bombers for comfort were already flying overhead. In such circumstances, towing a damaged ship at slow speed would be an invitation to disaster. Fortunately, the Rear Admiral held the same view and his terse, 'Sink HMS *Airedale*' forestalled the need for any signalling.

The order was passed to HMS *Airedale*. Most of her crew either swam to the waiting destroyers or paddled across in rafts and floats. Transferring her wounded was a more protracted affair which was made to seem even longer by the ever present threat of air attack. After what appeared to be an interminable time to those waiting, the last boat was ready to leave. The seacocks were opened and her Captain made a final inspection to ensure that all the living had left. Then he, too, departed, watching his ship with unspoken grief, like a dog owner bidding farewell to a well loved pet. We were now ten miles astern of the convoy.

We opened fire immediately, expecting this unpleasant task to be soon finished. Some salvoes burst inside HMS *Airedale*, causing even fiercer fires to rage below decks; others passed clean through her hull, playing ducks and drakes on the water beyond; others burst short, splaying her with splinters. But HMS *Airedale* showed not the slightest intention of sinking. Then HMS *Aldenham* joined in, while HMS *Hurworth* kept aerial guard, but her salvoes merely fanned the flames without disturbing her stability. HMS *Airedale* seemed determined to stay afloat.

I was growing really anxious. The convoy, accompanied by a devil's tattoo of shell bursts and bomb explosions, had disappeared behind a haze lining the eastern horizon. Already, our small force had tarried too long in an area full of bomber formations awaiting their turn to attack. A number of Stukas, some in obvious difficulties, had just flown out of the east and a fresh group was circling overhead. Torpedo bombers and shadowers were flying backwards and forwards and, to keep them at a distance, our guns had frequently to be diverted from the surface target. It was only a matter of time before some aircraft were attracted by this less dangerous target so a report that the Italian Battle Fleet was reversing course brought little comfort.

A harsh whine followed by three plumes of water close alongside proved that one aviator, at least, had made up his mind. But HMS *Airedale* still refused to sink. Her survival was either a tribute to her builders or a reflection on the quality of our ammunition. *Airedale* was now holed like a colander; smoke and flames billowed from her interior. This attracted more and more aircraft which hovered above like vultures waiting to pounce. Our guns kept switching from ship to bombers so hits on HMS *Airedale* were becoming so infrequent that we feared they would never sink her.

We had one more weapon so I called to Brewer, 'Tell HMS *Aldenham* to use a torpedo.'

The signal was passed. HMS *Aldenham* slowly aligned herself parallel to HMS *Airedale*, took aim and fired. The torpedo seemed to take so long to travel the few hundred yards that we were beginning to fear it had missed when, to our relief, HMS *Airedale* was shaken by a violent explosion. For a few seconds nothing further happened and an anxious voice muttered, 'God! Even a torpedo can't sink her.'

Then, having tormented us long enough, she rolled slowly on her side and sank.

The three destroyers, now at least ninety minutes behind the convoy, pounded eastward at full speed. We had barely left HMS *Airedale* when half a dozen bombers pounced out of the sun and dropped their bombs close enough to shake the ship from stem to stern. A few minutes later, four torpedo bombers punched through our barrage and released their torpedoes at such short range that the ships scarcely had time to comb their tracks. Both attacks had been so swift and accurate that a terrible fear that we had tarried too long kept hammering at my brain.

'My God', I thought. 'We'll never make it.'

The high level bombers joined in. They were almost invisible above the heat haze but their bombing became more and more accurate until it seemed only a matter of time before one of us was hit. By then, every man's heart was longing for the doubtful companionship of the convoy and we silently implored the engines to go faster.

Then suddenly the Commander in Chief signalled from Alex, 'Now is the time to get to Malta.'

Thornycroft frowned. 'How many hours to Grand Harbour?' He demanded.

'About fifty,' the Pilot retorted without even looking at the chart.

'Our ammunition won't last half that time,' Thornycroft emphatically stated. He paused and pointed towards the east. 'Just look at that. It'll be the devil's own job to turn the convoy with all that stuff flying around.'

The convoy was still out of sight but the horizon ahead was blackened by shell bursts as one attack after another was beaten off. Gunfire continued without respite as masts and upperworks became barely visible amongst the haze which was deflecting the rays of the sun, now sinking slowly towards the west. It was only too evident that the attacks on our detached force were no more than diversions from the main assault. As we drew closer, a mass of torpedo bombers swept in but was pulverised by gunfire before reaching decisive range. A few individual aircraft bravely struggled on, dropped their torpedoes haphazardly then beat a hasty retreat, leaving some blazing piles of wreckage to mark the graves of some of their number. High level bombers were overhead even before the torpedo planes were out of range.

Another signal from the Commander in Chief demanded a report on the amount of anti-aircraft ammunition remaining. By itself the signal would have been unexceptional; in due course it would have established that the fleet's ammunition had been reduced to thirty percent, quite insufficient for another attempt to reach Malta. But, following the 'get to Malta' signal, it gave another hint of uncertainty and aroused a suspicion that the Joint Headquarters was out of touch with the real state of affairs.

Speculation was interrupted by Godfrey calling up his voice pipe from the wireless office, 'Signal from Flag. HMS *Paladin*, HMS *Eridge*, HMS *Hurworth* and HMS *Aldenham* stand by HMAS *Nestor*.'

'What the hell's happening now?' I growled.

Brewer thumbed through the operation orders until he found the screening diagrams.

'HMAS *Nestor's* on the outer screen, ahead of the convoy,' he announced.

'Not any longer,' a signalman interrupted. 'She's off our port bow.'

He was staring through binoculars towards the convoy, still several miles ahead. It was still buried beneath the muck of battle. But, as it moved eastward, a destroyer lying motionless and listing heavily, slowly emerged. It was the Australian destroyer HMAS *Nestor*. HMS *Paladin* was already preparing to take the disabled ship in tow.

The three 'Hunts', cursing their extension outside the gunnery zone, joined HMS *Paladin* just as the sun was dipping below the western horizon. In the deepening twilight, the murk around the convoy seemed to be growing thicker but our detached group, being in the clear, was starkly silhouetted against the afterglow. Our guns were trained on the darker horizon and we waited tersely while the shades of night closed around us so gradually that they seemed determined to torment us. But, even though time seemed to be stationary, darkness, except for a sliver of moon, was moving imperceptibly nearer and we were beginning to breathe more freely when, without the slightest warning, a formation of JU 88s dived on HMS *Paladin*. They were almost invisible but tracers were stabbing the sky from all directions then the last bomber to attack suddenly dissolved into an obscene ball of fire, before plunging into the sea to a roar of frenzied cheering.

In the meantime, the convoy battle had faded over the horizon, leaving HMAS *Nestor* and her consorts alone in an empty and unnaturally silent sea. Presently the young moon set and darkness closed around us so tightly that it seemed determined to deny us any contact with the world beyond. Nevertheless, we did intercept a garbled signal from Malta reporting the arrival of HARPOON's two surviving supply ships although several escorts had been mined in the approaches to Grand Harbour. Nothing further had been heard of our own dash to Malta so we guessed that shortage of ammunition had caused it to be abandoned. By no stretch of the imagination could the arrival of two ships out of seventeen be claimed a success and, on this depressing thought, I wrapped myself in a rug, dropped wearily onto a chair and fell into an uneasy doze. In other parts of the ship, the hands, having supped and grumbled over the usual unappetising sandwiches, were resting despondently at their action stations, painfully aware that all their efforts had been in vain. Down in the engine-room, the gloom was lifted for a brief period to celebrate the twenty-first birthday of Hulme, a recently joined artificer. His health was drunk in lime juice and was followed by stoker Maltman's rendering of 'Happy Birthday' which aroused some caustic observations from those trying to sleep on the deck above.

Our progress, that night, was almost negligible. HMAS *Nestor's* heavy list was causing her to yaw so violently that HMS *Paladin* could only tow at dead slow speed. Even so, sometime during the middle watch Thornycroft's quiet voice awakened me to report that a surge more savage than usual had snapped the towing hawser. I flung off the rug, rose reluctantly and leaned against the bridge canopy, fighting desperately to keep awake. The night was pitch black and the ship seemed to have the sea to herself except where a shapeless mass, darker than the night itself, indicated the whereabouts of HMS *Paladin* and HMAS *Nestor*. A million stars were twinkling in a cloudless sky; not a ripple disturbed the surface of the sea and only the swish of the bow wave broke the silence of the deep, unfathomable night. It was so peaceful that, for the moment, one could imagine the ship was enjoying a pleasure cruise.

I was dropping into a peaceful doze when, all of a sudden, I was wide awake, feeling a dreadful premonition of disaster. A second later, a brilliant flash briefly illuminated the far distance. This was followed, many seconds later, by a dull boom.

'My God!' An awed voice muttered.

'Looks like an ammunition ship,' another muttered.

Then followed the usual anxious wait which always preceded the receipt of bad news. After several long minutes, a telegraphist called up the voice pipe, 'Signal from HMS *Beaufort*. HMS *Hermione* sunk by U-boat. Am picking up survivors.'

We tried not to think about this new disaster while another tow was being passed. Then the slow crawl to the eastward recommenced and, somehow, the long night wore imperceptibly away. But just as the sky was paling in the east, heralding the dawn of another calm, hot day, the tow again parted. HMS *Eridge* was then zigzagging broad on HMS *Paladin's* bows and some minutes elapsed before the after look-outs realised the two ships were not following. On hearing their report, the Gunner, now the officer of the watch, reduced speed to drop back on HMS *Paladin* and the telegraphs were still clanging harshly in the wheelhouse when he became uneasily aware that the ship was no longer alone.

'Alarm ahead,' he yelled.

I jumped up in time to see three E-boats slipping silently out of the twilight. All three seemed unprepared for such a chance encounter and swerved away as if taking up positions for an attack. Rayner, dozing uncomfortably at the pom-pom, was startled into wakefulness by our swift acceleration just as a long, slim craft glided across his line of sight. His hand closed automatically on the trigger and a stream of tracer flowed into the dawn, splaying around the leading hull. The E-boat, followed by her two consorts, immediately swung away with HMS *Eridge* in hot pursuit.

The E-boats quickly slipped back in the semi darkness but our game of hide and seek was swiftly interrupted by HMS *Paladin's* peremptory, 'Rejoin at once. Air attack imminent.'

We turned back regretfully, even though we had little chance of catching the faster craft, and concentrated on HMAS *Nestor*. An air attack seemed highly probable as we were miles outside the range of our fighters. We could now see that the damaged ship was practically on her beam ends and was so obviously foundering that HMS *Paladin* was embarking her crew. She had reached the end of the road but, having struggled for twelve hours to save her, we hated to lose her.

As soon as HMAS *Nestor* had been abandoned, HMS *Paladin* steamed slowly past and dropped a pattern of depth charges. So great was her damage that she merely shivered; then turned gently over, like a tired dog rolling on its back, and slid beneath the sea. As she was disappearing, Tobruk broadcast a 'red alert' which, at the time, we regarded as a usual anxiety-provoking warning. In fact it was a very special one because it was the last HMS *Eridge* was to hear: never again would the nerves of her company be shaken by another 'Red Tobruk'.

We reached Alexandria sometime during the night and secured alongside an oiler with HMS *Paladin*. Our gloom was reflected throughout the fleet. Everyone had been angered by the RAF's exaggerated claims which had so raised our hopes. They had caused the convoy to mark time within easy reach of enemy air bases but, even so, only two destroyers and two supply ships had been lost by air attack. We reckoned that we had held our own in the air and sea battle, only to be thwarted by the Italian Battle Fleet. So why had the RAF not made a more determined effort to attack? Surely the Middle East had more bombers than a few Liberators and Beauforts? Why had they not supported this major effort to replenish Malta, which was vital not only to the Navy but to the other services? It was being openly stated that Admiral Cunningham would not have tolerated such paltry support for his Fleet; he would have fought tooth and nail to ensure that such an important operation was given its proper share of the Middle East's air resources. But instead the desert battle on land had been given priority. The least the Army could do to heal our indignation was to hold their Gazala position and thereby retain possession of some of the Libyan airfields. But on 21 June 1942 Tobruk fell and the forward airfields were all lost.

In spite of our failure, the Commander in Chief was determined to supply Malta. But, before another convoy could sail, all ships had to embark ammunition, stores and fuel; several ships, including HMS *Eridge*, had been so heavily engaged that the linings of their gun barrels had to be replaced. Even so, the force detailed was weaker than the original. Apart from ships sunk, HMS *Centurion*, HMS *Birmingham*, HMS *Newcastle* and several destroyers had been damaged so the new covering force would consist of no more than five cruisers and fifteen destroyers. To offset that, the opposition was expected to be weaker. One battleship, while returning to Taranto, had been hit by a torpedo and twenty-five bombers destroyed by ships guns alone. Thus the opposing forces would be similar to those in the March convoy, MW10, although the British, the weaker fleet, could not expect any help from the weather. Moreover, during the unavoidable delay in sailing, the moon had been getting brighter. Very soon the nights would be light enough for night bombing attacks, against which our guns would be less effective. VIGOROUS had been much shorter than the long drawn out March operation but, since then, our mental stamina had been weakened and we hated the thought of another attempt. At the same time, we well knew that Malta had to be replenished and that pride and honour demanded some effort to avenge our defeat and the lives which, so far, had been lost in vain. Consequently, as the moon waxed nightly brighter, we chafed at the delay, wanting to start at once and get the ordeal over before daybreak.

Several post mortems into VIGOROUS were held during the waiting period before the next planned Malta convoy. One staff officer observed that, 'HMS *Eridge* should not have ordered the expenditure of a torpedo on a damaged ship when the enemy battlefleet was at sea', which would have been reasonable only if followed by advice on how to get rid of a ship which refused to be sunk by gunfire. Without such advice, the criticism convinced many of those present that some staff officers, at least, were out of touch with reality; that they had no conception of the threat building up around our detached force. The staff officer only had to read. The war at sea had already provided them with numerous examples of the fate of detached ships operating close to hostile air bases without fighter cover.

CHAPTER EIGHT

Incident off Matruh

Throughout June 1942 fighting in Cyrenaica was continuing with unabated fury. The Desert Army, having won some initial successes, had been confident of the ultimate result. But, after some savage fighting, the Afrika Corps had overrun the pivot of the British defences, and then cut off and destroyed the bulk of the British armour in the disastrous battle at Bir Hacheim, south of Tobruk. The garrison of the fortress was promptly reinforced and the Navy was reconciling itself to a resumption of the 'beef and spud' run when, during the course of a catastrophic few hours, Tobruk was captured. The news was so incredible that, at first, it was disbelieved. But, all too soon, the dreadful rumour was confirmed by the reappearance in the BBC news of all those places which marked every advance and retreat in the Desert – Bardia, Sollum, Halfya Pass, Sidi Barrani, Mersa Matruh – the names rolled inexorably eastwards towards Alexandria. Our bitterness was now transferred to the Army. The German and Italian air forces had been diverted against VIGOROUS, thereby easing pressure on the land battle; but the Army had failed to take advantage and got themselves into a proper mess.

In such circumstances, Alexandria became a hotbed of rumours. Enemy tanks were approaching; militant Egyptians were planning to rise against us; all dockyard stores were to be destroyed; saboteurs were infiltrating into Cairo and Alexandria. These rumours, starting in the bazaars and alleyways were passed from mouth to mouth until they were sweeping the city like a prairie fire. A successful conclusion to the war seemed very remote in those grim days.

One evening, I went to HMS *Cleopatra* to find out the situation in the land battle. The duty Staff Officer glanced up from a pile of signals and grunted, 'Not very cheerful, I'm afraid. The Army's falling back to a defensive position at Alam Halfa.'

'Never heard of it.'

The staff officer shrugged his shoulders. 'I'm not surprised. It's just a heap of sand between Alex and Matruh.'

A Malta convoy was now clearly out of the question after a retreat which had yielded all the advanced air bases. Moreover, the fleet in Alex would obviously become a priority target for bombing attacks which would endanger the city and dockyard.

To avert this, the fleet and its auxiliaries were dispersed to the rear bases in Haifa, Beirut and the Canal Zone, then our energies were taken up with moving everything which would float. First the two battleships HMS *Queen Elizabeth* and HMS *Valiant*, still suffering from their winter damage after the daring Italian attack, were escorted to Port Said. These were followed by the supply ships which had failed to reach Malta, then the depot ships which had not raised anchor for months and finally by the damaged vessels, dredgers, lighters, tugs and anything they could tow. For several days the coastal waters between Alex and Port Said were crowded with shipping, which naturally attracted a concentration of submarines. They achieved only one success but that, being the submarine depot ship HMS *Medway*, was a serious loss.

Having finished this depressing task, HMS *Dulverton*, HMS *Eridge*, HMS *Beaufort* and HMS *Hurworth* formed a striking force based at Alex, which was now deserted except for a few ships too severely damaged to be moved. The following weeks were amongst the busiest of the whole year. By day, all four ships remained at immediate notice for sea; by night, they patrolled the approach channels or swept along the coast, hoping to intercept amphibious forces or barges supplying the enemy's forward positions. In such a routine, ships were lucky to get a few hours leave every ten days or so before proceeding on night patrol. On those occasions, the gay life of Alex seemed very remote. It was a matter of consuming enough beer to last until the next distant run ashore. Naturally, the more hardened drinkers continued until the last possible moment when an Olympic sprinter might, with a little luck, just catch the liberty boat; not being in that class, the panting pack usually reached the jetty in time to see the boat vanishing into the distance. But, somehow, they got onboard by cadging lifts, commandeering feluccas and even swimming. Technically, having missed the boat, they were leavebreakers when the ship was under sailing orders. But, by their efforts, they had reached the ship before sailing so an admonition to forego the final pint in future seemed more appropriate than the harsh penalties prescribed for such an offence. Anyway, I was in no position to adhere too strictly to the letter of the law.

Dull day followed dull day until it became apparent that the enemy had no intention of using the sea for an assault landing or for supplying his troops. The striking force was then switched to more offensive action, commencing with a bombardment of Mersa Matruh. Before sailing, the commanding officers met in Petch's cabin onboard HMS *Dulverton* to discuss the bombardment and the action to be taken in various circumstances. As we were about to leave, Petch said, 'E-boats have been reported in Matruh. If they attack, we'll stick to the planned bombardment but keep a good look out for them. I don't expect any other targets but, if any are sighted, HMS *Eridge* and HMS *Beaufort* will deal with them.'

We sailed in daylight but managed to avoid detection before nightfall. It was a starlit night, warm and breathless. Phosphorescence foamed around the ships' bows and their white wakes unrolled astern in a straight line towards Alexandria. The rigging was silent: the smooth hum of machinery and the gurgle of water alongside were the only signs of progress through the calm sea. Such a night, in spite of an undercurrent of excitement at the prospect of offensive action, soothed everyone into silence. I was leaning against the bridge canopy, straining my eyes on HMS *Hurworth*, the ship ahead. Beside me, the Pilot gazed dreamily at the sharp forefoot cleaving through the bow wave and Brewer stared, more intently, in the direction of HMS *Dulverton's* unseen bridge, waiting for a flicker of her signal lantern. Down below, action cooks were mustering in the galley to draw the cocoa ration for their companions standing or lying at their action stations.

We were approaching Ras Kanaris, well behind the enemy's front line, when the silence was unexpectedly shattered by the shrill note of the wireless office bell. Brewer jumped across the bridge, hauled up the carrier and disappeared behind the chart canopy where he could safely switch on his torch. His voice, muffled and low was barely audible.

'Immediate form HMS *Dulverton*. Enemy convoy reported ten miles north-west of Matruh at 2200 hrs. Good hunting.'

It was well after midnight so the convoy should be safely inside Matruh. Nevertheless, we hauled out of line and HMS *Beaufort* was ordered to follow at twenty-five knots. Y gun's crew, dozing around their mount, felt the more violent vibration of the propellers and staggered to their feet, hoping to discover the reason for the increase in speed. They watched HMS *Dulverton* fading into the darkness astern and, in a very few minutes, HMS *Eridge* and HMS *Beaufort* were alone in the silent, starlit night. They were making wild guesses as to why we should be leaving our consorts when the communication number sang out, 'All guns provide twenty rounds of surface ammunition. HMS *Eridge* and HMS *Beaufort* are searching for a convoy.'

For some minutes the crews worked silently around the ammunition chutes, hoisting up the new ammunition and placing it in the ready use racks. Then Petty Officer Gibson, gun captain at Y gun, confirmed that everything was correct and ordered the communications number to inform the control that his gun was ready. Most of the crew then joined the Doctor, who was leaning against the splinter proof plating watching the gloomy looking coastline. Ras Kanaris was just visible on the port beam and low lying sand hills were stretching towards Matruh, still some miles ahead. Now that they were facing the possibility of action, the gun's crew was feeling nervous and time seemed to be moving very slowly as the ships drew nearer Matruh.

Now that land was so close, speed was reduced to lessen the conspicuous bow and stern waves. As the vibration eased, the wide, white wake became less and less pronounced until only a slight turmoil was bubbling around the stern. HMS *Beaufort* was slow in following our reduction and gradually overhauled us until her bow was almost touching our stern. Then HMS *Beaufort* sheered off to starboard. As her bow swung through north-west her fixed, forward pointing radar picked up a contact. Her report was still being transmitted when one of HMS *Eridge's* bridge look-outs called excitedly, 'There's a ship or something bearing green 50.'

In the same instant, HMS *Beaufort's* searchlight blazed into the night, pointing briefly into the sea. Then it flicked upwards and steadied on a large merchant ship.

The alarm screeched throughout the ship. 'Alarm starboard. All guns load. Follow director.'

Cartridges were slammed into breech blocks with a metallic clang. McCall continued his control orders in a slow, precise manner. Gibson followed the director pointer and chafed with impatience.

'Get a move on, for God's sake,' he muttered. 'Beat bloody HMS *Beaufort*.'

HMS *Beaufort's* pom-pom thudded into action and tracers flowed towards the target. Some, hitting the hull, snuffed out abruptly, as if they had passed through a thick curtain, while others ricocheted in all directions, carving strange patterns in the sky. Then her main armament opened fire only seconds before our first salvo.

Able Seaman Kidman, now thoroughly experienced in night actions, had swung his back towards the mounting of Y gun to avoid the worst of the flash. His nerves were quivering in anticipation of the salvo but his eyes, staring subconsciously at the dark water, suddenly focused on something vague and indefinite which caused him to blink and look again more urgently. Simultaneously, both barrels leaped backwards and an ear splitting crack pounded against his ear drums just as a cloud of acrid smoke swept across his mounting, biting into his throat and lungs. So great was his concentration that he had failed to close his eyes and was now quite blinded by the flash.

'Pull yourself together, man', Petty Officer Gibson roared at him. 'Stop dreaming and get another shell.'

Kidman, quite impervious to the peremptory order, continued to stare at the sea, struggling to regain his vision which was so slow in returning that each second's delay seemed like an eternity. For several moments he feared his imagination had been playing tricks and half turned to meet Gibson's angry curses. Then something caught his eye again. He riveted his gaze on the spot and glimpsed two white patches of foam which bubbled briefly and then disappeared. A second later, a swirl of broken water followed by flakes of phosphorescence hardened into two small objects speeding swiftly towards the ship. Then they were blotted out by the second salvo paralysing his sight. He had no further doubts.

'E-boats attacking from the port quarter,' Kidman roared.

'Get that to the control,' Gibson snarled at the communication number. 'God help you, Kidman, if you're wrong.'

'Up 400, right four, shoot,' the communication number chanted, as he continued relaying the director's movements.

'Stop that bloody bleating and obey my order,' Gibson hissed.

'They won't – ,' the other man began.

'Don't argue, pass it.'

A frightening thought hit Gibson. Neither the control nor bridge could react for several seconds and, by then, it might be too late.

'Local control,' Gibson yelled. 'Bearing Red 140. Barrage short; commence.'

The gun captain of X gun heard the sighting report and Gibson's orders. Determined to join in the action, he ordered his own mounting to assume local control.

'Aim over the stern,' he shouted at his trainer, guessing the ship would turn away from her attackers.

The sighting report was received on the bridge just as A gun fired at the supply ship. A second later, X and Y gun opened fire independently. They were out of step with the director's controlled firing and their initial detonation caused a momentary fear that the ship had been torpedoed. Then the continuous barrage confirmed that the gun crews were using their initiative.

No one on the bridge, presumably because of its height, had seen the E-boats but an order was immediately given to signal to HMS *Dulverton*, warning her of their presence. By using their greater speed, assuming they were undamaged, they could swiftly overhaul us: McCall kept the two after mountings trained on the quarters while he controlled the forward mounting against the supply ship. As we closed her, a small lifeboat was sighted ahead. Its sole occupant was a large, fat man, clad only in vest and pants, who plunged into the sea bellowing for help. His ship was now being repeatedly hit. Under the double assault from the two 'Hunts', minor explosions were ejecting coloured tracers and rockets. Small fires burning in her superstructure gradually merged into one enormous inferno which completely engulfed her upperworks. Her hull glowed white hot; streams of tracer and rockets became thicker and more frequent until the detonations sounded like the rapid firing of a pom-pom. Steadily the explosions concentrated into one gigantic holocaust; more and more rockets, flares and tracers hurtled skywards and the sea glowed alternately white, green and vivid red. The flames grew fiercer until the sea for miles around was illuminated so brightly that HMS *Dulverton* and HMS *Hurworth*, far to the southward, were clearly visible. Then the supply ship disintegrated and the blazing furnace inside her was briefly sighted before the whole mass soared hundreds of feet into the air. A few moments of complete silence was followed by a blast of hot air which swept across the sea seconds before a deafening explosion hit us. The great, blazing ball reached its zenith and hovered for a moment. The sea hissed and boiled as flaming lumps of red hot metal plunged below its surface and snuffed out like candles. Eventually the last one sizzled out leaving the night blacker than ever.

As soon as the ceasefire gongs had sounded, speed was increased and course altered to the north-west. A convoy could contain any number of ships so, in the absence of definite information, it was prudent to assume there would be more than one and this would be their probable direction of escape. We were feeling little elation at the ship's destruction, which had been so gruesome that we were painfully reminded that the roles could so easily be reversed. Consequently, ammunition was replenished in complete silence and subdued gun crews kept an even sharper look out for E-boats. As these were somewhere between us and the shore, they must have sighted all ships in the glare of the explosion. But we knew about them and were prepared, whereas they were ideally placed for attacking the bombarding force. A friendly aircraft was already dropping flares to illuminate the target and the flashes of their opening salvo suddenly flickered along the horizon, followed, seconds later, by the dull boom of their guns. Beyond, shore batteries were firing at the flare dropper.

'HMS *Dulverton's* been warned of E-boats, I suppose?' I asked Brewer.

'Not yet, sir. Her reception appears to be out of order.'

My heart thumped with dismay. 'Have you tried HMS *Hurworth*?'

'No, sir.'

'Well, do so. That E-boat report is vital.'

Our inability to warn HMS *Dulverton* was a shock. She and HMS *Hurworth*, concentrating on the shore, would be open to attack from the disengaged side. Even if our gunfire had damaged our two attackers, others might be at sea and our present course had carried us too far away to help. The trouble was that HMS *Eridge's* experience of E-boats was limited. We knew that they were very fast and manoeuvrable and VIGOROUS had proved their effectiveness. We were wary of them and our inability to help our consorts aroused a nagging anxiety which drove me around the bridge like a caged animal. The slow, mechanical bombardment seemed endless and I hardly dared watch, even when an ammunition dump detonated with an explosion which started a fierce blaze beyond the harbour. I realised that, for the first time at sea, my nerves were playing up.

The shrill note of the wireless office bell almost jerked me out of my skin.

'Immediate from Commander in Chief,' Godfrey called up the voice pipe from the wireless office. 'Clear area by 0230 hrs.'

We were far to the westward, behind enemy lines, but an immediate change of course could just achieve this. Instead, some mad impulse to prove to myself that I could conquer my nerves, urged me to press on. So the ship continued to forge through the calm sea until a longer silence warned that the bombardment was at last completed. The shore batteries ceased firing; the last friendly flare fell behind Matruh and, a few minutes later, HMS *Dulverton* signalled that HMS *Beaufort* had joined and that all three ships were returning to Alex. They had obviously avoided the E-boats and some of my anxiety lifted. But we were now entirely alone, at least a dozen miles from where the supply ship had sunk. In the time available, a typical supply ship could not have steamed further to seaward so it really was time to return.

Astern, the fire ashore was staining the sky for miles around. Ahead, sea and sky were meeting so softly that it was difficult to distinguish one from the other. The Pilot was still laying off the course for Alex when a brilliant ball of light flared unexpectedly in the sky ahead and was followed by two more, forming a line across our bow. The wireless office bell again screeched.

'Immediate from Commander in Chief,' Godfrey called. 'Do not, repeat not, proceed west of 27 10'E.'

'A bit late,' the Pilot's muffled voice grumbled from the chart table. 'We're probably beyond that, already.'

I was now worried as well as nervous and could not stop an explosive, 'You're looking at the bloody chart. Check it', even though he was already doing so.

Course was altered to windward to give as wide a berth as possible to this dangerous area. The enemy must know by now that the bombarding force was to the east of Matruh, returning to Alex. Consequently the only logical explanation for this search, so far to the westward, was that the flare dropper was cooperating with E-boats which were still stalking us. So much for my effort to prove that I could control my nerves. It was not even possible to claim that it had achieved something. At the least, it had exposed the ship to attack not only by E-boats but also by aircraft.

'We're ten miles west of the Commander in Chief's longitude,' the Pilot's muffled voice called from the chart table. 'It's also 0230 hrs. Course for Alex is 080.'

I was about to order the Coxswain to turn to 080 when the first flare hit the water and fizzled out, leaving the others slowly descending. The area beneath them was as bright as day and the director and forward look-outs were anxiously scanning it. Then a dark blob, several miles beyond the lighted area, seemed to rise out of the sea and harden into a ship with a tall, slim funnel – from which a plume of smoke was trailing to leeward. The second flare hit the water. As the third flare fell closer to the sea, its illuminated area contracted until darkness once more enveloped the ship. But she had stood out so clearly during the few seconds she had been visible that the look-outs' lack of reaction was astonishing.

'Did anyone see anything?' I asked, trying to hide my surprise.

There was a short silence; then a chorus of hesitant noes followed by a more emphatic 'no' from the director.

Course was altered, not towards Alex but back towards the distant ship, and a murmur of surprise rippled round the bridge at this unexpected change of direction. The Pilot withdrew his head from the chart table and I guessed he was watching me, wondering if his course for Alex had not been heard. Within minutes, HMS *Eridge* was again forced to turn to windward to avoid another line of three flares. It was eerie watching these brilliant balls of light bursting silently in the sky. This line was at a different angle to its predecessor but the final flare might possibly illuminate the target. I kept silent about the ship. I wanted positive confirmation by look-outs unaware of, and therefore uninfluenced, by my own sighting. I ordered a look-out bearing and waited. My nerves had now been calmed by the excitement of a hunt. At the same time, excitement was tempered by the reality of the situation. The ship was out of range and could not be engaged for many minutes. Consequently, HMS *Eridge* would be penetrating deeper into unfriendly waters while the night was slowly passing away. That meant she would be increasingly exposed to attack, not only in the immediate future but also during the long haul back to Alex, mostly in daylight within easy range of enemy air bases.

These flares seemed to take an unconscionable time to fall. The bridge team stared intently at the lit area, no one more anxiously than myself, as it steadily contracted after the first and second flares had hit the water. The third hovered tantalisingly in the sky. Beyond the light was a kind of smudge. If it was a ship, the look-outs still remained silent.

'Come on, come on,' I muttered impatiently. 'You're not drifting fast enough.'

The flare's parachute seemed to collapse, while the smudge was still beyond the circle of light, and it plunged vertically into the sea.

'Any hydrophone effect?' I asked Davey in the anti-submarine cabinet.

'Only our own, sir.'

'Anything on the screen?' I asked the radar office.

'No, sir.'

Before course could be altered towards the target, a third line of flares burst in the sky. This was more or less parallel to the first so it should be more revealing. The bridge team was growing restless. They were unaware of my sighting so, as far as they were concerned, the ship was aimlessly zigzagging after two direct orders had been ignored. Such disobedience could only be justified if we were definitely in contact with an enemy ship. But were we? We anxiously awaited the answer to that question while the flares floated slowly downwards and hit the water one by one. This time they revealed an empty sea.

I remembered Shorty's remark about imagination, made to me long ago, after *Chakdina* had been sunk. I also remembered our experience with an E-boat in the Sicilian Channel. On that occasion the E-boat had failed to see us because we lay beyond a flare's pool of light. In my mind's eye, this ship was beyond the lit area. Therefore, she should have been invisible or, at best, a shapeless blur. But I had seen a blob. Had my imagination turned it into a ship to justify my stubborn dalliance in the area? Neither look-outs or equipment had supported me so it would be foolish to persist.

'I thought I saw something but must've been wrong,' I told the bridge team. 'We'd better go home.'

The operation had been a success but my own role in it gave me no satisfaction. For the first time, my nerves had failed at sea. Hitherto, worrying about forthcoming operations had invariably stirred up an attack of nerves but, on proceeding to sea, this had always calmed down; that is, if impatience could be regarded as normal behaviour. On this occasion, the clash with the E-boats and our failure to warn our consorts had aroused an apprehension which had clouded my judgement. To clear the area by 0230 hrs, course should have been reversed immediately after the receipt of that order. Instead, to convince myself that I was not afraid, I had continued further than was prudent on the north-westerly course. By doing so, I believed I had sighted another ship. I remembered

Shorty's remark about the captain being the ship's best look-out. Perhaps I had sighted one in spite of all the negative reports. But, right or wrong, I should have had the courage of my convictions and carried out a more thorough search. Instead, I had used the negative reports as an excuse to break off the search. This meek acceptance worried me because it was the first personal decision I had ever doubted. It was a sign of fatigue, both mental and physical. Although the possible sighting of a ship had never been mentioned, the bridge team had been aware that something was amiss. Fortunately, they misinterpreted the symptoms and spread the rumour that the Captain, in addition to missing the ship on occasions, had become a little, but not dangerously, eccentric. This way reputations are made.

Next morning, aerial reconnaissance reported extensive damage in Matruh. Only two E-boats were in the harbour and both were on slipways – damaged. The initiative shown at the after guns had obviously been successful so my fears about E-boat attacks had been exaggerated. No Axis supply ships were in the harbour but that did not prove that mine had been a fictive. She could have departed before our arrival, perhaps to make room for the one we had sunk. But one thing was certain; whether my ship was real or imaginary would never be known.

The bombardment had been so successful that it was repeated a few days later. But Axis supply ships continued to use Matruh so it was decided to block the harbour. To achieve this, the striking force was to escort a merchant ship to Matruh, neutralise the opposition while she was being scuttled and then remove her crew. Owing to the block ship's comparatively slow speed, much of the passage would have to be made in daylight. If detected – and that seemed highly probable – the enemy would have little difficulty in guessing her destination so, even if she survived the inevitable bombing, the harbour defences would have been fully alerted. It promised to be a grim operation.

We knew the operation would be a big blow to the ships' morale. The Allied propaganda machine had been reiterating that the army's retreat was only temporary, to extend the enemy's lines of communication, and that a counter attack would soon push him back. In that event, every man in the striking force knew that the army would need Matruh as a supply base and as such the harbour would have to be useable once it was recaptured. Instead, we were going to be blocking the harbour, a sure signal no counter attack was in the offing. We would have to convince our ships' companies that blocking the harbour was an essential operation. But they were beyond the Crimean state of not reasoning why. Amongst themselves they would debate the reason for having to undertake such a hazardous task and would reach only one logical conclusion: there would be no advance in the near future. Propagandists could argue that the term 'near' covered an indefinite period but that would bear little weight with men whose morale would undoubtedly suffer if they ceased to believe what they were being told. This situation was eventually avoided, thanks to the RAF who sunk a ship in the approaches and rose highly in the estimation of at least one commanding officer. Thankfully, to preserve secrecy, the ships' companies had not been briefed before the operation was abruptly cancelled. To claim that the commanding officers were relieved would be an understatement.

In late July 1942, the striking force was relieved by another four 'Hunts' and split up. HMS *Eridge* then became the senior ship of four more 'Hunts' heading for Haifa. The withdrawal of the fleet to the Canal Zone, Haifa and Beirut had caused a great increase in shipping movements along the Levant coast, to which U-boats were naturally attracted. The purpose of our presence in Haifa was to combat this increased threat. We enjoyed those patrols. The weather was warm. There were no 'Red Tobruks' and air activity was minimal. We were given complete freedom of action and had great fun trying to anticipate a U-boat's movements, particularly at morning and evening twilight when we hoped to sight one surfaced against the lighter horizon. Several submarines were to be sunk during the next few weeks but HMS *Eridge* was ordered to return to Alex only a few days after our arrival.

On reaching Alex, we were informed that the Pilot and Doctor were being relieved forthwith. It was a double shock. Having served since commissioning, they were part of the ship and would be sadly missed. Of the two, I would feel more the loss of the Pilot. At sea, we had spent so much time together on the bridge that I knew him better than the other officers. Moreover, by being the target of my impatience, he had acted as my safety valve. That relieved my feelings but the poor Pilot had suffered and, sometimes, his life must have been far from happy. Perhaps a less quiet and more forceful approach on his part might have curbed my impatience; but it was a waste of time to think on those lines. Our natures would never change and I knew that, however hard I tried, tolerance would never be one of my virtues. A change was clearly in his best interest and, when he said farewell, I apologised for my behaviour and wished him a happier time in his next appointment.

The Doctor's relief was a young doctor, recently qualified. The new navigating officer was a reserve Lieutenant who immediately assumed his predecessor's title of Pilot. He was a tough extrovert who quickly adapted to the ways of the ship and his fellow officers. He seemed quite imperturbable and it was obvious that my patience was about to be tested by an entirely different personality. Perhaps it might even persuade me to count up to ten before exploding.

The routine was similar to that in our first attachment to the striking force – permanently at short notice for sea and patrolling most nights to the west of El Daba. There was some movement by coastal craft so ships were always at action stations. It was wearisome work but, fortunately, my nerves showed no signs of repeating their lapse off Matruh.

In mid August, HMS *Eridge* was allowed a night in harbour so the Chief, McCall and myself had dinner ashore to celebrate the anniversary of our departure from Gibraltar. We were all tired so we returned early to be greeted by the almost forgotten figure of Evans, who announced that he had been discharged from hospital. He was still looking terribly frail: his only recognizable feature was that familiar peeling nose. But his return put me in a quandary. Every First Lieutenant worth his salt had his own method of running a ship and our ship's company had become accustomed to Thornycroft's way during Evans' four month absence. During that period, many personnel changes had occurred owing to advancements, training courses and sickness. Consequently, if Evans replaced Thornycroft, those newcomers would have to make virtually a fresh start and I reckoned that was asking too much from a weary ship's company, even for an officer of Evans' calibre. My heart was heavy while explaining to Evans why he could not expect to resume his old appointment. Naturally, he was upset but, being loyal and chivalrous, he put the ship before himself and accepted his fate without demur. Bidding him farewell was one of the most depressing moments of the commission but, thanks to his generous nature, he bore no malice and, in the years ahead, our friendship was never affected during his progressive rise to flag rank.

CHAPTER NINE

El Daba

By the end of August 1942, the striking force consisted of HMS *Eridge*, HMS *Aldenham*, HMS *Croome* and HMS *Hursley*. The latter three were comparatively new to the station and their commanding officers were my juniors. The ship's company immediately assumed that the newcomers were being placed under the wing of the most experienced ship in the flotilla and had no hesitation in explaining this to their mates, who paid little heed to their boasting.

This was the period of Rommel's final preparations for his thrust towards the Suez Canal and the striking force was ordered to bombard his concentration area at El Daba. In fact, our salvoes could truthfully be described as the opening shots of the battle of Alam Halfa – one of the decisive battles in the struggle for North Africa. We met with no opposition but a full moon, by turning night into day, denied us the comforting protection of darkness and kept us horribly naked and exposed, reminding us forcibly of *Chakdina's* fate under similar conditions so many months previously.

Next day, aerial photographs revealed considerable damage so we were ordered to repeat the bombardment on the following night. These indirect bombardments, being highly specialised, were being conducted by John Hamilton, the Assistant Fleet Gunnery Officer, who was obviously revelling in his brief release from headquarters. He returned onboard in time for supper and, shortly afterwards, McCall, who was officer of the day, reported that an American war correspondent had joined the ship.

'Good,' I exclaimed. 'We could do with some publicity.'

McCall looked outraged. 'But this is Larry Allen,' he protested. 'He's a Jonah. Something happens to every ship in which he takes passage. He was onboard HMS *Galatea* and HMS *Naiad* when they were sunk.'

'Well, it's time the poor chap had a quiet passage,' I retorted, hoping I looked more cheerful than I felt. Sailors are superstitious and I knew what their reaction would be if they discovered our passenger's reputation. Inside, I silently cursed the staff officer who had sent him.

'Do you know the date?' Asked McCall, who seemed in a talkative mood.

'Yes. 27 August. What about it?'

'Oh, nothing really. But tomorrow's the anniversary of crossing the line on our journey round Africa. We've been eleven months in the Eastern Med.'

Eleven months! What a range of experience had been covered by those forty-eight weeks, nearly double the average life of a Mediterranean destroyer. In those weeks, long periods of strain and tension had steadily nibbled at men's nerves until many dreaded sleep because of the nightmares it brought. Spasms of intense fear had to be concealed by impassive expressions, even though death always seemed close, and the slowly moving seconds seemed to stretch for lifetimes. The ship's lack of casualties, despite involvement in so many dangerous Tobruk and Malta convoys, seemed incredible. Perhaps she had been launched under a lucky star, as so many of her company believed, and was destined to survive undamaged. But, even if that was so, we would never be sure of our future; fear of the unknown would always haunt us and, in time, this constant assault on our nerves was bound to have a cumulative effect, even on the least imaginative.

The force sailed at midnight. When clear of the swept channel, De Gruchy, the Chief Engine Room Artificer carried out a routine inspection of the after machinery spaces. In the gear room he was greeted by stoker Davies who was glad to see him. Davies was the only watchkeeper and was feeling very lonely in the small, hot compartment dominated by the huge boxes covering the rapidly revolving gears.

'Any problems?' De Gruchy asked.

'No. Everything's O.K.'

Leaving Davies he proceeded aft to the steering motor compartment to read the temperature gauges. Returning to the upper deck, he sat on the depth charges, breathing the cool night air. The broad, white wake was stretching astern like a great highway. It was pointing the way to Alex, thence to the Canal, round the Cape and, eventually, to far distant home.

It was the eve of the great land battle at Alam Halfa and the sky was full of aircraft – bombers, night fighters and reconnaissance planes. Probably the majority were friendly but some would be hostile and, as it was a bright, moonlit night, De Gruchy guessed the enemy would be aware of our presence and, most likely, of our ultimate destination. It was an unpleasant thought.

De Gruchy stood up and returned to the engineroom where he rejoined the Chief who had visited the boiler rooms. Artificers Berry and Woolacott were at the port and starboard controls respectively. But they had little to do – except drink copious draughts of lime juice – because HMS *Eridge*, being the leading ship, was maintaining a constant speed. In the background, a sound like a Gaelic lament was barely recognizable as 'When it rains, it rains'.

'Only Maltman,' leading stoker Blizzard explained. 'He's trying a lower key.'

'Tell him to grease his throat muscles,' the Chief grunted.

Speed was reduced to eight knots on sighting land at 0400 hrs and course altered to the westward when it was two miles ahead. Our aiming mark was clearly visible against the moon and, as soon as the spotting aircraft was ready to observe, the first salvo thundered towards the target area. Hamilton waited for a report of the fall of shot, corrected his range and deflection then signalled his new settings to the other ships. Of necessity, it was a leisurely shoot and those not actively engaged chafed at its slowness. Neither were we encouraged by the satisfying spectacle of hits because a range of sand hills was concealing the target. The passage of time was marked only by the blinding flash and heavy boom of each salvo.

In due course, the division reached the end of its westerly run, checked fire and reversed course in succession. Then the bombardment was continued at the same tempo. Each salvo was exactly the same – flash, boom, whistle, silence – until, after endless minutes, Hamilton reported that the shoot was completed.

The deck watch was then showing 0445 hrs so we had a good hour to morning twilight. By that time we should be well on the way to Alex which we should reach about 0900 hrs.

'Increase to twenty knots,' I told the Pilot. 'Then give me a course to Alex.'

He passed the order to the wheelhouse and Brewer signalled the new speed down the line. The Pilot was returning to the chart when every nerve in my body began to transmit an urgent, compelling warning. Instinctively, I called, 'Hard a starboard, full ahead port engine, alarm starboard.'

The Coxswain repeated the order, amid a clamour of ringing bells, while I stared anxiously towards the black shadow of a cloud. I could see nothing but my own alarm system was still tingling and I knew that my instinct was correct. Then a sinister, low lying craft glided out of the shadow, swung to port and passed HMS *Eridge* on a reciprocal course. In the same moment Leading Seaman Rayner spotted her; the pom-pom drummed into action followed instantly by an oerlikon and my fascinated eyes watched tracer hitting her hull and ricocheting off the water.

'Will the damn ship never answer her helm?' I wondered and glanced impatiently at the helm indicator, fearing the Coxswain had missed the order. No; the indicator was hard over and, while I was still looking, the ship started to turn, slowly at first but with increasing momentum until she heeled sharply under the rudder's influence.

Engine Room Artificer Berry, heaving open his manoeuvring valve, felt its spindle judder just as the pom-pom opened fire.

'That's a new target,' he was thinking when his little world exploded into blackness. Bruised and barely conscious, he realised he was lying on the upper gratings. He was only vaguely aware of the smell of oil and explosive and of the noise of inrushing water. But he was acutely and painfully aware of a choking sensation and of hissing jets of steam searing his flesh. He had no recollection of being blown onto the gratings but he knew that he had to get off them before he was broiled alive. Overhead, was a circle of lighter darkness which he guessed was the hatch. Gasping painfully for breath, he dragged himself towards it, praying that the ladder was intact. To his surprise, he seemed to be going downhill towards unseen water which was gurgling angrily just beneath his body. As he reached the ladder, water flowed over his grating as if determined to sweep him into the black pit below. He clutched the ladder to save himself and was thankful to find it still firmly secured. With rising water lapping at his heels, he hauled himself upwards, hand over hand, until he reached blessed fresh air. Stumbling over the combing, he collapsed on top of another man who had been knocked flat by a blast of pressurised steam from a ventilation trunk.

The noise was horrific. The safety valves had lifted, ejecting steam into the atmosphere with a thunderous roar. At the same time, the two sirens jammed open and their doleful shrieks were adding to the bedlam, making thought and speech difficult. But no shouted orders were needed. Every man knew what he had to do. Together Thorneycroft and the Chief assessed the extent of the main damage, finding that the torpedo had exploded between the engine and gear rooms. Both compartments were flooded, all auxiliary machinery destroyed or immobilised and the starboard gear complex had been hurled across the compartment, causing a heavy list to port. Under the impact, the gear room's after bulkhead had buckled allowing seawater to flow into the adjacent Petty Officers' mess. Seeing this the Shipwright knew that the compartment's after bulkhead had to be held firm. He directed his shores into the shellroom astern, where the ammunition party was shifting heavy shell cases to make space for the great balks of timber. Engineroom Artificer Pattinson, guessing he was now the senior Engine Room Artificer, carried out a hasty inspection forward, plugging some blown rivet holes with anything to hand. He then made his way aft, bumping into other men, tripping over bits of the whaler and getting entangled in fallen wireless aerials. When he finally reached the steering compartment he found the rudder jammed hard to starboard. Collecting the, now unemployed, boiler room crews and a threefold purchase, he set them the arduous task of hauling the reluctant rudder amidships. The Coxswain, too, having exchanged a useless main steering position for an equally useless secondary steering one, was organising more purchases and handlers to give the ship some steering capability. In the stern, the torpedomen were ditching depth charges after the Gunner and Petty Officer Paine had removed the primers. Over all this activity, the gun crews were keeping a vigilant watch.

The Doctor had been watching the bombardment. He was about to return to his sickbay when he was startled by the harsh clamour of the alarm bells followed by the close range weapons thudding into action. Moments later, a brilliant flash amidships temporarily blinded him. The ship bucked as if she was leaping and a pillar of discoloured water amidships jerked high into the air. As it sluiced across the upper deck, the ship slumped back into the water with a hard, sickening crump. For a few seconds, she shivered like a stricken animal and then settled down with a heavy list to port. Calling to Morgan, the sick berth attendant, to bring his medical bag, he struggled, like Pattinson, through a detritus of disaster until he collided with two men attending to Berry.

'He'll be OK,' one of them told him. 'We've given him a shot.'

'Well done. Where did he come from?'

'Engineroom.'

The possibility of finding more survivors needing his attention overcame the Doctor's natural reluctance and he clambered over the hatch combing into the engineroom, whilst Morgan made his way into the neighbouring gear room. Almost at once the Doctor's feet encountered water. Halting, he dipped his head beneath the hatchway into a stench of oil and cordite. It was still very hot and thick, swirling dust clawed at his throat and lungs, almost choking him. Holding his breath, he was rummaging for his torch when the ship gave a sudden lurch and, for one frightening moment, he feared she was turning over. But, to his relief, she settled down again, trembling slightly causing the water beneath him to slosh from side to side. Having found the torch, he switched it on and swung the beam round the compartment. A few days earlier, the Chief had shown him round and they had admired the shining brass and clean paintwork and marvelled at the great turbines and maze of pipes. Now it was unrecognisable. A dirty mess of oil and water was completely covering the port turbine, the control platform and much of the starboard turbine. Paintwork above the water level was hidden beneath an oily scum and the pipes had been twisted into fantastic shapes, some still leaking steam. Only the upper end of the sloping grating could offer sanctuary. It was empty. Somewhere below, De Gruchy, Woolacott, Blizzard and Maltman were lying in their steel tomb. Never again would 'When it rains' compete with the more harmonious sound of smooth running machinery. The compartment looked ugly, sinister and the Doctor, feeling profoundly shaken, was glad to clamber back into cool, clean air.

Conditions in the gear room were similar, if not worse, and Morgan knew at once that stoker Davies would have no chance of survival. Further aft, a little group was gathered round the hatch to the Petty Officers' mess, paying out a line to a seaman who was descending the ladder.

'Who's down there?' Morgan asked.

'Damage control. Three men.'

Thinking he might be needed, Morgan followed the seaman into a black pit. The ladder was situated where the water came up to his waist. Clinging to a rung, his head only just above the water, was a semi-conscious stoker.

'Get him up,' Morgan told the seaman. 'I'll look for the others.'

The seaman slipped a running bowline under the man's armpits and called to his mates to haul him up. As he rose through the hatch, Morgan waded to port through deepening water. To his left, the bulkhead was creaking and groaning, warning that it might collapse at any moment. He would have to hurry. But movement in the darkness was difficult and he kept bumping into floating stools and tables or grazing his shins against sunken objects. The water was up to his chest when he reached the side. He then felt his way along the plating and was satisfied that no one was trapped on the port side. Using the after bulkhead as a guide, he waded to starboard with growing ease as the water became shallower. Behind the bulkhead he could hear heavy thumps, where preparations were in hand to shore up the bulkhead.

Near the starboard side his knee hit something less painful than some of his earlier bumps. He thrust out a hand and encountered the legs of a man sprawled across a locker. Moving a little further, he found a second man sitting on the deck, his back supported by a locker. Both were unconscious, the second man's head was only just above water. Returning to the first man, Morgan jammed him in a corner, praying that he would not slip beneath the water. He then half dragged, half carried the other casualty to the seaman. The bulkhead was now protesting violently and the depth of water was steadily increasing as he waded back to starboard. Reaching the last casualty, he turned him on his back and swam towards the ladder desperate to reach it before the bulkhead gave way. The seaman met him halfway and slipped the running bowline over the casualty. The gang on deck hauled away and the unconscious man was hoisted aloft like a sack of potatoes. The seaman followed upwards and finally Morgan started to climb the ladder.

'Anyone down there?' A voice demanded.

'Yes – Morgan,' the seaman replied.

'Poor devil,' the voice continued, then paused before adding: 'What the devil was he doing down there? That's not his action station.'

At that moment, Morgan's head rose above the combing. The speaker shot backwards and uttered a startled yelp as if he was looking at a ghost.

What the hell do you think I'm doing?' Yelled an unamused Morgan. 'Taking a voluntary bathe?'

The bridge was more or less isolated, all communications, both internal and external, except for Brewer's aldis, having been destroyed. Not that this mattered at the moment; the other ships had already started a circular patrol and, for the time being, could do little else. Onboard, remote advice or demands for information would needlessly distract those trying to assess or limit the damage, so it was an advantage to be deprived of the means of being tempted to interfere. Besides, my immediate task was to decide our action when the damage reports had been collated by First Lieutenant Thornycroft. I expected these by 0500 hrs but, whatever the damage, only one question really mattered at the moment. Would the ship remain afloat or was she slowly sinking? The decision would be easy if she was doomed – the crew would be transferred and her destruction expedited. After our experience with HMS *Airedale*, there would be no messing about with guns. HMS *Aldenham* would be instructed to use a torpedo. That would enable the surviving ships to be heading for Alex at full speed by sunrise and rapidly draw closer to effective fighter cover.

The situation would be more complicated if the ship was expected to remain afloat and some hard thinking was needed. But mental concentration was almost impossible owing to the roar of escaping steam and the shriek of sirens. I tried to block out the barbaric noise while noting that the ship had swung in a semicircle and come to rest facing west, her bow pointing towards the still unseen headland of El Daba. A towing destroyer would, therefore, have to steam towards the headland while working up sufficient speed to achieve steerage way. She would then have to turn 120 degrees to starboard to get on course for Alex. That should pose no problem because HMS *Eridge* would tend to swing to starboard – her least immersed side. We had faced a similar problem a year earlier. On that occasion, it had taken three hours to get HMS *Firedrake* heading for Gibraltar, including a turn through 270 degrees. Now we had a shorter turn and HMS *Eridge's* favourable list should enable the towing ship to gain steerage way at a lower speed. The time taken to get on course should, therefore, be considerably reduced.

Even this saving gave little cause for satisfaction. The ships would still have no chance of starting to leave the area before sunrise. Until then they would be lying little more than two miles from a hostile coastline, after which a slow passage of ten to twelve hours, mostly within easy range of enemy air bases, would lie ahead of them. So was I justified in exposing the division to this danger and risking the lives of the 700 men in the four ships? There were occasions, as we well knew, when scuttling a ship was the only option. But those ships had been far from a friendly base whereas HMS *Eridge* was less than 100 miles from Alex and surely within range of some degree of fighter cover. In such circumstances, the option of scuttling was out of the question. Whatever the hazards ahead, a tow to Alex had to be faced and I sensed, from the reaction around me, that the ship's company would heartily support that decision. Having made it, I could only wait with as much patience as possible while the noise of escaping steam was mercifully dying away to a whimper.

Shortly after 0500 hrs, Thornycroft's head rose above the hatch combing. Before he could speak, I demanded, 'Will she float?'

'Yes,' was the brief retort.

'Good. Prepare to be towed. Brewer, tell HMS *Aldenham* to take us in tow. Ready in ten minutes.'

The situation immediately began to get out of control. The towing hawser should have rolled smoothly off its reel; instead, it seemed to be jammed solid. Cursing softly, the Chief Bosun's Mate dropped on his belly and peered under the reel. To his dismay, he saw that the deck plating had buckled thereby twisting the reel out of alignment. Praying that the damage could be overcome, he detailed men with crowbars to try to straighten the reel and ordered others to operate a purchase to drag the hawser off its reel, fathom by fathom. It was a slow, laborious task. The ten minutes stretched to twenty, then thirty and forty while our consorts patrolled impatiently around us. Every second of the agonizingly slow additional minutes seemed to chide me for making the wrong decision. Not until the sky was paling in the east could the eye of the hawser be passed to HMS *Aldenham*, where it was shackled to her towing pendant.

HMS *Aldenham* steamed ahead slowly to prevent any strain on the hawser while it was being paid out from our focs'le. By the time its 900 feet were outboard, the other ships were visible and the headland at El Daba was beginning to take shape. The inboard end of the towing hawser had been secured to the cable, two shackles of which were now being veered to add weight to the tow. Cable and hawser were forming a steep catenary between the two ships when we heard an aircraft. We were expecting early reconnaissance planes, hopefully not before sunrise, but this, barely visible against the lighter eastern horizon, was a dive bomber.

The early appearance of one of these menaces was a shock and every gun opened fire with a desperate urgency. Probably the bomber had only a rough idea of the ships' whereabouts but it promptly dipped into a power dive, dropping almost to sea level before swooping upwards. It was flying landwards when a tall column of water jerked out of the sea directly between HMS *Eridge* and HMS *Aldenham*.

'Christ it's hit the hawser,' Brewer muttered.

His instinctive comment seemed only too probable and never was a hawser watched with such apprehension as when HMS *Aldenham* moved slowly ahead. For what seemed an unconscionable time both ends continued to dangle in the water as if the hawser had parted. But, as HMS *Aldenham* moved further away, the wire began to form a more noticeable catenary. It was, at least, behaving normally which suggested that its unseen bight was undamaged.

HMS *Aldenham* continued to accelerate by a couple of engine revolutions at a time. It was a slow but prudent procedure and, in comparison, daylight was approaching at an alarming rate. Enemy traffic on the coast road was now visible. El Daba, against the darker background looked sombre and forbidding. But when the sun rose majestically out of the sea its rays shone briefly onto the headland: it looked so alarmingly close that individual rocks and shrubs were recognizable. A staff car had stopped by the roadside and its occupants, typical Panzer officers, were watching the ships through binoculars. One of them was speaking into a radio telephone.

Aircraft were becoming increasingly active. A succession of fighter bombers were diving out of the sky, dropping their bombs and scurrying back to base. They appeared not to be working to a coordinated plan but were carrying out haphazard and not very accurate attacks, more irritating than effective. The real attacks were still to come.

The Pilot was burning the confidential books and ciphers on the signal deck so McCall had abandoned his now useless director to relieve him on the bridge. There was little he could do except act as an additional look-out or keep an eye on HMS *Aldenham*. He was doing this with increasing impatience as she drew steadily closer to El Daba.

'For God's sake, turn,' he muttered.

I was sharing his anxiety. HMS *Aldenham* had got steerage way by now. In fact she had made several attempts to turn because I had seen her bow faltering two or three degrees to starboard before swinging back. HMS *Eridge* had never looked like following and that was contrary to all the rules of seamanship. She should have turned easily to starboard so the explosion had obviously caused damage, not easily visible, which was producing this unusual behaviour. Could it have twisted the hull so that the stern was acting as a giant rudder, turned slightly to port, I wondered? In the absence of any other explanation, it was worth testing but it would have to be done swiftly otherwise the coastline curving towards El Daba would be too close for a turn to port. For that matter, if we failed to change our present course, we would run aground below the headland.

'Try the other way,' Brewer signalled.

HMS *Aldenham's* helm was reversed. Slowly, very slowly, her bow swung to port and, to our great relief, we followed quietly in her wake. Then, without the least warning, HMS *Eridge* surged unexpectedly to port like an uncontrolled paravane, dragging HMS *Aldenham's* stern with us until our momentum took charge and both ships began to swing at an increasing speed. We swept through 180 degrees without faltering. Lieutenant Stuart-Monteith, HMS *Aldenham's* captain, vainly manoeuvred his helm and engines but our dead weight astern was relentlessly pulling his ship through east. It was not until her bow was swinging towards north that the wild surge was slowed down. When finally halted both ships were heading west again so, thirty minutes after sunrise, we were still trapped in the bombardment area. We were falling far behind my timetable and the only consolation was that our erratic behaviour had confused the hit and run bombers whose aim had become very uncertain.

But from that moment onwards, air attacks became better coordinated. HMS *Aldenham* had just started her second attempt to turn when three fighter-bombers swooped overhead. The ships were still shuddering from the concussion of their bombs when another Stuka dived almost vertically onto HMS *Aldenham*. A terrific barrage burst around it, blowing it off course, then the Stuka released its bombs which missed their target by half a cable. The upheaval had barely subsided before another three fighter bombers dived out of the sun. This attack was followed by a brief, unnatural silence which was suddenly broken by a vicious whine. This coincided with a tall column of water rising leisurely on our starboard beam.

The rays of the sun were glistening and scintillating off the calm sea while a steady stream of shells shrieked over the bridge or burst just short of the ship. Stuart-Monteith was now keeping the turn so well under control that, to anxious eyes, the swing seemed barely perceptible. But this was increasing the turning circle. Both ships were so close to the shore that they had become the target of a shore battery, though the battery's continual misses were no credit to the gunners. Near the shoreline were two small objects – the two boats that had successfully attacked us earlier. One was now an abandoned wreck; the second was our other attacker on which a man was working with desperate urgency. As we drew closer, a Messerschmidt skimmed low over the water and unexpectedly sprayed this man's craft with cannon fire, forcing him overboard, angrily shaking his fist at the retreating fighter. Our situation was far too serious for laughter but the fact that the enemy airmen could be stupid enough to mistake a friendly assault craft for a hostile destroyer, gave some consolation.

Spectators were gathering in groups along the coast road. Behind them, flashes in the dunes marked the position of the battery, now pumping out shells with increasing accuracy. From time to time HMS *Croome* sprayed the area with high explosive, forcing the gunners to keep their heads down and warning spectators that their ringside view was dangerous. Every few minutes small formations of bombers kept diving out of the clear sky, some faltering in the face of our barrage; others pressing resolutely through it. The whole force, under attack from land and air, hampered by a cripple and with hours of daylight ahead, was hopelessly compromised. The risk of a ship being hit was making it increasingly difficult to retain any confidence in my decision. Nevertheless, it was too late to change it. We could only press on, hoping for fighter cover which, to anxious minds, already seemed long overdue. In the meantime, El Daba was becoming so familiar that its grim features would be printed indelibly on our minds for the rest of our lives.

HMS *Aldenham* at last steadied on the course for Alex and, to our great relief, HMS *Eridge* followed docilely astern without displaying any tendency to surge to port. I glanced at my watch; then put it to my ear hoping it had stopped. No! Not yet 0800 hrs. It was still ticking and no more than three hours had elapsed since being torpedoed. To strained nerves that time span seemed to cover a lifetime. Owing to our unexpected mishaps, we had only equalled the time taken to get HMS *Firedrake* on course: the division, instead of being miles closer to Alex, were still in the bombardment area. Something like this must surely have happened to Moses when time stood still.

A whisper of sound in the east grew steadily into the hum of approaching aircraft. The divisions' guns swung swiftly towards the bearing, HMS *Eridge's* hand-operated mountings following with difficulty. Anxious eyes scanned the heavens and nerves tautened when six fighters became visible. But these were behaving differently to their predecessors. They were flying at cruising speed at a moderate height and McCall suddenly shouted, 'Friendly fighters. Do not fire.'

The tension which had been steadily mounting since the early attacks, due partly to our inability to offer more than a token defence, instantly dissolved into cheers of relief. The Hurricanes approached in arrowhead formation. As they flew overhead, they waggled their wings in a welcome which was reciprocated by every man onboard. Their presence was an inspiring reminder that the bombers would now have to contend with a more powerful defence.

Suddenly the heavens were filled with the babel of brutal battle. A dozen Messerschmidts had also arrived but at a much higher altitude and they swooped onto the unsuspecting Hurricanes. The sky seemed to be filled with fighters twisting, turning, climbing, diving. Such was the confusion that ships dared not open fire and their gun crews could only watch in helpless frustration while the unequal fight was reaching its inevitable conclusion. That did not take long. Within minutes of their arrival, the Hurricanes, some belching oily smoke, others with lowered undercarriages were limping towards their base while their victors, to add insult to injury, flew a triumphant circuit around the ships before climbing back into the high heavens.

The arrival of the fighters had so cheered everyone that their sudden, unexpected defeat had a thoroughly depressing effect. Once again I was assailed by doubt. If fighters were unable to help, our situation was even more precarious and our survival would be dependant on the accuracy of our gunfire. I comforted myself with the reminder that the 'Hunts' had successfully repelled numerous aerial attacks and although HMS *Eridge*, without a control system or power, would hardly excel in marksmanship, her consorts could damn well do so again. One danger, at least, had receded because the battery was now screened by a spur of the sand hills.

'I suppose the spectators will be returning to their dugouts,' McCall mused. 'I hope they feel like a football crowd whose team has just been beaten. Neither the gunnery or bombing will've impressed 'em.'

McCall's comment was followed immediately by the roar of aircraft. The sound was so menacing that the possibility of friendly fighters never entered our heads. All guns were immediately trained towards the dangerous sector and were pumping out high explosive seconds before six fighter bombers dived in to sight. They seemed surprised by their reception and dropped their bombs hastily without bothering to take accurate aim.

When the aircraft had vanished from sight, I climbed wearily onto a high stool, noting thankfully that El Daba was becoming blurred behind a heat haze. The day had become unbearably hot and, soothed by the gentle swish of water alongside, I kept falling asleep. For a time I struggled to keep awake but I had nothing to do but think and, being utterly exhausted, leaned more and more heavily against the compass pedestal until I slipped into a troubled doze. It seemed no more than a few seconds before Brewer's yell of, 'Look out! They're diving,' jerked me awake.

I hoped I was dreaming because the frightful noise certainly seemed part of some horrible nightmare. Then memory flooded back and I was shocked to see a sky seemingly full of Stukas. By then, every gun in the force was firing as rapidly as possible and their deeper rumble mingled with the tormented scream of diving engines, the high pitched shriek of falling bombs and their deafening detonations, first to one side and then the other. We seemed to be isolated in some dark corner of Hades where a huge giant was tossing us back and forth like a shuttlecock. We were imaginary persons, utterly remote from the civilised world, against whom was concentrated all the fury and hate of the nether regions.

Our guns thundered defiantly as plane after plane dived into the barrage. Overhead, fumes and high explosive were drawing a dark veil across the sky and, above it, the sun looked as if it had lost most of its brilliance. Tall, black splashes jerked into the air, remained suspended for a moment and then subsided into circular patches of scum on the deep, blue sea. It was quite impossible to think sanely amid such bedlam and a man, wherever he was stationed, could only carry out the automatic motions of a well drilled team. After an eon, McCall realised that the harsh scream of diving Stukas was diminishing. Reason flooded back and his eyes became locked on HMS *Croome*, above whom a solitary bomber was diving almost vertically through the haze. Its approach was too swift for the guns so its plummet-like fall was unchallenged. HMS *Croome*, however had spotted the danger and turbulence beneath her stern confirmed that she was working up to full speed.

The bomber was diving so low that its pilot seemed to be either dead or crashing deliberately onto his target. Even if he could pull out of so steep a dive, his bombs would never miss from such a low altitude. It seemed this was the moment of disaster which had been haunting the ship all morning and catastrophe seemed more certain than ever when the bomber swooped upwards just before HMS *Croome* vanished amongst a turmoil of explosions. I was desperate to learn what was happening beyond the cataclysm which seemed determined never to subside. Then HMS *Croome's* bow emerged from the black compound of seawater and high explosive: her bridge followed; then her funnel and after superstructure; finally the whole ship, steaming at full speed, broke clear. Miraculously, every bomb had missed.

McCall glanced at me and let out an explosive sigh. Feeling far too thankful for speech, I glanced around, subconsciously noting that the hated headland was no longer in sight. Our consorts seemed to be undamaged but, beyond them, a pile of wreckage smouldering on the sea marked where one of the bombers had crashed. Further away, five, ten, fifteen Stukas were forming up in line astern before returning to their base. They were offering a wonderful target for fighters but, alas, the only fighters in sight were German. Sometimes it was very difficult to believe that we had an air force.

Our reporter Larry Allen had watched the preparations for being towed and the determined defence against air attack from the signal bridge. After the Stuka attack, he decided to walk round the ship to inspect the damage and to form an opinion of her company's morale. He was left in no doubt about the determination to reach Alex.

'You're going to get her back, aren't you?' Allen said to stoker Edwards.

'You bet, we will,' Stoker Edwards retorted with a grin. 'You're in good hands.'

The ships continued their slow withdrawal and the sand hills sank, almost imperceptibly, below the horizon until the latter was girded entirely by the sea. Air attack, for the time being at least, had petered out; there was not a plane in sight except for an occasional glimpse of the German fighters rotating high overhead, as if acting as our escort. I walked to the after end of the bridge, curious to survey the damage but dreading what I might see. The forward end of the ship seemed intact but, just abaft the pom-pom, a deep crater had been blown out of the side and upper deck. Above it, the searchlight was hanging at a drunken angle from its platform; the bow and stern of the motor boat were dangling from sagging davits while the greater part of its hull was nestling snugly beneath the shattered whaler on the opposite side of the ship. Steel plates were twisted into improbable shapes; smashed floats and rafts were swinging limply from their stowages and jumping ladders hung untidily over the side. The damaged area was scorched by heat and deeply coated in oil, leaving a slick in the wake astern. Not much would be holding the stern to the ship and the jarring jolt of gunfire could easily snap it off. Despite this, at X gun, Hambrook, as solid as the Rock of Gibraltar, was staring into the sun, waiting for the next attack. Beside him Rowson was tenderly massaging a broken nose. The rest of his crew, barely recognisable beneath a film of grime, were at instant readiness for action. They were fully alert, almost eager for the next attack, and I envied them, knowing the misery of being inactive at such a time. To deprive them of this, by ordering the after guns not to fire, was too cruel to contemplate. Moreover, such a policy would have a disastrous affect on morale, not only amongst the gun crews but the whole ship's company. The stern and, with it, the ship would have to take its chance.

The Doctor, having made his casualties – mostly suffering from shock – as comfortable as possible, was talking to Thornycroft on the signal bridge below me. Since passing the tow, Thornycroft and the Shipwright had been shoring up bulkheads and plugging holes in the hot, airless compartments below decks; Thornycroft was covered in oil and dirt, through which rivulets of sweat were dribbling onto the deck below and forming round, discoloured stains. Beside them, Larry Allen was lying on the deck, trying to make himself as comfortable as an inflated life jacket would allow. Beyond him, the Pilot was still feeding a small bonfire with the codes and ciphers. He looked like a Buddhist monk kneeling over an incense burner. The Pilot had seldom spoken to Allen, being too intent on not burning himself for conversation. But he had noted Allen's pale, strained face and the pile of cigarette butts beside him gave some indication of his nerves. The Pilot felt sorry for the reporter. He was not a fighting man but had volunteered to join us merely to write a story for strangers, thousands of miles away, to read with their breakfasts.

A telegraphist called out, 'The fighter direction receiver's working again! HMS *Croome's* using some shocking language.'

I picked up the handset. Lieutenant Commander Rupert Egan, HMS *Croome's* captain, whose language was always expressive, was using the transmitter himself and the atmosphere was blue with his complaints about the lack of fighters. Not a man in the division would disagree with his vitriolic remarks. We knew the position where the armies were facing each other, some fifty miles west of Alex, and the ships had never been more than a short flying distance from the advanced fighter bases. Their absence was inexplicable. We felt abandoned but more determined than ever to save the ship without outside help.

The messman, looking in his life jacket like a woman with a well developed bust, arrived on the bridge with a plate of sandwiches and some bottles of warm beer. I suddenly felt both hungry and thirsty and that made me much happier, believing it to be a good sign. The Pilot, who had returned to the bridge, was trying to estimate our position while munching a sandwich. No land was in sight and our speed was anybody's guess but we were obviously passing from clear, blue water into the muddy outflow from the Nile so he reckoned the ship was more than halfway home. It was hotter than ever and the air was so uncannily still that the events of the morning before seemed like the memory of bad dream.

This had been our longest period without an attack but, just as we were beginning to hope that we had seen the last of the bombers, the hum of aircraft jerked us back to reality. We had every excuse for hoping that these were the long awaited fighters but a heat haze had drifted across the sky and the planes crossed unseen, flying into the sun. The noise of their engines steadily receded in a southerly direction and then remained constant for a few seconds, as if the aircraft were turning. Our emotions were still alternating between hope and fear when their engines suddenly accelerated with a huge roar.

Our opening salvoes were still bursting raggedly in the sky when the noise changed into a menacing whine and six fighter bombers dived into sight. They had already reached their bombing position and the close range weapons could do no more than fire a few ineffectual rounds before some huge giant seemed to be shaking the ship. But once again we survived the explosions.

The expended ammunition had barely been replaced before the roar of engines warned of another attack. The bombers, unseen above the haze, repeated the earlier tactics of turning into the sun and then diving through our barrage. Their bombs shrieked seawards in graceful curves and one hit the water, just off our bow, without exploding. Relieved, we watched the ripples spreading round the spot where the bomb had disappeared. The ship seemed barely to be moving but slowly, very slowly, the bridge drew level with the turbulence which, foot by foot, dropped astern to the funnel and thence to X gun. Its perimeter lapped against the hull with a gentle slap, slap until it drew level with the quarterdeck. Then the bomb unexpectedly exploded; it was either defective or operated by a delayed fuse. The explosion was so deep that the surface of the sea vibrated as if it had been electrocuted. The ship gave a violent shudder and heeled over so far that water flowed across her waist. A sickening crunch of jagged pieces of metal grinding together sounded like the stern breaking away. We watched apprehensively while the ship was struggling to right herself. The stern gave a couple of uneasy waggles before settling down with another ugly crunch. It was holding.

The seaward end of the swept channel to Alex was always patrolled by a trawler. Look-outs were already hopefully scanning the horizon, eager to be the first to spot her, and a wave of elation swept through the ship when her mast eventually poked above the horizon. That harmless looking vessel was our first cheerful sign since the brief appearance of the Hurricanes and all our doubts and uncertainties immediately vanished into thin air. We were still three hours away from Alex but we were now convinced that nothing would prevent us reaching harbour. The same thought apparently occurred to our unwelcome escort of German fighters because they dived low, waggled their wings in farewell and flew off westwards. Within minutes, they had been replaced by a squadron of Hurricanes which began to circle overhead with such a display of importance that they appeared to be boasting that they, alone, were responsible for our survival. No wonder that the cheers which greeted them sounded a little hollow.

Nevertheless, it was comforting to be under our own fighter cover and we began to relax. After all, this was a fine summer's day in which the sun was shining gaily on the white horses breaking gently against the hull. A porpoise, playing off the bows, crossed and re-crossed our track, as if determined to be cut in half. A few gulls flew past, reminding us that even sea birds avoided the grim headland of El Daba. Already the day's events were looking less horrifying, although the fixed expressions on the tired, grey faces of the ship's company warned that they would never be forgotten.

And so HMS *Eridge*, with her dead and dying, returned for the last time to the base from which she had sailed so often. Having passed the Great Pass Beacon, the familiar panorama slowly unfolded before our eager eyes – El Gabbari, the crowded anchorage, the bored, glum faces of the Vichy Frenchmen, a racing yacht running before a freshening breeze, Ras El Tin and, in the background, the tall, white buildings towering above the harbour. Almost with disbelief we realised that life here, with its curious mixture of peace and war, had carried on, completely oblivious to the horror of the past fifteen hours. Our thoughts had been so concentrated on our own danger that we had felt that everyone must be sharing our ordeal. But this normal, well known scene was so remote from it that, once again, I half believed we had dreamed it. Then I looked at the tired, haunted faces around me; it had happened.[14]

Two tugs relieved HMS *Aldenham* and began to edge HMS *Eridge* towards the dockyard. The slipping of the tow severed our final link with those tense, frightening hours and was greeted by an upsurge of elation which peaked while the Commander in Chief was circling each ship in turn, calling to us, 'Well done; well done. Half a Hunt is better than no Hunt.'

Then, as our adrenalin gradually faded, a strained, exhausted ship's company secured their battered ship alongside a jetty where ambulances were already waiting for the wounded. While they were being carried ashore a signal informed us that accommodation had been arranged at the naval barracks.

'We'll have to leave some ship keepers onboard,' Thornycroft told the officers.

'That's already fixed,' the Chief interposed. 'The dead are engineroom ratings and they'd want their mates to be with them. I'm staying onboard with some stokers.'

Thornycroft noticed that the Chief was nearly in tears. He looked old, frail and drained of all vitality and Thornycroft hated the thought of him staying onboard this lifeless hull in such a condition. But when he started to remonstrate, a stubborn expression spread over the Chief's face, warning Thornycroft that nothing would alter his determination to keep this vigil.

After the ship's company had disembarked, I bade farewell to Hamilton and Larry Allen and returned to my cabin which was looking drab and inhospitable without its pictures and ornaments. I had no idea how I intended to spend the night – I might even remain in the chair onto which I had collapsed.

The most horrible experience of my life lay behind me but my memory was still reliving every incident of that long, endless day so, to calm it, I drank two large, neat whiskies in rapid succession. A pleasant, warm drowsy feeling began to creep through my body. To accelerate the cure, I drank a third. Perhaps a quarter bottle of whisky on an empty stomach was unwise because the cabin started to revolve with an uneasy, jerky motion. I made no effort to fight the sensation and was drifting into a welcome state of forgetfulness when I began to suspect that I was no longer alone. Opening my eyes, I saw two figures, both of which seemed to be saying something, floating around the perimeter of the cabin. I blinked rapidly and the revolving figures gradually came to rest, merging into a single marine orderly who was trying to explain that Flag Officer, Alexandria, was expecting me to dine and sleep at his house. By then, I was in no condition to meet an Admiral. I was even worse after he had plied me with a couple of stiff gins and, at dinner, I alternated between mumbling unintelligible gibberish and falling asleep, like the dormouse at the Mad Hatter's tea party. But the Admiral was very tolerant and, having made me eat some solid food, promptly put me to bed.

Next morning, the ship was placed in a dry dock. Her damage was far more extensive than we had imagined and any amateur naval constructor could see that she was unlikely to go to sea again. Apart from the demolished compartments and the great, gaping gash in her side and upper deck, an ominous split almost encircled the hull and the stern was only held by a single plate. Already the bitter sweet tang of death was hovering over the ship and the waist was the scene of noisy activity; acetylene burners were cutting away plates to enable cranes to lift the mangled machinery off the dead within the engineroom. Thank God. We had no doubt that all had died without suffering.

As I watched the five canvas covered bodies being lifted out, I could not help wondering if the risk of saving the ship had been justified. No questions would ever be asked because we had reached harbour but one hit on another ship would have endangered the whole force and that would have been very different. Then I thrust the doubt aside. It would never be wrong to fight against odds even if an easier alternative was available. Victory would never be won if we took the easier course instead of forcing the enemy to fight. This we had done, destroying at least one bomber without any other ship suffering more than superficial damage.

Later that day, I reported to the Commander in Chief who made some appropriate remarks before adding, 'I was delighted to see HMS *Eridge* safely in harbour. I nearly ordered her to be scuttled.'

I muttered, 'I'm glad you didn't, sir' and meant it. For better or for worse, a local decision had been made quickly and, thenceforth, every man in the force had been fully aware of the task. Although that decision had been made without any knowledge of the availability of fighters, it had been swift whereas the Staff, way back in Alex, would never have appreciated the pros and cons before it was too late to scuttle in darkness. In such circumstances, that order would have been thoroughly unhelpful and I dared not think how it would have been handled.

The Commander in Chief then asked a number of searching questions before explaining, 'I'm digging into all this detail because the RAF deny it ever happened. They are claiming that only a few long range bombers from Crete attacked you.'

This was such an outrageous statement that I lost my temper.

'What the hell do they know about it?' I hotly demanded. 'Apart from the early morning, no fighters came within miles of us so they haven't the slightest idea of what attacked us. I can produce records of more than seventy bombing attacks, all by short range aircraft.'

He held up his hand.

'I know, I know,' he replied in a quiet voice. 'But don't forget you were hit close to the enemy's front line where there's so much aerial activity that it's not easy to distinguish specific targets amongst the general activity. Anyway. You've got witnesses. I've read your reporter's description. It's grim reading and Hamilton confirms it.'

'Couldn't fighters be sent?' I asked.

The Commander in Chief smiled briefly but grimly. 'At this moment the RAF is deployed to fight a battle on which the fate of the Middle East may depend. In that context, your's was a very minor affair.'

I was still not mollified. Those attacks had happened. They were not a figment of some super sensitive imagination and I wanted an assurance that the Commander in Chief intended to put the record straight with the RAF. But, as I looked at his kind but firm face, I knew I would never get it. He might be sympathetic enough to make a reasonable but courteous protest in his own time and manner – in fact he had probably done so already. But he would never give a junior officer the impression that he was condoning interservice bickering and a slight chill in his manner warned me to drop the subject. Then I noticed signs of strain lurking behind his eyes. This surprised me because we were inclined to believe that Commanders in Chief had to be tough, nerveless men who would greet success and failure with equal equanimity. But here was one suffering just as we lesser mortals suffer: my anger melted away and I vowed not to add to his difficulties by spreading the RAF's accusation. I felt quite certain that the ship's company, if they knew it, would half kill any airman unlucky enough to cross their path.

He stood up, as if ending the conversation, but unexpectedly added, in such a quiet voice that he might have been talking to himself, 'This won't last forever you know. One day, we'll return home to enjoy the fruits of our labours.'

Then followed several days of funerals. The dead were buried in three separate services. During one of these Scruffy, who had never shown the slightest fear of bombs or gunfire, was so startled by a rifle volley that, much to the embarrassment of his human friends, he nearly fell into an open grave. This was an unhappy period during which it was impossible to live a normal life and not a man amongst us was untroubled by the thought that he was lucky not to be amongst the casualties. Luckily, everyone sincerely believed that no negligence had contributed to our mishap so the deaths of these brave men did not prey on anyone's conscience. Nevertheless, it was not easy to accept the loss of so many shipmates.

Like all survivors, every officer and man optimistically expected a quiet, restful period in which to recuperate in a rest camp or amongst the flesh pots of Alex. Poor, simple souls. Survivors were God's gift to the drafting authorities, who now had a pool of unattached men from which to fill vacancies in ships and shore establishments. Within days the ship's company had been considerably reduced. The departure of so many was very sad because each man took with him a spark of HMS *Eridge's* spirit, reducing her steadily nearer to the status of a hulk. We had been so proud of her. In her, we had often been wet, tired and frightened but never had anyone felt the slightest uneasiness that either the ship or any man in her would let the others down. Both ship and crew had done well. Sixteen decorations for gallantry and several mentions in despatches had been won in actions which had destroyed or damaged one U-boat: one supply ship; four E-boat types and many aircraft. We had also escorted many supply ships safely to their destinations. Now it was all over but it seemed inconceivable that her spirit would not survive amongst her disbanding ship's company, even though they were being dispersed amongst not only the Mediterranean but also the Eastern Fleet.

Soon I was appointed in command of the HMS *Javelin*. I was still mentally weary but it was exciting to be given a modern fleet destroyer. On the day of my departure, while some seamen carried my luggage to a waiting taxi, I took a final nostalgic look around the cabin which had been my home for the past eighteen months. Apart from one brief visit by my wife, shortly after commissioning, no woman had ever entered it. It had been a man's refuge. In it, I had lived through the most vital and nerve wracking months of my life and had tasted the whole gamut of emotions – failure and success, pride and humility, hope and fear, sadness and, to be fair, some happiness which had so tempered my character that, at times, I barely recognised myself. All had been felt so keenly that some of my personality must surely be trapped within this steel shell. I wondered who its next occupant would be. The ship was already condemned so it would never be some young officer waiting with pride and nervousness to take his first command to sea. More probably it would be some weary traveller, thrust here through lack of accommodation elsewhere, who would grumble at its discomfort without even sparing a thought for its previous occupant. As if answering my thoughts, the door swung open and in stalked the cat which jumped onto the settee where she glared at me as if saying, 'I've had to wait a long time for this'. Then she turned her back and started to wash her face.

I went slowly on deck, my heart heavy with the knowledge that a major milestone in my life was being left behind forever. The remaining seamen and stokers, wearing the shy, embarrassed expression of men trying to pretend they were present by accident, had gathered in little groups around the gangway and each muttered a gruff farewell as I was passing. 'Scruffy', contemptuous to the end, brushed past and raced across the gangway to cock his leg against the taxi. I followed more slowly and paused on the gangway to gaze for the last time on my first command. She was looking so forlorn, as if grieving at her separation from so many old friends. But, while I was looking, the faces of the dead flashed before my eyes. These men, my faithful companions in so many dangers, had crossed the frontier from which there was no return and the termination of this particular episode of my life suddenly seemed trivial by comparison. A lump rose in my throat and I had to swallow vigorously to choke back tears. I waved to the waiting men, jumped into the taxi and nodded to the driver. The vehicle jerked forward with a clash of gears before gathering speed. HMS *Eridge's* focs'le dropped below the dockside leaving visible only her bridge, masts and funnel. These too, suddenly vanished behind a shed and my thoughts, as if acting in sympathy, turned from the past to look forward to the future. I never saw her again.

The Desert Army, now named the Eighth Army under General Montgomery, had successfully repulsed the Axis assault on the Eighth Army's defensive position at Alam Halfa in early September 1942. By the end of October 1942, the Eighth Army started their offensive, the final battle of El Alamein. The fleet maintained an off shore patrol where the continuous rumble of gunfire was clearly audible. On the night of 4-5

November the Eighth Army offensive broke the Axis resistance. For the next few days our excitement was maintained by intercepting almost continuous reports from exuberant fighter-bomber pilots, as they bombed or strafed the endless columns of tanks, troop carriers and lorries trying vainly to escape along the hazardous coastal road.

Then, on the 8 November, our radios began to receive BBC reports of Allied landings in French North Africa. Our spirits soared as if a great load had been lifted from our shoulders. The whole of the Mediterranean's southern coast was under Allied attack. The situation had completely changed. We had at last assumed an offensive role and an end to the war now seemed credible.

Malta had become the Navy's priority. Some fast ships had reached the island with vital stores during the confusion following the break through at El Alamein but the siege could only be lifted by the arrival of a convoy. This was planned for the third week in November when a degree of fighter cover would be provided. I was looking forward to the first convoy in which the odds would be in our favour. But it was not to be. All the flotilla commanders decided that I had had enough and advised the Commander in Chief that I should go home. Just before the convoy's departure I was transferred to command the destroyer HMS *Janus* which was being sent to the UK for repairs. We made an uneventful passage and, in due course, reached the Tyne where she was berthed at Swan Hunters yard. Jean, through intercepted signals, was aware of the ship's destination so, having obtained leave from the WRNS, was able to join me in Newcastle; we were together in the town we had left two years earlier. We had travelled full circle.

Postscript – D-Day

In the spring of 1943 I was appointed to Norfolk House, the Headquarters of the Joint Staffs which had planned the 1942 invasion of North West Europe, an operation that was to have been carried out only in the event of disaster on the Eastern front. This invasion was finally given the go ahead by President Roosevelt and Churchill at the May 1943 Quebec Conference and was scheduled for Normandy in the summer of 1944. I was appointed as the senior staff and training officer at the Naval Headquarters for Group G, tasked with landing the 50th Division on what would be known as Gold Beach on D-Day. One day, shortly after my arrival, the Commander of the Group unexpectedly asked me, 'What do you expect your job to be during the invasion?'

'Duty officer onboard the headquarters ship, I suppose', I replied in some surprise.

'Don't you believe it', he laughed. 'You're going to be the Principal Beachmaster.'

I gaped at him in horror. The first task of this character was to land during the assault phase with a few beach commandoes, erect beach signs, survey the beaches, mark obstructions and generally control the beaching of subsequent waves of landing craft. My brief experience as a planner had taught me that seventy-five percent casualties were expected amongst the assault troops and the prospect of being one of them hardly improved my morale. I argued vehemently that, if I had wanted to fight on land, I would have joined the army, not the navy. It was useless, of course.

The first half of May 1944 was spent driving around the pleasant countryside, which looked so peaceful that war seemed very remote, ensuring that all our landing craft were fully stored and operational: checking the loading arrangements at the various hards and ports and welcoming our infantry and tank landing ships from the Mediterranean and America. Then came the briefing of senior officers and their staffs by the Commander in Chief , the Task Force Commander and, finally, by our own Assault Force Commander, Commodore Douglas Pennant.

During this period, the Assault Divisions of the British, Canadian and American armies began to converge on the south coast. Almost overnight the peaceful countryside vanished and every road, for miles and miles, was lined by endless convoys of tanks, guns, armoured assault vehicles, troop carriers, armoured cars, recovery vehicles, bulldozers, trucks, mobile kitchens, communication vehicles and jeeps. Every one of our joint exercises had involved a heavy movement of military vehicles but this was out of all proportion to its predecessors; it seemed impossible that the enemy would not spot such a fantastic concentration and guess its significance. But they failed to do so and, by 4 June, the whole force was loaded into thousands of ships and craft which filled Southampton Water, the Solent and most of the harbours in Southern England.

Then the weather deteriorated and sailing had to be postponed. It was a frustrating anti-climax for fit, active, highly trained troops to remain cooped up onboard overcrowded craft and time also weighed heavily on the staff waiting in their idle headquarters. Having told Jean that we would be exercising for a few days, I dared not return home so I spent some of the slowly moving hours in a cinema, trying not to think of the future.

During the night, the weather showed signs of moderating. It was to be a temporary improvement only but General Eisenhower made the brave decision to go ahead. It was the moment most of us had been secretly dreading for months. I embarked in the *Empire Halberd,* one of our merchant ships converted to carry an infantry battalion. As I left the shore I could not help wondering if I would ever set foot again in England.

The infantry ships sailed shortly after dark on 5 June and headed for an area south of St. Catherine's Point. From there onwards, we were in the midst of an enormous armada, the very size of which pushed fear into the background. But no one slept much that night; we were facing a battle which was expected to be the bloodiest of the war. In any case, breakfast was to be served at 0200 hrs. I was looking forward to a large helping of the usual bacon and eggs, a luxury which had always been served on our merchant ships during exercises. Consequently, I felt cheated when the steward slapped down a plate of liver and onions, a horrible mixture to offer in the middle of the night, to men who would be eating their last decent meal for days or, perhaps, for ever. Sitting next to me was a young Subaltern in the East Yorks who looked little older than a schoolboy. He was obviously nervous, because he talked incessantly, like a young boy trying to hide his feelings before his first appearance for the school fifteen. I often wondered what happened to him because so many officers who sat down to that meal were to become casualties during the hard fighting in the days ahead.

After breakfast, we mustered alongside our assault craft. It was a dark, silent night except for the normal noises of the ship and the drone of bombers overhead. Those same bombers had already awakened Jean and parents and wives all over southern England, warning them that their menfolk were embarked on the long awaited invasion. Far to the eastward, silent gun flashes were flaming along the horizon which suddenly erupted into a gigantic sheet of flame followed, seconds later, by a growl like distant thunder. It was the Norwegian destroyer *Svenner* blowing up. We tried hard not to think about the possibility we would meet a similar fate while checking over our equipment. Having struggled into mine, I looked a sorry caricature of a sailor encumbered, as I was, by khaki battledress, steel helmet, haversack, revolver, ammunition, waterproof watch, French currency, signalling torch, maps, beaching plans, operation orders, flags. I also had a kit bag containing the most vital items of all – bottles of gin and whisky.

The infantry ships anchored seven miles off shore and the assault units embarked in their landing craft. As each man went over the side he was handed anti-seasick pills and a vomit bag which seemed a curious contradiction. The planner responsible obviously knew his pills because the bags were in constant use during our slow, wet passage through a choppy sea, which was distinctly rougher than it had looked from the high decks of our large infantry ship.

Hundreds of craft were now closing the shore between Ouistreham and the Cherbourg Peninsular. Our view to the flanks was restricted by the heaving sea and flying spray but we were in the midst of a group of infantry assault craft near the head of an endless column flanked by destroyers and gunboats. Later these would shoot up the beaches from close range but they were currently guarding their flocks like faithful sheep dogs. Just ahead were some small tank carriers which were to disembark swimming tanks before H hour so that they could provide covering fire while the infantry were crossing the beaches. Almost alongside us were the rocket craft and more tank carriers loaded with self propelled guns, which had a role to play in the pre H hour bombardment. Behind them, assault craft, large infantry carriers and tank landing craft stretched back towards the horizon, entirely blocked by a huge shadow which, as a blustery day slowly dawned, gradually became recognisable as a solid mass of shipping. Amongst it were battleships and cruisers which began to bombard the coastal batteries with slow, deliberate salvoes, their smoke covering the anchorage with a thin haze of cordite: their shell bursts tossing up gigantic mushrooms of muck and dust. Overhead, a continuous stream of heavy bombers was flying southward, blasting the defences with high explosive. As a huge pall of smoke spread over the coastline, it seemed impossible that anyone could survive such a battering. The noise was terrific. The naval and air bombardments were so continuous that one's stunned senses gradually accepted that the flashes ashore were our shell and bomb bursts alone. But, from time to time, gigantic columns of water would rear skywards near the assault waves, proving that the battery at Mont Fleury was still in action. But, by then, the visible signs of overwhelming power had made one feel such a tiny cog in so mighty a machine that one had no sense of fear, only confidence that no shell could find one individual amongst so many.

As the coast line became clearer, I felt a curious sensation of having been there before. In a way, I suppose that was true because, beneath the smoke, the panorama unfolding before our eyes was the original of the model on which we had been briefed. On our extreme left was the village of La Riviere. From there, stretching westwards towards Arromanches, lay a ribbon of golden sand backed by low dunes. Behind these, the land rose in a gentle slope chequered by meadows and cornfields which were bisected by a road running inland from the beach. On the crest of this hill were the light house and coastal batteries at Mont Fleury. Behind La Riviere stood a large, white farm house.

As the leading waves drew closer to the shore, the heavy bombers were replaced by light bombers which, in turn, gave way to fighters diving vertically onto selected targets. Five minutes before touch down, the naval and air bombardments were shifted inland. The touch down at 0725 hrs had been so timed that the beach obstacles – parallel lines of horrible looking steel hedgehogs with mines attached – would be above the tidemark. This was to allow time for naval demolition teams to destroy them before the bulk of the force was due to beach. That meant the infantry would have to cross about 500 yards of open beach before reaching the shelter of the dunes. Support, just before and during this vital period, was provided by the self propelled guns until their craft had to turn away to prepare the guns for disembarkation. Two minutes before touch down, the rocket craft opened fire, blasting the back of the beach with heavy concentrations which exploded with an ear splitting 'whoomph', 'whoomph', 'whoomph'. By then, the Dragoon Guards' swimming tanks should have been taking up positions. But we could see that the landing craft were having great difficulty in launching their tanks, few of which looked likely to ever reach a position from which they could help the infantry. It was even more apparent that the heavy westerlies of the past few days had so piled up the sea that the obstacles were already too deeply covered for the clearance parties to have a hope of destroying them. Several craft from the first wave had already fallen foul of this armed barrier and their shattered hulls were wallowing helplessly in the shallows. Our own craft, yawing dangerously from side to side, heading first for an obstacle and then for a gap, was slowly approaching these armed lumps of metal. The Coxswain was spinning his wheel continuously, trying to steer a safe course, when a following sea caught our stern, flinging the craft parallel to the shore and sweeping her broadside towards the obstacles. Their horrible, sharp fangs were horribly mesmerising and each successive sea was carrying our helpless craft sideways towards them. There was a rending, grinding crash of metal against metal and water gushed into the boat. We held our breath, staring mutely at each other, waiting for the mines to explode. One, two, three seconds passed; then we came alive again and, leaving all but inessential equipment, jumped overboard just as the hull vanished below the surface.

We were wading shorewards when a badly scared soldier ran toward me, calling, 'Give me a lift to a ship, Jack'. I was surprised that he could recognise a sailor beneath so much camouflage. Until then we had been completely unaware of any resistance but we now realised that several badly wounded men were clinging weakly to beach obstacles, against which the flood tide was brutally battering them. Closer inshore, a number of dead were lying in the shallows, their bodies rolling wearily back and forth as the sea flowed and recoiled over them. Higher up the beach, little heaps which, from a distance, had looked like piles of sand also proved to be khaki clad casualties of the assault. Of the living there was no sign. The several hundred troops who had just landed had vanished into the dunes, as if the sand had swallowed them. Only the continuous rattle of small arms fire showed where they were advancing.

It was shortly after 0730 hrs when we struggled ashore. The commando had been divided amongst several landing craft, each man having been allocated a specific task on landing; Mitchell, the other Beachmaster, went west and I turned east to ensure that everything was going according to plan. I ran along the half tide mark, looking for runnels or other obstructions. To my right, the battle amongst the dunes was still continuing although it was barely audible amid the general noise of aircraft, naval guns, landing craft and shouting men. To my left some tank carriers were discharging armoured assault vehicles and I had a vague impression that some of these were being diverted from their planned role to provide infantry support in place of the missing Dragoon tanks. One of these was standing disabled on an otherwise empty beach ahead of me and, as I reached it, one of the crew called out, 'Look out for that gun!' From the briefing, I knew exactly what he meant and, shortly afterwards, spotted its vicious, black barrel protruding out of an anti-tank bunker near the outskirts of La Riviere. I ran even faster, trying to convince myself that no trained gun crew would waste a shot at a single man, and had almost reached the village (fortunately unaware that it was still held by the Germans) before spotting the flank marker planted to show the edge of the landing zone. The men who had erected it were presumably sheltering in the dunes so I turned back. A commando was placing a marker on the disabled tank, which was already surrounded by water and would soon be a dangerous hazard unless it could be towed away. Beyond it, assault craft which had landed the reserve battalion were turning away from the beach, leaving the usual quota of damaged craft.

A temporary control post had been established near one of the beach exits, where an assault vehicle had hit a mine. No one was moving it; neither was anyone searching for mines and, as I joined the little huddle of communication ratings, an angry voice was shouting, 'Where the hell are those bloody sappers?' Down on the beach, large troop carriers were beginning to disembark the reserve brigade's infantry, who were advancing up the beach and pushing roughly through a motley collection of pale faced, haggard beach defenders. These men seemed to have assembled without any apparent supervision: most of them turned out to be Russians serving in the German army.

On landing, the sea had been about 450 yards from the high water mark. By now it had encroached a further 100 yards, completely covering the obstacles and entirely surrounding the damaged tank. There was not much more than two hours before the ebb commenced and, during that time, we had to disembark about 3,000 vehicles. The reserve brigade was still wading ashore when the first wave of tank landing craft were sighted, heading for the shallows. In exercises, these had always been comparatively clear but they were now cluttered with wrecks. Through these wrecks the heavier craft pounded, with a grinding crunch of metal against metal, their wash sweeping the damaged craft further inshore, before coming to rest with their bows only a few feet from dry land. Their vehicles were still wading shorewards when the second wave plunged into the gaps, piling the damaged craft into an even more compact mass. With them, further adding to the congestion, came the craft carrying the vital self propelled artillery which had already played a part in the preliminary bombardment.

More than 400 vehicles were now ashore or wading towards it. But, owing to casualties or the diversion of assault vehicles, only a few exits had been cleared and the planned flow of tanks, guns and trucks into the open countryside was being reduced to a mere trickle. Conditions offshore were just as bad: the shallows were blocked by wrecks and unloaded craft trying to back off the beach into the teeth of a strong westerly wind. Prudence demanded that the third wave of tank landing craft should defer beaching for a few minutes.

'Tell 'em to wait offshore for ten minutes,' I told the Yeoman of the Signals.

Signalmen semaphored, flashed an aldis and chattered on the radio. But we might have been talking to the moon for all the good they did. The third wave piled into the flotsam and disgorged another 200 vehicles which rolled to the back of the beach, where they came to a grinding halt amongst the waiting queue.

This latest influx completely blocked the control post's view of the sea. Not that this seemed to matter because no one had paid the slightest attention to our one attempt at control. I decided to join the beach parties, which were doing their utmost to guide craft into the least blocked stretches of beach and then get them to sea before the large tank landing ships arrived. These deeper draughted vessels, carrying the bulk of the division's vehicles, were running a race with time because the tide was now a further 150 yards up the beach and only a short hour of flood remained in which to discharge their huge loads and then escape the ebb. The squadron of twelve was already approaching, slewing vigorously from side to side in an attempt to avoid the smaller craft backing, turning and working their way seaward. They had little chance of grounding on the beach party's leading marks. Bulldozing a passage through this armada, they skidded along the gently shelving beach amid a surge of piled up water which compressed the abandoned craft into an even more compact mass. One after another the ships came to rest with their bows about fifty yards from dry land. Their vehicles were thus faced with a comparatively long wade, at the end of which an unbroken barrier of battered wrecks was barring them from the beach. Not even a Hercules seemed capable of clearing a passage. The tide was still advancing at about six feet each minute so any vehicles delayed in the water would be swiftly overwhelmed and a frightening vision of losing these vital reinforcements flashed before my eyes. Luckily two bulldozers were standing near the water's edge.

'See if you can move some of these wrecks,' I called to the drivers.

The drivers, glad of something to do, willingly charged into the shallows and crushed the wreckage into heaps of scrap metal. Some vehicles managed to squeeze between these heaps but space was still inadequate so we were thankful to see the tide driving the ships further and further inshore, forcing them relentlessly through the wreckage, until, by high water, their ramps were virtually on dry land. Meanwhile, the beach controllers were cursing and cajoling the drivers of trapped vehicles to park bumper to bumper, side by side, thus clearing sufficient space for the ships to discharge onto a strip of beach now less than fifty yards wide.

At this stage, the dazed defenders of La Riviere began to recover their nerve and a steadily increasing number of mortar bombs fell amongst the packed vehicles, causing fires and minor explosions. The assault infantry were now a mile or two inland so Colonel Humphreys, the Beach Group Commander, gathered together his infantry element. They then spent a grim couple of hours winkling the Germans out of the ruined village; these men had bitterly resented the loss of their fighting role and eagerly accepted the unexpected task. But few others knew what was happening and most feared that the mortars were heralding a counter attack which had penetrated the infantry screen, still lacking its armour and artillery. In fact, the only Germans capable of such a stroke were several miles inland, pinned down by the heavy bombardments from sea and air.

Meanwhile, the sappers were searching the exits and eventually enough were cleared for the traffic controllers to disentangle the knot of vehicles. Then the tanks, guns, personnel carriers, trucks and jeeps of the British Second Army began to roll off the beach and thrust up the gentle slope to the crest of the hill. Here, the fighting vehicles deployed into the fields and disappeared amid clouds of dust. This was the first stage of their drive to Bayeux and thence to the outskirts of Caen. It was a most thrilling spectacle.

Back on the beach, the tide was now ebbing rapidly. A number of tank landing ships and craft were still struggling to unbeach, churning up the sand like enormous whales floundering in the shallows. Luckily all the ships got away but a few tank landing craft were stranded until the next tide, amongst scores of minor landing craft and drowned tanks, guns and trucks – which were quickly towed away to the recovery park. As the tide continued to fall, the demolition parties began to make up for lost time by destroying the surviving obstacles in a series of ear splitting explosions which nearly startled us out of our wits.

During this low water period, massed beaching at timed intervals was impracticable. But the continuous growl of guns to the southward confirmed that the Army was using a prodigious amount of ammunition and supply was maintained by coasters drying out and discharging direct into lorries. Further out to sea, merchant ships carrying motor transport were unloading onto huge, unwieldy 'rhino' ferries which sometimes landed up on their correct beach. In the reverse direction, a steady stream of wounded was reaching the beach and waiting, with all the patience in the world, to be evacuated.

As soon as their evacuation was proceeding satisfactorily, I set off along the beach to estimate how many damaged craft might be salvaged at the next tide. Amongst a group of wrecks I recognised my own craft and the recollection of its cargo reminded me that a strong drink would be highly beneficial. A nasty mixture of oil and water was partially covering my kitbag in which I found a sodden mess of clothes, writing paper and paperbacks. There was not a sign of any gin or whisky. This so shocked my faith in human nature that I promptly relieved my feelings in a verbal dual with the captain of an American landing craft which, for some reason or other, had strayed into British territory. Before leaving the beach, I had a look inside the anti-tank gun bunker and earmarked it as the permanent beach headquarters. It was an eerie feeling inside that dark, concrete bastion, its gun still pointing in the direction in which it had fired its last shot: its floor littered with empty shell cases. Hand to hand fighting must have occurred in and around the position but there were no dead, no signs of its defenders' fate. In fact, although I saw many British dead, I never saw a dead German throughout the whole of that day.

On my way back to the control post, a stoutish soldier near me on the dunes unexpectedly fell down. By then, my good humour had been restored and, thinking he had tripped, I burst out laughing. But laughter suddenly changed to horror at the sight of a trickle of blood on his temple. At the same time, something pinged angrily past my ear and I realised we were being sniped from a cornfield. In such circumstances, it seemed only prudent to dig in the control post so we borrowed the Beach Group's picks and shovels. An airman just behind me swung his pick into the ground. There was a blinding flash and my brain went black. When I came to I found myself lying on the ground, about ten feet from gruesome bits of flesh and bone which had once been a man. This incident and the sniping naturally made us cautious so when the village priest, breathing benevolence and bonhomie, arrived on the scene, the poor fellow was treated as a potential fifth columnist and given a very cool reception. He was last seen returning towards the ruins of his church, obviously ruminating on the strangeness of the so called liberators.

As night fell, enemy aircraft made their first appearance and the anchorage was suddenly illuminated by vivid gun flashes flickering along the horizon. More flashes far to the eastward warned of a skirmish between our light forces and surface raiders. Ashore, patrols surrounded our corn fields and slowly winkled out the snipers. Sometime after midnight, having confirmed that the wounded were being smoothly evacuated, I scraped a hole in the sand. It was a cold night. During the past twenty-two hours, I had been in and out of the water and had eaten only a biscuit and a bar of chocolate. I was cold, wet and hungry and badly in need of alcoholic refreshment. But having none, I shivered in my foxhole, contemplating my loss which, I was convinced, was the work of pongos because no sailor would be so dishonest. Shortly before dawn, I dropped into an uneasy doze.[15]

To be honest, I had disliked being a Beachmaster. At heart I remained a destroyer officer, always jealous of our escorts and resentful of my khaki battledress. Unfortunately I did not return straight to sea after D-day. Instead, as I was apparently regarded as something of a specialist in amphibious operations, I joined Combined Operation Headquarters. In this capacity the Chief of COHQ, General Laycock, asked me to accompany him to a meeting where future operations in the Far East would be discussed. So, in January 1945, I boarded the Cunard liner *Franconia*. We knew we were heading to the USSR for a meeting between the 'Big Three' – Churchill, Roosevelt and Stalin – to coordinate the final operations of the war, but our final destination remained a mystery. Not until *Franconia* was well clear of the Irish coast did she turn south and thereby indicate that she was bound for the Black Sea. We were heading to the Crimean resort of Yalta.

My part in the Yalta Conference was regrettably insignificant. In fact, I can truthfully boast that I did less work than anyone in the combined delegations. That was because amphibious operations were never discussed, the Russian Generals being uninterested and the American Admirals unwilling to hasten the arrival of British forces in their sphere of responsibility. Returning to London from Yalta I found lodgings near Buckingham Palace which I shared with a Brigadier. Together we celebrated VE day, the end of the war in Europe, on 8 May 1945. But the war with Japan had not ended and COHQ continued work preparing amphibious operations. Unfortunately, the strain of the last few years was beginning to take its toll and I became increasingly unwell until I eventually collapsed and was taken to the Royal Masonic Hospital. I was to spend three months in hospital suffering first from glandular fever and then pneumonia. I shared a ward with three other officers who were too busy writing their memoirs to engage in more than brief bouts of conversation. That suited me. I was taking a drug which had a very depressing effect and not even news of the Japanese surrender aroused any enthusiasm.

In 1947 I was appointed to command a destroyer again, HMS *Constance*, in the British Pacific Fleet. But the pleasure of commanding a destroyer in peacetime was all too brief and in 1949 I was transferred back to the Admiralty in London. My last twelve years in the Navy would be on the staffs, away from the junior officers and ratings one can mingle with at sea. It was interesting work but after the responsibility of commanding a wartime destroyer it seemed a little trivial.

After a joints staffs appointment in Singapore and a period as Naval Attache in Ankara my final appointment was in Malta in 1958. The appointment bore the grandiose title of Chief Staff Officer (Intelligence) to the Commander in Chief, Mediterranean and carried responsibility for the collection of area intelligence and for its dissemination to the fleet and Admiralty. There was still a mystique about intelligence and if, at a staff meeting, I announced that the Kurds were revolting against the Iraqi government, members always believed that the information had been supplied by a secret source and not by the latest edition of *The Times*. I did nothing to disabuse them.

In Malta it was clear that this was the end of an era. The great British Fleets which had dominated the oceans of the world had vanished. The battleships had gone to the ship breakers, the aircraft carriers, their successors, were being phased out. Soon all that would be left would be a depleted Navy of submarines and small ships.

From time to time, the Malta based ships were still reinforced by an aircraft carrier or a cruiser. One of these was the HMS *Tiger*, a ship full of complicated equipment, which bore little resemblance to the old battlecruiser I had joined in 1927. It was more than thirty years since I had served in her but walking round her successor and seeing once more the familiar silver was a sentimental journey. It seemed appropriate that the last ship to be visited before retiring should bear the name of my first ship. The years following the HMS *Tiger* had been exceedingly fortunate. As a lieutenant, I had spent eight years as second in command of a gunboat and of several destroyers. Then had followed another eight years, mostly in command of destroyers. That period had covered the war when the preservation of one's ship and her company had frequently depended on instant reactions and decisions – the zenith of responsibility. I could never forget the HMS *Eridge* and her crew. HMS *Eridge* had been my first command, and I was to be her only Captain. The most vivid experiences of my life were nearly all bound up with her, and the crew and I had been through so much together. Unfortunately post war appointments always seemed trivial by comparison. But it was useless to pine for something which had been irretrievably lost. Far better to look back with pleasure on a wonderfully happy and satisfying career in the Royal Navy, even though, alas, HM ships are no longer found in every corner of the globe.

Notes

1. Fleet destroyers were designed for offensive action, usually against other fighting ships, with the main battle fleet, as opposed to escort destroyers which were designed to protect convoys from submarine and air attack.
2. The Admiralty in fact credited HMS *Jaguar* with downing one the attacking planes, a fact unknown to Gregory-Smith until many years after the war.
3. Gregory-Smith was awarded the Distinguished Service Cross for his part in the towing of HMS *Firedrake* to Gibraltar. The citation reads: 'The safe arrival of 'Firedrake' at Gibraltar can be attributed largely to the fine seamanship, courage and determination shown by Lieutenant-Commander Gregory-Smith.'
4. East Libyan coastal region.
5. HMS *Barham* was torpedoed and sunk by U-331 on 25 November 1941. Only 396 of her crew were saved from a compliment of 1,258.
6. On 10th December 1941 the battlecruiser HMS *Repulse* and the battleship HMS *Prince of Wales* were attacked and sunk by Japanese aircraft off Malaya. It was one of Royal Navy's worst disasters in the entire war.
7. The cruiser HMS *Neptune* and destroyer HMS *Kandahar* were sunk, and the cruiser HMS *Aurora* was badly damaged.
8. Site of RAF airbase outside Tobruk.
9. HMS *Jaguar* was sunk by U-652 off Sidi Barrani on 26 March 1942 with the loss of 190 of her crew.
10. Lieutenant Evans and three other seamen were awarded Bronze Medals by the Royal Humane Society for their bravery in repeatedly going over the side of the ship to rescue exhausted survivors from *Clan Campbell*.
11. Gregory-Smith received the Distinguished Service Order for his part in the Battle of Sirte. The citation reads: 'For outstanding services in the successful defence of the convoy against heavy and sustained air attack without the support of the Fleet Cruisers or Destroyers.'

12. In January 1942 Hitler instructed the Luftwaffe to crush Malta with devastating bombing raids. The campaign reached its peak during April when 8,788 sorties were flown against the island. At this point in the war, Malta was the most bombed place on earth.
13. Gregory-Smith received a Bar to his Distinguished Service Order for his part in the sinking of U568. The citation reads: 'For the efficiency and determination with which he conducted a prolonged hunt on 27th and 28th May, 1942, the enemy submarine being destroyed at 0400 upon the latter date.'
14. Gregory-Smith was Mentioned in Dispatches for 'Coolness and courage in the face of repeated air attacks after his ship had been torpedoed'.
15. Gregory-Smith received a Bar to his Distinguished Service Cross 'for gallantry, skill and undaunted devotion to duty shown during the landing of Allied Forces on the coast of Normandy in June 1944.'

Glossary

'A' Gun Most forward gun turret, 'B' Gun is the 2nd most forward. Guns at the rear are listed as 'X' and 'Y' with 'Y' gun being the rearmost

Abaft Towards the rear

Aft Rear

Artificer Engineer responsible for the ships mechanical equipment, primarily in the engineroom

Bosun Petty Officer in charge of deck hands and equipment

Chief Chief Engineer

Coxswain Seaman in charge of the helm

Combing their tracks Standard torpedo avoidance. Torpedoes are generally fired in groups. To reduce their large side-on target, ships turn towards the torpedoes to allow them to pass on either side of the vessel

Corvettes Small convoy escort vessels

Director Central weapons system on the ship allowing all the main armaments to be aimed and fired centrally if required

Dog Watch 4pm-6pm

E-boat Small, fast German torpedo boat

ERA Engine Room Artificer

Executive signal Instruction to proceed with existing orders. On ships orders are often given by flag signals and are only executed when the flags are dropped

Flag Officer Officer of the rank of Vice-Admiral and above

Focs'le Forward section of the ship

Forenoon 8am-noon

Grog Watered down rum

Gunner's Mate Petty Officer assisting the gunnery officer

Gunwales Upper edge of the side of a ship

Gyro Gyrocompass – a non-magnetic direction finder

Lascar Sailors from the East Indies. Many served on merchantmen during the war

Libertymen Men ashore off the watch

Middle Watch   Midnight–4am

Midshipman   Trainee officer

Paying off pendant   Very long thin flag flown from the topmast of Royal Navy ships on leaving foreign stations for home and on the return to home port. The pendant is the length of the ship and increased in proportion to the extra length of service

Petty Officer   Naval non-commissioned officer, the equivalent of corporals and sergeants in the army

Pilot   Navigation officer

Pom Pom   Rapid firing quadruple 2 pounder cannon, mainly used for anti-aircraft

Pongo   Naval nickname for the infantry

Port   Left

Provost Marshal   Head of the military police

Quarterdeck   Section of the upper deck behind the main mast

Quartermaster   Petty Officer in charge of ships stores

Oerlikon   Rapid fire 20mm calibre cannon

RAF   Royal Air Force

Starboard   Right

Stern   Rear end of a ship

Wardroom   Officers communal rest and living area

Warrant Officer   Intermediary rank between Petty Officers and Officers

Watchkeeping Certificate   Certificate allowing an officer to take charge of a vessel on any given watch

'X' gun   2nd rearmost gun turret

'Y' gun   Rearmost gun turret

Index